The Certificate in Education and Training

Ann Gravells and Susan Simpson

SAGE | LearningMatters

Los Angeles | London | New Delhi
Singapore | Washington DC

064832
SC 370.711 GRA
EDUCATION
TEACHING
CET

S.C. CAC

Learning Matters
An imprint of SAGE Publications Ltd
1 Oliver's Yard
55 City Road
London EC1Y 1SP

SAGE Publications Inc.
2455 Teller Road
Thousand Oaks, California 91320

SAGE Publications India Pvt Ltd
B 1/I 1 Mohan Cooperative Industrial Area
Mathura Road
New Delhi 110 044

SAGE Publications Asia-Pacific Pte Ltd
3 Church Street
#10–04 Samsung Hub
Singapore 049483

Editor: Amy Thornton
Development editor: Jennifer Clark
Production controller: Chris Marke
Project management: Deer Park Productions,
Tavistock, Devon, England
Marketing manager: Catherine Slinn
Cover design: Wendy Scott
Typeset by: C&M Digitals (P) Ltd, Chennai, India
Printed by Henry Ling Limited at The Dorset Press,
Dorchester, DT1 1HD

MIX
Paper from
responsible sources
FSC
www.fsc.org FSC™ C013985

© Ann Gravells 2014

Library of Congress Control Number: 2014930440

British Library Cataloguing in Publication data

A catalogue record for this book is available from the
British Library

ISBN: 9781446295878
ISBN: 9781446295885 (pbk)

CONTENTS

ACKNOWLEDGEMENTS

The authors would like to give a special thanks to the following subject experts who have helped and contributed towards this book. They have freely given their time, knowledge and advice, which has resulted in some excellent contributions.

Sharron Carlill Head of Services to Business at Rotherham College.

Professor Ian Favell of Accredited Training International (ATi)

Special thanks go to both authors' family members for their patience and support.

The authors would like to thank their editor Jennifer Clark for her continued support and excellent guidance.

Special thanks go to Amy Thornton from Learning Matters (which is part of SAGE Publications Ltd) for her advice, encouragement and tremendous patience with all our questions, e-mails and telephone calls.

Thanks go to the Education and Training Foundation for permission to use the Professional Standards for Teachers and Trainers in England.

Every effort has been made to trace the copyright holders and to obtain their permission for the use of copyright material. The publisher and authors will gladly receive any information enabling them to rectify any error or omission in subsequent editions.

Ann Gravells
Susan Simpson

AUTHOR STATEMENTS

Ann Gravells

Ann is a director of her own company *Ann Gravells Ltd*, an educational consultancy based in East Yorkshire. She specialises in teaching, training, assessment and quality assurance for the Further Education and Skills Sector.

Ann creates resources for teachers and learners such as PowerPoints and handouts for teaching and assessment qualifications. These are available via her resource website www.anngravells.co.uk/resources

Ann is a consultant to The University of Cambridge's Institute of Continuing Education. She has worked for several awarding organisations producing qualification guidance, policies and procedures, and carrying out quality assurance of teacher training qualifications. She has been teaching in further education colleges since 1983.

Ann holds a Master's in Educational Management, a PGCE, a Degree in Education, and a City & Guilds Medal of Excellence for teaching. Ann is a Fellow of the Institute for Learning and holds QTLS status.

She is often asked how her surname should be pronounced. The 'vells' part of Gravells is pronounced like 'bells'.

She is the author of:

- *Achieving your Assessor and Quality Assurance Units (2014)*
- *Delivering Employability Skills in the Lifelong Learning Sector (2010)*
- *Passing Assessments for the Award in Education and Training (2013)*
- *Passing PTLLS Assessments (2012)*
- *Preparing to Teach in the Lifelong Learning Sector (2012)*
- *Principles and Practice of Assessment in the Lifelong Learning Sector (2011)*
- *The Award in Education and Training (2014)*
- *What is Teaching in the Lifelong Learning Sector? (2012)*

She has edited:

- *Study Skills for PTLLS (2012)*

Susan Simpson specialises in teaching, training, assessment and quality assurance for the Further Education and Skills Sector. She has been teaching since 1980.

Susan is the Lead for Communities and Partnerships for North East Lincolnshire Council. Susan was previously the Head of Community Learning Services, and has worked as a curriculum manager for Education and Training, ICT, Business Administration and Law. She developed, managed and taught adult education programmes in Botswana for ten years. Susan has also presented at regional level for teacher training and nationally for ICT Skills for Life.

Susan holds a Post Graduate Diploma in Management Studies, BA (Hons) in Further Education and Training, and a Certificate in Education (Hons) in Business Studies and Economics.

Ann and Susan have co-authored:

- *Equality and Diversity in the Lifelong Learning Sector (2012)*

- *Passing Assessments for the Certificate in Education and Training (2014)*

- *Passing CTLLS Assessments (2011)*

- *Planning and Enabling Learning in the Lifelong Learning Sector (2010)*

- *The Certificate in Education and Training (2014)*

Ann and Susan welcome any comments from readers; please contact them via Ann's website: www.anngravells.co.uk

PREFACE

Teaching qualifications in post-compulsory education seem to change regularly. This is not only because of government regulations, but to reflect different approaches to teaching, learning and assessment, and to keep pace with the influence of new technology.

This book was first published in 2008 and was called *Planning and Enabling Learning* to reflect the core unit of the Level 4 Certificate in Teaching in the Lifelong Learning Sector (CTLLS). It was successful due to its plain English approach and ability to put complex theories into language new teachers could understand. A second edition was published in 2010 to refresh the content.

This edition of the book has been fully updated to cover the content of the revised qualification, now called the Level 4 Certificate in Education and Training. One of the units from the Award in Education and Training is also part of the Certificate in Education and Training. There is therefore some duplication of content in the text which supports the Award in Education and Training, and this textbook.

The appendices contain all the learning outcomes and assessment criteria for the mandatory units which can be taken to achieve the Certificate. They also include the minimum core personal skills which should be evidenced by teachers throughout their time taking the qualification, and the Professional Standards for Teachers and Trainers in England.

Learners taking the Certificate in Education and Training would also benefit from the companion book *Passing Assessments for the Certificate in Education and Training*. This book, also by Ann Gravells and Susan Simpson, gives key advice on completing written and practical assessments to help achieve the qualification.

INTRODUCTION

In this chapter you will learn about:

- the structure of the book and how to use it
- teaching in the Further Education and Skills Sector
- the Certificate in Education and Training
- the minimum core
- academic writing, study skills and reflective practice
- the historical perspective of the sector
- educational abbreviations and acronyms

The structure of the book and how to use it

This book will help you if you are working towards a teaching qualification, for example, the *Certificate in Education and Training*, or just wish to know what it is like to teach in the Further Education and Skills Sector. It has been written in accessible language and without too much educational jargon to help anyone fairly new to their teaching role. It is structured around the units of the qualification. However, the content will be valuable whether you are currently teaching or not.

The sector includes those aged 14 and upwards who are in:

- adult education
- armed, emergency and uniformed services
- charitable organisations
- community learning
- further education (FE) colleges
- higher education institutions and universities
- immigration and detention centres
- on-site learning centres
- prisoner and offender centres
- private sector learning
- probation services
- public and private training organisations
- schools and academies
- sixth form colleges
- voluntary sector learning
- work-based learning

At the end of this chapter you will find a useful table listing many of the educational abbreviations and acronyms you might come across. At the end of all chapters is a *theory focus* which lists additional texts and websites to help inform your learning further. Within the chapters are examples of templates you could use for various teaching, learning and assessment activities.

The chapters relate to the full process of teaching, learning and assessment and cover the content of the mandatory units which contribute towards the Certificate in Education and Training. The book is also applicable to anyone working towards units of other qualifications such as those known as *Learning and Development*. Throughout the book, the term *Certificate* will be used to denote the Certificate in Education and Training.

At the end of each chapter is a cross-referencing grid showing how the chapter's contents relate to the units of the Certificate in Education and Training, and the Professional Standards for Teachers and Trainers in England.

Throughout the book, the terms *teacher* and *trainer* are used, even though you might carry out a different role, for example, *assessor, coach, counsellor, facilitator, instructor, learning co-ordinator, lecturer, mentor, presenter, staff development manager, supervisor* or *tutor*. The term *learner* is used in the book and refers to other terms such as *apprentice, candidate, delegate, employee, participant, pupil, student, studying professional* and *trainee*. The term *programme* is used to refer to courses and events which do or do not lead to qualifications.

You can work logically through the book by starting with Chapter 1, or you can just look up appropriate topics in the index (at the back of the book) to access aspects relevant to your current area of study or interest. There are *activities* to enable you to think about how you will teach and assess, and *examples* to help you understand the process of teaching, learning and assessing. At the end of each chapter section are *extension activities* to develop, stretch and challenge your learning further. These are aimed at helping you work towards the requirements of the Certificate.

While this book covers the theory required for the Certificate, the companion book *Passing Assessments for the Certificate in Education and Training* by Ann Gravells and Susan Simpson will help you put theory into practice and structure your work to meet the qualification's requirements.

Some of the regulations and organisations referred to in this book might only be relevant in England. If you are teaching nationally or internationally, you should check what is current and applicable to where you work.

Appendices 1–5 contain the learning outcomes and assessment criteria of each of the units which make up the Certificate.

Due to the structure of the units of the Certificate, there are aspects in this book which also appear in the *Award in Education and Training* (2013) by Ann Gravells.

Teaching in the Further Education and Skills Sector

Teaching is about helping someone reach their full potential, whether this is for personal or professional reasons. The Further Education and Skills Sector in the UK can include learners from age 14 upwards; therefore you have the opportunity to help make a difference to someone's life and career, which can be very rewarding.

If you are new to teaching, this could be because you are contemplating a change of profession or you are required to take a particular teaching qualification because of your job role. Perhaps you have a hobby, interest, a trade or a profession you would like to teach others; you know you are good at it and feel you have the skills, knowledge and experience which you could pass on to others. If you have been teaching for a while, perhaps you are reading this book to help you achieve a teaching qualification. While this book will guide you through the process of teaching, learning and assessing, it is up to you to ensure you are current with your particular specialist subject knowledge. Depending upon where and what you are going to teach, you may not need to be qualified in your specialist subject, but may need to be able to demonstrate appropriate skills and knowledge at a certain level. Some subjects require you to have a level above that which you will teach, for example, holding a level 3 qualification to teach it at level 2. Others might not require you to hold a subject qualification at all, but just have the necessary skills and knowledge. If you are teaching towards qualifications in the UK, there will be a *Sector Skills Council* or *Standards Setting Body* responsible for your subject. They, along with the awarding organisation who accredit and certify the qualification, will decide what is required to deliver and assess in your subject area.

Not all programmes, courses and events will lead to qualifications; some are for leisure, for example, home maintenance, some are for work, for example, to help employees improve their skills and knowledge, and others are to help people improve their confidence or health and well-being. There are many programmes available for different reasons to fulfil certain needs, for example, those aimed at reaching vulnerable people and deprived communities. Programmes are often known as *vocational* (work or employment related), *non-vocational* (leisure or interest related) and *academic* (theory related). Records of achievement or attendance, or an informal certificate might be issued to learners who complete programmes which are not formally accredited by an awarding organisation.

The most important aspect of teaching is to ensure that learning is taking place. If you are currently teaching, your delivery methods might be based on experiences of how you were taught in the past, or how you think people will learn. However, there are many different approaches you could use and this book will hopefully give you new ideas to engage, encourage and motivate your learners. Teaching is not just about delivering to groups in a classroom; it can take place in many different environments such as training in the workplace, public, private or voluntary settings, delivering sessions indoors, outdoors, or online. It can also be on a one-to-one basis, remotely via the internet, or using another appropriate method.

Professional Standards for Teachers and Trainers in England

In 2014, The Education and Training Foundation introduced new Professional Standards for Teachers and Trainers in the Further Education and Skills Sector in England.

The Standards encompass the following areas:

- Professional values and attributes
- Professional knowledge and understanding
- Professional skills

The chapters in this book are cross referenced to each of the areas and can be seen in Appendix 9. The purpose of the Standards is to:

- set out clear expectations of effective practice in education and training

- enable teachers and trainers to identify areas for their own professional development

- support initial teacher education

- provide a national reference point that organisations can use to support the development of their staff

http://www.et-foundation.co.uk/supporting/programmes/professional-standards-review/ date accessed 11.04.14

The Certificate in Education and Training

The Certificate in Education and Training is a teaching qualification achievable at level 4 on the Qualifications and Credit Framework (QCF) in England and Northern Ireland. You will find more information on the QCF in the next section of this chapter, along with the Scottish Credit and Qualifications Framework (SCQF).

The Certificate is made up of different units, each with a *credit value*. You need at least 36 credits to achieve the qualification. The time taken to achieve the credits is normally calculated as one credit being approximately ten hours of learning; therefore 36 credits equates to 360 hours of learning. This will consist of a certain amount of *contact time* with a teacher such as attending sessions and being assessed. It also consists of your own time, known as *non-contact time*, which can be used for reading, research, completing assignments and gathering evidence of work towards meeting the requirements of the qualification.

The Level 4 Certificate is made up of two types of units known as *mandatory* and *optional*. Mandatory units are those which you must achieve, and can be taken in any order. Optional units are those which you can choose, providing they meet certain rules, to meet the requirements of your job role and the qualification.

Mandatory units

The first unit of the Certificate is at level 3 and is also part of the Award in Education and Training. If you have taken the Level 3 Award prior to working towards the Level 4 Certificate, you will not need to repeat this unit.

The mandatory units are:

- Understanding roles, responsibilities and relationships in education and training (3 credits, level 3)

- Planning to meet the needs of learners in education and training (3 credits, level 4)

- Delivering education and training (6 credits, level 4)

- Assessing learners in education and training (6 credits, level 4)

- Using resources for education and training (3 credits, level 4)

This book covers all the requirements of all the mandatory units of the Certificate; you can see each unit's content in the appendices. However, you are responsible for keeping up to date with the subject that you wish to teach. While the book will help you with ideas for teaching, learning and assessing in general, you will need to adapt these to suit your subject and the environment within which you will teach.

Working towards the Certificate

The Certificate can be delivered in different ways depending upon where you choose to take it, for example, a series of evening classes, daytime classes or an online programme.

How you are assessed will differ depending upon who you are registered with. The organisation you are taking the qualification with will register you with an awarding organisation. Each awarding organisation will specify how you will be assessed, for example, assignments, written work and projects. Some might have a more academic focus, i.e. require formal writing and the use of research and referencing. Others might assess holistically, i.e. assess aspects of more than one unit at the same time. You will need to find out how you will be assessed before you commence, to ensure you can meet the requirements. While the delivery and assessment methods might differ, the content of the qualification will be the same no matter who you are registered with.

If you haven't applied to take the Certificate yet, you might like to find out where it is offered, how it is delivered and how it is assessed before you apply.

If you are currently teaching, this is known as *in-service*, and if you are not yet teaching, this is known as *pre-service*. Throughout your career, you might be known as a *dual professional,* i.e. a professional in the *subject* you will teach, as well as a professional *teacher*.

Optional units

To achieve the Certificate, you need to choose optional units to the value of 15 credits. Many optional units are available, at different levels and with different credit values. However, not all organisations offer them all. You therefore need to consider which units you are capable of achieving, which are relevant to your job role, and which are available for you to take. You might already have achieved some of the units elsewhere; therefore, if they meet the *rules of combination,* you will not be required to repeat them. The rules govern which optional units you can take to meet the requirements of the Certificate at level 4. You will need to discuss these with your assessor to ensure you are taking the correct units, at the correct level, with the correct credit values. You will need to consider how long it will take you to achieve the units, using the method of one credit value equalling ten hours of learning. Table 0.1 lists some of the optional units which can be used towards achievement of the Certificate. This book does not cover the content of the optional units as there are so many to choose from. The organisation you are taking the Certificate with should support you with the content of the optional units.

Table 0.1 Some of the optional units available as part of the Certificate

Title	Level	Credit value
Action research	5	15
Assess occupational competence in the work environment	3	6
Assess vocational skills, knowledge and understanding	3	6
Delivering employability skills	4	6
Deliver and prepare resources for learning and development	4	6
Equality and diversity	4	6
Evaluating learning programmes	4	3
Inclusive practice	4	15
Internally assure the quality of assessment	4	6
Preparing for the coaching role	4	3
Preparing for the mentoring role	4	3
Quality procedures within education and training	4	6
Understand the principles and practices of internally assuring the quality of assessment	4	6
Working with the 14–19 age range in the learning environment	4	9

The above list includes some of the optional units which are available. The full list can be found in the document *Qualification Guidance for awarding organisations: Level 4 Certificate in Education and Training, available at: www.excellencegateway.org.uk/node/65.*

Teaching practice

As part of the Certificate, you will need to undertake at least 30 hours of teaching practice with learners. Even though you might not feel you are *practising* teaching, you are putting theory into practice each time you are with your learners. You will be observed on at least three separate occasions. However, some optional units have additional observation requirements, for example, the unit *Assess occupational competence in the work environment.* As this unit is also part of the Learning and Development suite of qualifications, further observations will be necessary.

Your observer will be looking to see that you achieve the criteria as stated in the qualification. However, they might also be observing your progress towards meeting certain Ofsted criteria for teachers. Ofsted is the Office for Standards in Education, Children's Services and Skills and they inspect and regulate services which care for children and young people, and those providing education and skills for learners of all ages. If your observer uses the Ofsted grading characteristics, they might give your session a grade of 1, 2, 3 or 4, grade 1 being the highest. Alternatively, they might state that your session was outstanding, good, requires improvement or was inadequate. Whichever method they use, the feedback you receive should be invaluable to help you improve. You can find more information regarding observations and Ofsted grading characteristics in the companion book *Passing Assessments for the Certificate in Education and Training* by Ann Gravells and Susan Simpson.

Teaching is a chance to use your newfound skills and knowledge with your learners. Never be afraid to try something new, or do something differently if it didn't work the first time. No teaching situation is ever the same as you may have different learners on different occasions. What works for one learner or group might not work with another.

The Level 4 Certificate in Education and Training Qualification Guidance states:

An effective teaching practice experience should ideally include:

- *different teaching practice locations/settings/contexts*

- *teaching across more than one level*

- *teaching a variety of learners*

- *teaching individuals and groups*

- *experience of non-teaching roles*

- *gaining subject specialist knowledge through workplace mentoring*

(2013, page 8)

You should aim to meet the above requirements throughout your time taking the Certificate.

Progression

While working towards the Certificate, it would be extremely beneficial for you to have a mentor, someone who can help and support you, not only with teaching skills, but also with your specialist subject knowledge. If you are currently teaching or training, your mentor could observe you and give you developmental feedback as to how you could improve. Conversely, you could observe them to gain useful ideas and tips for delivering your subject based on the approaches they use with their learners.

You will find it a valuable experience to keep a reflective learning journal as you progress through your programme of learning. It is a bit like keeping a diary of what you have learnt and how you have put theory into practice. Reflection is about becoming more self-aware, which should give you increased confidence when teaching and assessing learners. Please see the end of this chapter for more information regarding reflection.

When you are nearing completion of the Certificate, you may find it useful to summarise your learning and create an action plan for your future development. This could be a list of your strengths and achievements so far, aspects you would like to develop or improve, and how you aim to work towards accomplishing them.

After achieving the Level 4 Certificate, you might wish to progress further and work towards a higher level teaching qualification such as the Level 5 Diploma in Education and Training. It is possible to take the Diploma without taking the Certificate first, but this would depend upon how skilled and knowledgeable you are at the time, and the requirements of your job role.

The Diploma's content is the same as the Certificate in Education (or Professional or Postgraduate Certificate in Education (PGCE)) for anyone holding a degree. However, these qualifications are usually accredited via universities rather than an awarding organisation and are at a higher level.

Qualifications and Credit Framework

The QCF is a system for recognising skills and qualifications by awarding credit values to units of qualifications in England and Northern Ireland. The equivalent for Scotland is the SCQF, and for Wales the Credit and Qualifications Framework for Wales (CQFW).

These credit values enable you to see how long it would take an average learner to achieve a unit. For example, the *Understanding roles, responsibilities and relationships in education and training* unit is 3 credits which equates to 30 hours. These hours include *contact time* with a teacher and assessor, and *non-contact time* for individual study and assignment work.

There are three sizes of qualifications on the QCF, each with a title and associated credit values:

- Award (1 to 12 credits)

- Certificate (13 to 36 credits)

- Diploma (37 credits or more)

All qualifications on the QCF use one of the above words in their title, for example, the *Level 2 Certificate in Women's Hairdressing*, the *Level 3 Award in Customer Service,* or the *Level 5 Diploma in Education and Training*. The level of the qualification defines how difficult it is to achieve and the credit value defines how long it will take to achieve.

You don't have to start with an Award, progress to a Certificate and then to a Diploma as all subjects are different. The terms Award, Certificate and Diploma relate to how *big* the qualification is (i.e. its size), which is based on the total number of credits. For example, a Diploma with 75 credits would equate to 750 hours of learning and is therefore a bigger qualification than a Certificate with 36 credits and 360 hours of learning.

The QCF in England and Northern Ireland has nine levels; ranging from an Entry level through to level 8, for example, level 3 would be easier to achieve than level 5.

A rough comparison of the levels to other qualifications is:

1. GCSEs (grades D–G)

2. GCSEs (grade A*–C), Intermediate Apprenticeship

3. Advanced level (A level), Advanced Apprenticeship

4. Vocational Qualification level 4, Higher Apprenticeship

5. Vocational Qualification level 5, Foundation Degree

6. Bachelor's Degree

7. Master's Degree, Postgraduate Certificate and Diploma

8. Doctor of Philosophy (DPhil or PhD)

The SCQF in Scotland has 12 levels instead of 8; you can see these at the weblink shortcut: http://tinyurl.com/pvexa8c

It is anticipated there will be a European framework and eventually a worldwide framework. This will make the recognition of qualifications much easier for people applying for jobs internationally or when moving between countries.

The minimum core

The minimum core consists of four elements: literacy, language, numeracy and information and communication technology (ICT). As part of your teaching role you should be able to demonstrate these elements to at least level 2. This will enable you to support your learners with English, maths and ICT (known as functional skills). It will also ensure you teach your area of specialism as effectively as possible.

The minimum core aims to:

- promote an understanding that underpinning literacy, language, numeracy and ICT skills may be needed for learners to succeed and achieve their chosen qualification

- encourage the development of inclusive practices to address the literacy, language, numeracy and ICT needs of learners

- raise awareness of the benefits to learners of developing embedded approaches to teaching, learning and assessment of English, maths and ICT

- provide signposts to useful materials which will support collaborative working with specialist teachers of literacy, language, numeracy and ICT in understanding how to integrate these skills within other areas of specialism (LLUK, 2007, page 6)

The four elements of the minimum core are integrated into the mandatory units of the Certificate which are at level 4. You won't want to make mistakes in front of your learners as this will give a bad impression; therefore you need to demonstrate your competence in the four elements when you are with your learners.

> The introduction of the minimum core will provide a foundation upon which all teachers can develop their own skills as well as their ability to identify when it is appropriate to work with subject specialists.

> (Skills for Business, 2007 [revised 2013], page 4)

Developing and improving your skills in the four elements will enable you to consider how to best teach your subject in ways that also support the development of your learners' functional skills. You need to be prepared to meet the needs of your learners whose levels of literacy, language, numeracy and ICT skills might otherwise jeopardise or hinder their learning. You therefore need to ensure your own skills are adequate, to help improve those of your learners. For example, you might encourage your learners to use the internet as a research tool, but not feel confident about using it yourself. Have a look at Appendices 6, 7 and 8 at the back of this book to familiarise yourself with the *personal skills* in each element. Personal skills are those you will be required to demonstrate as part of your teaching practice, and will enable you to effectively fulfil your role as a professional teacher. The knowledge and understanding required to demonstrate your competence in the personal skills will be taught as part of the Certificate programme and are often referred to as

Part A, with the personal skills referred to as *Part B*. This is due to the referencing of the sections in the document within which they are listed.

If you are not competent or confident with the personal skills, you might make errors and not know any different. When planning and delivering your sessions, consider how you will demonstrate the four elements. Also consider which aspects you want your learners to demonstrate, for example, the use of language when they are writing. When reviewing learners' work, you could comment on any errors of spelling, grammar and punctuation to help them improve. This is demonstrating your own skills and also helping your learners to understand any mistakes they have made. If you don't point them out, they might remain unaware of their mistakes.

If you took the Award in Education and Training, you will have already embedded English, maths and ICT skills within your teaching, and will therefore be familiar with enabling your learners to demonstrate these skills.

Some examples of integrating elements of the four skills into your sessions are:

- Literacy – reading, writing, spelling, grammar, punctuation, syntax

- Language – speaking, listening, role play, interviews

- Numeracy – calculations, interpretations, evaluations, measurements

- ICT – online learning, e-learning, word processing, use of a virtual learning environment (VLE), e-mails, using new technology, video conferencing

You might like to take additional learning programmes if, for example, your computer skills need further development or you feel your spelling and grammar need to be improved. When you are teaching, your learners will want to trust and believe you. If you spell words incorrectly in a handout or a presentation, your learners will think the spelling is correct because you are their teacher and they believe what you say and do.

Academic writing, study skills and reflective practice

If you are working towards the Certificate in Education and Training, you may be required to produce written work in an appropriate writing style and with references to quotations from relevant texts, journals, websites and other sources. This section will briefly cover how to do this, as well as how to improve your study skills and reflect upon the effectiveness of your practice. However, you should seek guidance from your assessor beforehand as to how they recommend you approach your work. You wouldn't want to spend a lot of time working on an assignment, only to find out you haven't produced it in the required way. There might be an expected word count for some work; if so, you should aim to be within 10 per cent of this, either above or below the required figure.

Referencing work

Referencing your work is about correctly inserting a quote from, for example, a relevant text, journal or website, into your own writing. You should relate the quote to what you are discussing at the time, for example, stating why you agree or disagree with it. You would then reference it in a particular way so that you are not just copying the work of others, but giving them credit for it. If you are required to do this, you will need to check with your assessor which writing style to use, and whether it is mandatory or optional to use it. The *Harvard* system is the style that is generally used and standardises the approach to writing and referencing. However, other styles could be used within your writing; just make sure you are consistent throughout your work.

It is important to reference your work correctly to:

- acknowledge the work of other writers, authors and theorists

- assist the reader to locate your sources for their own reference, and to confirm they are correct

- avoid plagiarism (i.e. using the work of others without acknowledging it)

- provide evidence of your reading and research

- use existing knowledge and theories to support your work (whether as a direct quote or paraphrased into your own words to validate your opinions)

Referencing a book

When using quotes from different sources, for example, a textbook, you need to insert the author, date of publication and page number after any quotation you have used. The full details of the book can then be included in a reference list at the end of your work.

For example, if you are describing ground rules, you could state:

> Ground rules should be agreed at the start of a new programme. 'Ground rules can be used to create suitable conditions within which learners can safely work and learn' (Gravells, 2013, page 100). It is important to establish these early to ensure the programme runs smoothly. If learners do not feel safe, they might not return again, or their learning could be affected.

Any quote you insert within your text should be within quotation marks, often known as speech marks. The name of the author, the year of publication of the book and the page number should be in brackets directly afterwards. At the end of your work, you should have a reference list in alphabetical order, giving the full details of the book you have quoted from. For example:

Reference list

Gravells, A (2013) *The Award in Education and Training.* London: Learning Matters SAGE.

Before inserting a quote, make sure you understand what the quote means and how it will fit within your writing. It could be that you agree with what the author has said and it supports what you are saying, or it could be that you totally disagree with it. If so, explain *why* you agree or disagree, along with what your point of view is and how it relates to your specialist subject.

Throughout your writing, you should refer to different sources and authors where applicable. The organisation with whom you are taking the Certificate should be able to give you advice on using quotes and referencing your work, and provide you with a reading list of relevant textbooks.

Reading more than one book will help you to gain the perspectives of different authors. You don't have to read the book fully; you can just locate relevant topics, usually by referring to the index at the back. If you have a look at the index at the back of this book, you will see all the topics are listed alphabetically, making it easy for you to locate relevant page numbers. This is useful if you want to dip into the book rather than read it cover to cover.

If the quote is longer than three lines of text, indent the paragraph from both margins. Three dots ... can be used to indicate words you have left out. Always copy the words and punctuation as they are in the original, even if there are mistakes. You can add [sic] after the mistake as this denotes you are aware of it, but are not changing it as that is the way it was originally written. Long quotes are always in single line spacing, quotes of three lines or less can be in the line spacing of the main text, for example, double line spacing.

If a quote is not used, but the author is still referred to, it will probably look like this:

Gravells (2013) advocates the use of ground rules with learners.

Again, the full book details will go in the reference list at the end.

Referencing a website

The quote should be inserted within your writing in a similar way to a textbook quote.

For example:

'There is no one single strategy for creating assessments suitable for learners who have difficulty communicating with others, due to the wide range of conditions and impairments that might lead to such a difficulty' (LSIS, 2012).

It would look like this in your reference list, along with the date you accessed it:

Learning and Skills Information Service (2012) *Assessment.* Available at: www.excellence-gateway.org.uk/node/320 (accessed 10.12.13).

The date you accessed it is important, as web pages often change or are removed.

Referencing an online report

The quote should be inserted within your writing in the same way as a textbook quote.

For example:

'Teacher educators have traditionally struggled with convincing learners to work on their portfolios, competing against more traditional assessment demands and the habit of putting the portfolio together at the last minute' (Hopper and Sanford, 2010, page 4).

It would look like this in your reference list, along with the date it was accessed:

Hopper, T and Sanford, K (2010) Starting a program-wide ePortfolio practice in teacher education: Resistance, support and renewal. *Teacher Education Quarterly*, Special Online Edition. Available at:

www.teqjournal.org/onlineissue/PDFFlash/HopperSanfordManuscript/fscommand/
Hopper_Sanford.pdf (accessed 10.12.13).

There are other ways of referencing different sources of information and you might like to obtain further information from relevant textbooks or websites to help you.

Study skills

When working towards the Certificate, you will need to be prepared to study in your own time (known as *non-contact time*) with activities such as research, reading relevant text-books and completing assessment activities. If you can, set aside time in a place where you won't be disturbed so that you can focus on what is required. If you are interrupted, dis-tracted, hungry or thirsty when studying, you probably won't be able to concentrate well. You will need to keep to any deadlines or target dates for submitting your assessments. Using a diary to forward plan when these need to be submitted will help when planning your time.

To help you study effectively, it is useful to know the best ways in which to learn. You will probably have a particular learning preference, a way that suits you best. For exam-ple, you might like to watch someone perform a task, and then carry it out for yourself, or you might just want to try it out for yourself first. There are several ways of think-ing regarding the ways people learn. A popular method is known by the acronym VARK. This groups people into four styles of learning: **v**isual, **a**ural, **r**ead/write and **k**inaesthetic. However, some might be multi modal, i.e. a mixture of two or more. If you have access to the internet, go to www.vark-learn.com and carry out the short online questionnaire. See what your results are for each of V, A, R and K and read how your preference can help you learn more effectively.

If you are attending a taught programme, it would be useful to make notes during your sessions to which you can refer later. This could be on handouts given by your teacher, or hard copies of a presentation. If you have a laptop or tablet, you could make notes electronically during the session (providing this is acceptable). When taking notes, try to remain focused, otherwise you might miss something. You could write quickly by cutting out vowels, for example, *tchr* for *teacher*. You could also cut out small words such as *an, are, at, is* and *the*. Whichever way you take notes, make sure you will know what they mean when you look back at them. If you are reading handouts, textbooks and/or journals, you might like to use a highlighter pen or underline certain key words, or use sticky notes to draw attention to key points. You could also make notes in the margins, but only do this on your own materials, not on ones borrowed from others or libraries.

During attended programmes, you might be required to take part in group work or give short presentations to your peers. Use this as an opportunity to work with others and to gain new skills and knowledge. If you are taking the Certificate via an online or distance learning programme, you might not meet your teacher or your peers in person. However, you should be able to communicate with them either by e-mail or through an internet-based system.

You might need support to help you improve aspects such as English, maths and com-puter skills. This might be available at the organisation where you are taking the Certificate, or you could attend other relevant programmes. There are some free online programmes available that you could access which are listed at the end of this chapter. If you don't have access to a computer at home, you could use one at a local library or internet cafe. If you are not very confident about using a computer yet, there are often free programmes you could take to help you, or you could ask for help from the organisation where you are taking the Certificate.

If you are unsure of anything while you are studying, or have any concerns, don't be afraid to ask for help. It is best that you get clarification prior to submitting any work for assessment, in case you have misinterpreted something.

Although this is a very brief guide to study skills, you might like to obtain further information from relevant textbooks or websites, some of which are listed at the end of the chapter.

Reflective practice

Reflection is a way of reviewing your own progress, which is often just your thoughts (which can be positive or negative) but can take into account feedback you have received from others. It is useful to maintain a reflective learning journal, a diary or a blog to note critical events; you can then refer to this when planning your future development and preparing your sessions. Reflecting upon the effectiveness of your practice is part of the four mandatory units of the Certificate which are at level 4. You will therefore need to keep evidence of your reflections throughout your time taking the qualification.

Reflection is about becoming more self-aware, which should give you increased confidence and improve the links between the theory and practice of teaching, learning and assessment.

A straightforward method of reflection is to have the *experience*, then *describe* it, *analyse* it and *revise* it (EDAR). This method incorporates the *who, what, when, where, why* and *how* approach (WWWWWH) and should help you consider ways of changing and/or improving.

Experience ⟶ Describe ⟶ Analyse ⟶ Revise

EDAR

- *Experience* – a significant event or incident you would like to change or improve

- *Describe* – aspects such as *who* was involved, *what* happened, *when* it happened and *where* it happened

- *Analyse* – consider the experience more deeply and ask yourself *how* it happened and *why* it happened

- *Revise* – think about how you would do it differently if it happened again and then try this out if you have the opportunity (Gravells, 2013, page 186)

Self-reflection should become a part of your everyday activities, enabling you to analyse and focus on things in greater detail. All reflection should lead to an improvement in practice; however, there may be events you would not want to change or improve as you felt they went well. If this is the case, reflect as to *why* they went well and use these methods in future sessions. If you are not able to write a reflective learning journal, mentally run through the EDAR points in your head when you have time. As you become more experienced at reflective practice, you will see how you can improve and develop further. The process of self-reflection and your own further development should help improve the quality of the service you give your learners. Reflection is covered in more detail throughout the other chapters of this book.

Historical perspective of the sector

You will experience perpetual change when working within the Further Education and Skills Sector. This will be regarding not only your job role, but also changes due to local and government initiatives and policies, funding, legislation and qualification revisions. The sector is also influenced by the requirements of employers, for example, those with skills shortages.

Historically, unlike teachers in schools, teachers in the Further Education and Skills Sector did not require a teaching qualification. In the 1960s the PGCE became the main teacher training qualification; however, this was primarily for teachers in schools. It was often taken at a teacher training college or university after achieving a degree. The Certificate in Education (Cert Ed) was available for those who did not hold a degree. It was followed in the 1980s by a work-based National Vocational Qualification (NVQ) for those who trained others in the workplace. Throughout this time, the Certificate in Education was still available and other teaching qualifications with different titles also became available, but none were government regulated and there was still no requirement for teachers of adults to gain a qualification.

This section will give you a brief chronological historical perspective regarding teacher training in England. There are slight differences for the other United Kingdom (UK) countries.

Table 0.2 Historical perspective of the sector

1970s	The Further Education Teachers' Certificate (FETC) became available, aimed at teachers of post-compulsory ages. This qualification was not mandatory.
1986	The National Council for Vocational Qualifications (NCVQ) was established as a result of a White Paper *Working Together – Education and Training* (1986) to co-ordinate training, education and qualifications for all people to ensure a competent workforce in Britain for the twenty-first century. NCVQ stated that FE teachers involved with the delivery and assessment of NVQs should be qualified.
1990	The Training and Development Lead Body (TDLB) was established to write standards for various teaching roles.
1992	The Further Education Unit (FEU) completed trials of the TDLB standards and recommended they should be used as a basis for teacher training.
1999	The TDLB standards were revised and incorporated into the Further Education National Training Organisation (FENTO) standards.
2000	The Department for Education and Employment (DfEE) issued a consultation paper *Compulsory Teaching Qualifications for Teachers in Further Education*.

(Continued)

Table 0.2 (Continued)

2001	It became mandatory for all further education (FE) teachers in England and Wales to work towards a teaching qualification, regardless of their job role.
2002	The Department for Education and Skills (DfES) published *Success for all – reforming further education and training*. This set out targets for all full-time and part-time FE teachers to be qualified and emphasised the importance of good specialist subject knowledge.
2003	An Ofsted survey, *The initial training of further education teachers*, found the current system of FE teacher training did not provide a satisfactory foundation of professional development for teachers. It recommended the standards would benefit from substantial revision.
2003	*The future of initial teacher education for the learning and skills sector – an agenda for reform – a consultative paper* triggered considerable discussion about a suitable model of teacher training to supply effective teachers in the diverse and developing sector.
2004	Lifelong Learning UK (LLUK) was established. They produced a proposal for developing a *threshold* qualification for teachers to address the DfES strategy in *Equipping our Teachers for the Future* (2004). LLUK had a remit to develop a Preparing to Teach in the Lifelong Learning Sector (PTLLS) Award by May 2006, ready for piloting in September 2006. Teachers would then progress to the Certificate in Teaching in the Lifelong Learning Sector (CTLLS) or the Diploma in Teaching in the Lifelong Learning Sector (DTLLS) depending upon their job role. Standards Verification UK (SVUK), a subsidiary of LLUK, were given the remit of endorsing all Initial Teacher Training (ITT) qualifications to ensure they met the requirements of the QCF.
2004	*A Licence to Practise* (LLUK) identified the components of a licence to teach for qualified teachers in the learning and skills sector.
2006	New Overarching Professional Standards for Teachers, Tutors and Trainers in the Lifelong Learning Sector came into effect, which replaced the FENTO standards.
2006/2007	PTLLS, CTLLS and DTLLS became available.
2007	The Further Education Teachers' Qualifications (England) Regulations 2007 were introduced for new teachers. Existing teachers who were already suitably qualified prior to the 2007 Regulations, and who fulfilled the FENTO requirements, did not need to take the new qualifications. New teachers must achieve Associate Teacher Learning and Skills (ATLS) or Qualified Teacher Learning and Skills (QTLS) status within five years of commencement of their role. The Further Education Teachers' Continuing Professional Development [CPD] and Registration (England) Regulations 2007 were introduced. This required compulsory registration with the Institute for Learning (IfL) and a declaration of an annual amount of CPD.
2011	The Learning and Skills Improvement Service (LSIS) became responsible for teacher training standards, having taken over from LLUK and SVUK which were no longer operational.

2011	The Wolf Report considered how vocational education for 14–19 year olds could be improved and put forward proposals to recognise QTLS status within schools. Therefore, anyone who held QTLS status should be accepted as having the equivalent to Qualified Teacher Status (QTS) to teach in a school.
2011/2012	PTLLS, CTLLS and DTLLS were revised and updated by LSIS.
2012	The Lingfield inquiry *Professionalism in Further Education Interim Report* recommended the deregulation of both the CPD and the Teaching Regulations, making the suggestion that they had not had the intended impact. The Department for Business, Innovation and Skills (BIS) published a research paper (Number 66), *Evaluation of FE Teachers' Qualifications (England) Regulations 2007*, which gave compelling evidence that the regulations and qualifications did have a positive impact on FE teaching and learning. The Further Education Teachers' Continuing Professional Development and Registration (England) Regulations 2007 were revoked in September.
2013	The Education and Training Foundation was launched in August. LSIS ceased operation. The Further Education Teachers' Qualifications (England) Regulations 2007 were revoked in September. It is now the responsibility of individual employers to decide what qualifications their teachers should hold.
2013/2014	The Level 3 Award, Level 4 Certificate and Level 5 Diploma in Education and Training became available.

Maintaining CPD is still good practice, as is holding a teaching qualification and registering with a professional body. This shows a commitment to the profession and will hopefully have a positive impact upon the teaching, learning and assessment process. The current teaching qualifications include the PGCE and the Certificate in Education, along with the Level 3 Award, the Level 4 Certificate and the Level 5 Diploma in Education and Training.

The Education and Training Foundation

The Education and Training Foundation came into being in September 2013 in the UK. The Foundation was set up to improve professionalism and standards in the Further Education and Skills Sector and is funded by the Department for Business, Innovation and Skills (BIS).

The Foundation sets the professional standards and provides support to ensure learners benefit from a well-qualified, effective and up-to-date professional workforce supported by good leadership, management and governance.

Although the Foundation is funded by BIS, it is *owned* by the Association of Colleges (AoC), Association of Employment and Learning Providers (AELP) and the Association of Adult Education and Training Organisations (known as Holex).

Educational abbreviations and acronyms

All working environments seem to use abbreviations and acronyms at some point. Education is no different and the ones used seem to be continually updated and added to.

Table 0.3 Educational abbreviations and acronyms

ACL	Adult and Community Learning
ADD	Attention Deficit Disorder
AET	Award in Education and Training
ADHD	Attention Deficit and Hyperactivity Disorder
ADS	Adult Dyslexia Support
AELP	Association of Employment and Learning Providers
AI	Awarding Institution
AO	Awarding Organisation
AoC	Association of Colleges
ASD	Autism Spectrum Disorder
ATL	Association of Teachers and Lecturers
ATLS	Associate Teacher Learning and Skills
BEd	Bachelor of Education
BIS	Department for Business, Innovation and Skills
BME	Black and Minority Ethnic
BYOD	Bring your own device
CCEA	Council for the Curriculum, Examinations and Assessment (Northern Ireland)
CET	Certificate in Education and Training
CETT	Centre for Excellence in Teacher Training
Cert Ed	Certificate in Education
CIF	Common Inspection Framework
CL	Community Learning
CLA	Copyright Licensing Authority
COSHH	Control of Substances Hazardous to Health
CPD	Continuing Professional Development
CQFW	Credit and Qualification Framework for Wales
CRB	Criminal Records Bureau
DBS	Disclosure and Barring Service
DCELLS	Department for Children, Education, Lifelong Learning and Skills (Wales)
DfES	Department for Education and Skills
DET	Diploma in Education and Training
DSO	Designated Safeguarding Officer
E&D	Equality and Diversity
EBD	Emotional and Behavioural Difficulties
ECDL	European Computer Driving Licence
EDAR	Experience, Describe, Analyse and Revise
EDIP	Explain, Demonstrate, Imitate and Practice
EFA	Education Funding Agency
EI	Emotional Intelligence
EHRC	Equality and Human Rights Commission
EQA	External Quality Assurance
ESOL	English for Speakers of Other Languages
ETF	Education and Training Foundation
FAQs	Frequently Asked Questions
FE	Further Education
FHE	Further and Higher Education
GCSE	General Certificate of Secondary Education
GLH	Guided Learning Hours
H&S	Health and Safety
HEA	Higher Education Academy
HEI	Higher Education Institute
HSE	Health and Safety Executive
IAG	Information, Advice and Guidance
IAP	Individual Action Plan
ICT	Information and Communication Technology
IfL	Institute for Learning
IIP	Investors in People
ILA	Individual Learning Account
ILP	Individual Learning Plan
ILT	Information and Learning Technology
IT	Information Technology
ITE	Initial Teacher Education

ITP	Independent Training Provider
ISA	Independent Safeguarding Authority
ITT	Initial Teacher/Trainer Training
IQ	Intelligence Quotient
IQA	Internal Quality Assurance
IWB	Interactive Whiteboard
LA	Local Authority
LAR	Learner Achievement Record
LDD	Learning Difficulties and/or Disabilities
LLUK	Lifelong Learning UK (no longer operational)
LRC	Learning Resource Centre
LSA	Learning Support Assistant
LSIS	Learning and Skills Improvement Service (no longer operational)
LSCB	Local Safeguarding Children Board
MLD	Moderate Learning Difficulties
NEET	Not in Education, Employment or Training
NIACE	National Institute of Adult Continuing Education
NLH	Notional Learning Hours
NOS	National Occupational Standards
NQT	Newly Qualified Teacher
NRDC	National Research and Development Centre for adult literacy and numeracy
NTA	Non-teaching Assistant
NVQ	National Vocational Qualification
Ofqual	Office of Qualifications and Examinations Regulation
Ofsted	Office for Standards in Education, Children's Services and Skills
PAT	Portable Appliance Testing
PCET	Post Compulsory Education and Training
PGCE	Post Graduate Certificate in Education
PLTS	Personal Learning and Thinking Skills
POCA	Protection of Children Act (1999)
PPP	Pose, Pause, Pick
PSHE	Personal, Social and Health Education
QCF	Qualifications and Credit Framework
QTLS	Qualified Teacher Learning and Skills
QTS	Qualified Teacher Status (schools)
RARPA	Recognising and Recording Progress and Achievement
RLJ	Reflective Learning Journal
RPL	Recognition of Prior Learning
RWE	Realistic Working Environment
SEAL	Social and Emotional Aspects of Learning
SCN	Scottish Candidate Number
SCQF	Scottish Credit and Qualifications Framework
SFA	Skills Funding Agency
SL	Student Loan
SLC	Subject Learning Coach
SMART	Specific, Measurable, Achievable, Relevant and Timebound
SoW	Scheme of Work
SP	Session Plan
SSB	Standard Setting Body
SSC	Sector Skills Council
SWOT	Strengths, Weaknesses, Opportunities and Threats
TA	Transactional Analysis
T&L	Teaching and Learning
TAQA	Training, Assessment and Quality Assurance
UCU	University and College Union
ULN	Unique Learner Number
VACSR	Valid, Authentic, Current, Sufficient and Reliable
VARK	Visual, Aural, Read/write and Kinaesthetic
VB	Vetting and Barring
VLE	Virtual Learning Environment
WBL	Work Based Learning
WEA	Workers' Educational Association
WWWWWWH	Who, What, When, Where, Why and How

Throughout this book, the first occurrence of any acronym in each chapter will always be in full, followed by the acronym in brackets. Table 0.3 on pages 18 and 19 lists most of those you will come across in your role as a teacher or trainer.

Summary

In this chapter you have learnt about:

- *the structure of the book and how to use it*
- *teaching in the Further Education and Skills Sector*
- *the Certificate in Education and Training*
- *the minimum core*
- *writing, study skills and reflective practice*
- *the historical perspective of the sector*
- *educational abbreviations and acronyms*

Theory focus

References and further information

Appleyard, N and Appleyard, K (2009) *The Minimum Core for Language and Literacy*. London: Learning Matters SAGE.

BIS (2007) *Evaluation of FE Teachers' Qualifications (England) Regulations 2007*. London: Department for Business, Innovation and Skills.

Castle, P and Buckler, S (2009) *How to be a Successful Teacher*. London: SAGE Publications Ltd.

Clark, A (2009) *The Minimum Core for Information and Communication Technology*. London: Learning Matters SAGE.

Clarke, C (2002) *Success For All – Reforming Education and Training – Our Vision for the Future*. London: DFES.

Directorate of Learning Resources (2010) *Harvard Referencing: Student Style Guide*. Sunderland: COSC Press.

DfE (2011) *Review of Vocational Education – The Wolf Report*. DFE-00031-2011.

DfES (1986) *Working Together: Education and Training*, White Paper. London: HMSO.

DfES (2003) *The future of initial teacher education for the learning and skills sector – an agenda for reform – a consultative paper*. London: DfES.

DfES (2004) *Equipping our teachers for the future: Reforming initial teacher training for the learning and skills sector*. London: DfES Standards Unit.

DfES (2005) FE White Paper *Raising Skills, Improving Life Chances*. London: DfES.

FENTO (1999) *Standards for teaching and supporting learning in further education in England and Wales*. FENTO.

Fisher et al. (2011) *Teaching in Lifelong Learning: A Guide to Theory and Practice*. Oxford: Oxford University Press.

Gravells, A (2013) *The Award in Education and Training*. London: Learning Matters SAGE.

Gravells, A and Simpson, S (2014) *Passing Assessments for the Certificate in Education and Training*. London: Learning Matters SAGE.

Gravells, J and Wallace, S (2013) *The A–Z Guide to Working in Further Education*. Northwich: Critical Publishing Ltd.

IfL (2008) *Code of Professional Practice: Raising concerns about IfL members*. London: Institute for Learning.

Lingfield (2012a) *Professionalism in Further Education – Interim Report*. London: BIS.

Lingfield (2012b) *Professionalism in Further Education – Final Report*. London: BIS.

LLUK (2006) *New Overarching Professional Standards for Teachers, Tutors and Trainers in the Lifelong Learning Sector*. London: LLUK.

LLUK (2007) *Inclusive learning approaches for literacy, language, numeracy and ICT*. London: LLUK.

LSIS (2007, revised 2013) *Addressing literacy, language, numeracy and ICT needs in education and training: Defining the minimum core of teachers' knowledge, understanding and personal skills – A guide for initial teacher education programmes*. Coventry: LSIS.

LSIS (2013) *Level 4 Certificate in Education and Training Qualification Guidance*. Coventry: Learning and Skills Information Service.

Machin et al. (2013) *A Complete Guide to the Level 4 Certificate in Education and Training*. Northwich: Critical Publishing Ltd.

Ofsted (2003) *The initial training of further education teachers: A survey*. London: HMI. 1762.

Ofsted (2004) *Framework for the Inspection of Initial Training of Further Education Teachers*. London: HMI. 2274.

Ofsted (2011) *The Framework for the Inspection of Initial Teacher Education 2012*. Manchester: Ofsted.

Ofsted (2012) *Common Inspection Framework for Further Education and Skills*. Manchester: Ofsted.

Ofsted (2012) *Handbook for the Inspection of Further Education and Skills*. Manchester: Ofsted.

Ofsted (2012) *Initial Teacher Education (ITE) Inspection Handbook*. Manchester: Ofsted.

Ofsted (2012) *The Initial Training of Further Education and Skills Teachers: Findings from 2011–2012 inspections of courses leading to awarding body qualifications*. Manchester: Ofsted.

Pears, R and Shields, G (2010) *Cite them right: The essential referencing guide*. Basingstoke: Palgrave Macmillan.

Peart, S (2009) *The Minimum Core for Numeracy*. London: Learning Matters SAGE.

Roffey-Barentsen, J and Malthouse, R (2013) *Reflective Practice in Education and Training* (2nd edn). London: Learning Matters SAGE.

Rushton, I and Suter, M (2012) *Reflective Practice for Teaching in Lifelong Learning*. Maidenhead: OU Press.

Skills for Business (2007) *Inclusive learning approaches for literacy, language, numeracy and ICT: Companion Guide to the Minimum Core*. Nottingham: DfES Publications.

Wallace, S (2011) *Teaching, Tutoring and Training in the Lifelong Learning Sector* (4th edn). London: Learning Matters SAGE.

Websites

Ann Gravells (information and resources) – www.anngravells.co.uk

Credit and Qualification Framework for Wales (CQFW) – www.cqfw.org

Department for Business, Innovation and Skills – www.bis.gov.uk

Education and Training Foundation – www.et-foundation.co.uk

English and Maths free support – www.move-on.org.uk

FE Advice – www.feadvice.org.uk/next-steps

Institute for Learning – www.ifl.ac.uk

Learning preference questionnaire – www.vark-learn.com

LLUK (2006) *New Overarching Professional Standards for Teachers, Tutors and Trainers in the Lifelong Learning Sector.* London: LLUK – http://tinyurl.com/b3k2r4o

Minimum Core – Inclusive learning approaches for literacy, language, numeracy and ICT (2007) – www.excellencegateway.org.uk/node/12020

Minimum Core Standards – http://repository.excellencegateway.org.uk/fedora/objects/import-pdf:93/datastreams/PDF/content

National Institute of Adult Continuing Education – www.niace.org.uk

Observations of teaching and learning – www.excellencegateway.org.uk/page.aspx?o=128948

Ofqual – www.ofqual.gov.uk

Ofsted – www.ofsted.gov.uk

Optional units for the Certificate in Education and Training – www.excellencegateway.org.uk/node/27271

Post Compulsory Education and Training Network – www.pcet.net

Qualifications and Credit Framework (QCF) – www.ofqual.gov.uk/qualifications-and-assessments/qualification-frameworks/

Scottish Credit and Qualifications Framework (SCQF) – www.scqf.org.uk

Sector Skills Councils – www.sscalliance.org

1 ROLES, RESPONSIBILITIES AND RELATIONSHIPS

In this chapter you will learn about:

- roles, responsibilities and relationships
- maintaining a safe and supportive learning environment
- promoting appropriate behaviour and respect
- working with other professionals
- legislation, regulatory requirements and codes of practice
- promoting equality and valuing diversity
- continuing professional development

There are activities and examples to encourage you to reflect on the above which will help you develop and enhance your understanding of the roles, responsibilities and relationships of teaching. If you are fairly new to teaching, you will benefit from reading *The Award in Education and Training* (2013) by Ann Gravells which will introduce you to the full role of teaching and training in the Further Education and Skills Sector.

At the end of each section within the chapter are extension activities to stretch and challenge your knowledge and understanding. A list of useful references, further information and website links can be found at the end of the chapter in case you would like to research the topics further.

At the end of the chapter is a cross-referencing grid showing how the chapter's contents relate to the units of the Certificate in Education and Training, and the Professional Standards for Teachers and Trainers in England.

Roles, responsibilities and relationships

Your main role should be to teach or provide training in your subject in a way which actively involves and engages your learners during every session, whether this is in the workplace, a college or other training environment. However, it is not just about *teaching and training*; it is about the *learning* that takes place as a result. You can teach as much as you wish, but if learning is not taking place then your teaching has not been successful. Most careers are quite challenging and demanding, and the role of a teacher or trainer is no exception to this. However, the role can be very rewarding, particularly when you see your learners' progress, achievements and success, which is a direct result of your contribution and support. This will present itself in very diverse and exciting ways depending upon your learners.

If you are new to teaching, you may find you are teaching in the same way you were taught at school, college or university, or in the way you prefer to learn. You won't yet know all the other approaches, methods and activities you could use to make learning interesting and engaging.

Sue Crowley of the Institute for Learning (IfL) stated:

> *Often new teachers teach as they were taught, then perhaps as they would like to have been taught, and finally they realise different people learn in different ways and a wider spectrum of teaching and learning approaches are needed and available.*

(LSIS, 2009, page 8)

As you become more experienced, your confidence will grow and you will be able to experiment with different approaches, as not everything you do will suit all your learners. When performing your role, you should act in a professional manner and give a good impression to your learners. This includes not getting too personal with your learners, maintaining good time-keeping, and dressing and behaving appropriately towards your learners and others.

Activity

Define the word professional and explain how acting in a professional way is important when you are with learners. Compare your response to a dictionary definition. Explain the professional roles and responsibilities you will carry out in an education and training context.

Being professional is about having the correct skills, knowledge and understanding to perform your role, and carrying out that role with the right attitudes, values, behaviours and beliefs.

The following is a list of examples of roles and responsibilities you might undertake, in alphabetical order. If there is anything you are unsure of at the moment, don't worry. As you progress through the chapters in this book it should all become clearer.

- acting professionally and with integrity

- attending meetings

- carrying out relevant administrative and monitoring requirements

- communicating appropriately and effectively with learners and others

- completing attendance records/registers (which is a legal requirement for many organisations)

- complying with relevant regulatory requirements, legislation, policies and procedures, and codes of practice
- creating high quality teaching, learning and assessment materials which are appropriate to your subject and learners
- differentiating teaching, learning and assessment approaches and materials
- ensuring assessment decisions are valid, reliable, fair and ethical
- ensuring learners are on the right programme at the right level
- establishing ground rules
- following health and safety, equality and diversity, and safeguarding requirements
- giving appropriate information, advice and guidance where necessary
- helping learners develop their English, maths, and information and communication technology (ICT) skills
- incorporating new technology where possible
- maintaining a safe, positive and accessible learning environment for learners and others
- maintaining records and confidentiality of such
- partaking in quality assurance processes
- promoting appropriate behaviour and respect for others
- referring learners to other people or agencies when necessary
- reflecting on own practice and partaking in continuing professional development (CPD)
- standardising practice with others
- teaching, training and assessing in an inclusive, engaging and motivating way
- using a variety of assessment types and methods to assess progress formally and informally, and giving feedback to learners (verbal and written)
- using appropriate equipment and resources
- using icebreakers and energisers effectively

When you are with your learners, you should always use clear language at an appropriate level and in terms they will understand. Although you know what you are talking about, this might be the first time your learners have heard it, therefore never be afraid of repeating yourself or going over aspects again. Think back to when you learnt something for the first time. Perhaps you didn't take it all in at once, and you need to know this will be the same for your own learners.

Petty states: *It is what the learner does, not what the teacher does, that creates learning, so the task is the key* (2009, page 587). You need to involve your learners by making your sessions and the learner tasks interesting, therefore engaging them in the subject, keeping them motivated and leaving them wanting to learn more. Ideally, you should be involved with all aspects from when your learners apply to take the programme, to when they leave. Your job role as a teacher or trainer will depend upon the subject you are delivering, i.e. whether it is a short event, a longer programme or a qualification containing several units. It will also depend upon the age and experience of your learners, the environment you are in and your organisation's requirements.

Becoming a good teacher or trainer includes being enthusiastic and passionate about your subject, being approachable, and taking pride in your work, which should all be conveyed to your learners when you are with them.

Example

Vic, a new trainer, always arrives early to his sessions. He ensures the training room is tidy and organises the furniture in a way that encourages communication between learners. He delivers his subject with passion and enthusiasm. He uses lots of examples and anecdotes to relate his subject to real life. He includes all his learners by addressing them personally and asking questions, yet he remains fair with the support and advice he gives. He always tidies up afterwards and offers to e-mail handouts and additional learning materials if required. His learners see how conscientious and professional Vic is and they begin to match this by being early, being polite and submitting work on time.

A good first impression will help you establish a positive working relationship with your learners. The way you dress, act, respond to questions and offer support will also influence your learners. They don't need to know anything personal about you, but they will probably make assumptions about you. If asked personal questions, try not to give out any information: by remaining professional, and not becoming too friendly, you should retain their respect. Most teachers are on first name terms with their learners. However, you will need to decide what is appropriate to your situation and the age range of your learners. Establishing routines will help your sessions flow smoothly, for example, always starting on time, setting and keeping to time limits for activities and breaks, and finishing on time.

The teaching, learning and assessment cycle

The teaching, learning and assessment cycle is a systematic process which helps ensure your learners have a positive experience and are able to achieve their goals. The process can start at any stage of the cycle and keep on going, however, all stages should be addressed for learning to be effective. Quality assurance should take place continuously to ensure all aspects are being delivered and assessed fairly and accurately, and to ensure learning is taking place.

Your role might follow the cycle, which includes aspects of quality assurance at each stage, and will briefly involve:

- **identifying needs** – finding out what your organisation's, your own, and your potential learners' needs are; finding out why learners are taking the programme and what their expectations are; carrying out initial and diagnostic assessments; agreeing individual learning plans; ensuring learners are capable of progressing to their chosen destination

- **planning learning** – preparing schemes of work, teaching and learning plans, and materials to ensure you cover the requirements of the programme; liaising with others as necessary

- **facilitating learning** – teaching, training and facilitating learning using a variety of approaches and resources

- **assessing learning** – checking your learners have gained the necessary skills, knowledge, understanding and behaviours at all stages throughout their time with you, using formal and informal types and methods of assessment

- **evaluating learning** – obtaining feedback from others; evaluating your role and all aspects involved with the teaching, learning and assessment process in order to make improvements for the future; evaluation could also take place after each stage of the cycle

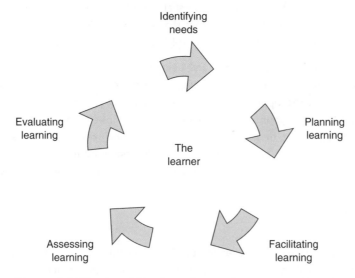

Figure 1.1 The teaching, learning and assessment cycle, focussing upon the learner

Running throughout the cycle is quality assurance. This is a system of monitoring and improving all aspects of teaching which occur with learners throughout their time of training, from when they commence to when they leave. Good practice for all programmes is to include a system of *internal quality assurance*. However, this might be a formal requirement if you are delivering and assessing towards a qualification. This means a colleague at your organisation will monitor and sample aspects of everything you do to ensure you are being fair to all learners, making correct decisions and following the relevant policies and procedures. If you are teaching and assessing a qualification, there might also be an *external quality assurance* system. This involves a person visiting from the organisation which awards the qualification, to ensure all staff are following the requirements correctly.

Most teachers and trainers follow the cycle from beginning to end. However, your job role might not require you to be involved with all aspects. For example, you might not carry out the *identifying needs* stage if other staff within your organisation do this. You will, however, need to liaise with them to obtain the information to help you plan your sessions. You might be training a member of staff in the workplace and only carry out the *planning learning* and *facilitating learning* stages, as someone else might assess their progress. Again, you would need to liaise with whoever else is involved with your learner.

To teach and train effectively involves not only the approaches you use to deliver your subject, i.e. discussions, group work, paired activities, questions and independent learning, but also many other factors that go before and after the taught session. This includes planning logically what you will cover in your sessions, preparing your materials and resources, assessing that learning has taken place, giving feedback, keeping records, and evaluating yourself and the experiences your learners have had. Never underestimate the amount of time you will need to dedicate to the role.

When teaching or training, your personality and mannerisms will be noticed by your learners. You might do things you are not aware of, for example, waving your arms around, clicking a pen or fidgeting. It is really useful to make a visual recording of one of your sessions. You may see things you didn't realise you did or things that you would like to change. If so, make sure you get the permission of your learners and explain that you are doing it to help you improve.

Personal qualities such as arriving early and being organised, and smiling when your learners enter, will help you all relax at the beginning of the session. Using your learners' names when you get the opportunity will make them feel you are getting to know them as individuals. Observing your learners' body language will help you to see if they are not understanding something, or not paying attention. You can then ask a question to bring them back on track. Don't be afraid of regularly recapping points and repeating aspects. Remember, you know your subject, but for your learners it is probably the first time they have seen or heard anything about it.

Boundaries

There are two aspects to boundaries for teachers and trainers: boundaries between your teaching or training role and other professional roles, and other aspects you are *bound by* which might hinder or challenge your role.

- Professional boundaries are those within which you need to work and it is important not to overstep these, for example, by becoming too personal or friendly with your learners. Boundaries are about knowing where your role as a teacher or trainer stops. You should be able to work within the limits of that role, but know that it is okay to ask for help. Don't try to take on too much, or carry out something which is part of someone else's role.

- Other boundaries include the things you are bound by, for example, policies and procedures, the amount of administrative work you are expected to complete, or a lack of funding or resources. These boundaries can often be interpreted as the negative aspects of your roles and responsibilities. However, these are a necessary part of your role, for example, the amount of documentation you need to maintain for audit purposes.

You might have other professional roles besides teaching, for example, you might interview learners and have to decide whether they can attend a programme or not. You might have difficult decisions to make. However, you should always be able to get the support of other staff at your organisation. Never feel you are on your own; find out who can help and advise you. If you make a decision not to accept a learner, you will need to justify your reasons, and make sure you keep records as to why. Records should always be factual and relate to the programme entry requirements. You should find out and follow all relevant organisational policies and procedures.

When you are with learners, you need to act professionally at all times. This includes remaining in control, being fair and ethical, and not demonstrating favouritism towards a particular learner, for example, by giving one more support than the others. You might want to keep in touch with your learners between sessions. Giving them your personal telephone number could be seen as encouraging informal contact, and you may get calls or texts which are not appropriate or relevant. Communication via e-mail would be more appropriate, as long as the tone is kept professional and not overly friendly. During a session, you might not want to take your break with your learners as it might blur the line between your professional role and a personal role. If you are asked to join learners' social networking sites they might see you as more of a friend than a teacher. Always remember that it is unprofessional to use bad language or to let your personal problems affect the performance of your role.

Teaching is not just about your professional role, it is about your professional values too. These values should be based on those of the organisation you work for, and those of any professional associations you belong to, for example, the IfL. *The professional values you hold will not relate exclusively to your teaching. They will inform the way in which you interact with colleagues and other professionals, your engagement with your specialist subject, and your relationship to the institution in which you teach* (Wallace, 2011, page 64).

Extension Activity

What other professional roles, besides teaching or training, do you think you might be required to carry out? What boundaries do you think you might have between these roles and other professional roles? How could you overcome them?

Maintaining a safe and supportive learning environment

You might be teaching in a variety of environments, indoors, outdoors or even as part of an online learning environment. There will be many aspects you will need to consider; which relate to the *physical, social* and *learning* environments. Each has an impact on the others, and all three aspects should be appropriate, accessible, supportive, relevant and safe for the subject you will teach, and for you and your learners (see Table 1.1 on page 30).

You have a duty of care to ensure your learners are able to learn and achieve in a safe and supportive environment, wherever this might be. Safe doesn't just relate to health and safety, but how safe learners feel to express their opinions, and how safe they feel in others' company.

Your learners need to know that their safety is of paramount importance to you and your organisation and that everyone has a responsibility for this. This information can be communicated to your learners in various ways, i.e. through staff and learner handbooks, marketing materials, induction procedures, learner contracts, tutorials, reviews, online and learner focus/involvement groups.

Example

Part of Sheila's job role was to update the organisation's learner handbook each year. Although safety and security was mentioned, she realised there was not enough information which related to how learners can remain safe from aspects such as bullying and harassment. Sheila therefore revised the content to include this. All learners are given a hard copy when they commence and have access to an electronic version.

Table 1.1 Examples of physical, social and learning aspects of the environment

Physical	Social	Learning
Ensure adequate heating, lighting and ventilation	Use a suitable icebreaker to put learners at ease and create a rapport	Have clear aims and objectives/learning outcomes of what will be covered and plan what will take place during each session
Ensure ease of access to all learning areas	Agree ground rules to help promote appropriate behaviour and respect	Engage and motivate learners; give support and encouragement
Ensure the layout of the room, tables and chairs are suitable or adjust if possible (e.g. to ensure all learners can see and hear)	Communicate effectively (speaking, listening, body language, eye contact)	Make the session interesting and relevant; summarise and recap regularly
Ensure toilets and refreshment facilities are accessible	Use paired and group activities; draw on learners' skills, knowledge and experiences	Use a variety of suitable teaching, learning and assessment approaches
Ensure safe use of equipment, materials and resources	Encourage learners to listen to you and each other	Differentiate for individual needs; refer learners elsewhere if necessary
Carry out risk assessments and minimise hazards; know who the first aider is	Use learner names and eye contact; include all learners in activities and when communicating	Assess progress and achievement on an ongoing basis (formally and informally)
Know where fire extinguishers and emergency exits are	Give adequate breaks at appropriate times	Provide ongoing constructive feedback
Make sure the room is tidy before and after use	Challenge inappropriate behaviour	Keep records of what has been taught, and the progress of all learners

Safeguarding

Safeguarding is a term used to refer to the duties and responsibilities that those providing a health, social or education service have to carry out/perform to protect individuals and vulnerable people from harm. Following the publication of the Safeguarding Vulnerable Groups Act in 2006, a vetting and barring scheme was established in autumn 2008. This Act created an Independent Barring Board to take all discretionary decisions on whether individuals should be barred from working with children and/or vulnerable adults. In 2006, the Department for Education and Skills (DfES) produced a document called *Safeguarding Children and Safer Recruitment in Education*. This guidance was aimed at local authorities, schools and further education (FE) colleges in England who are responsible for promoting the welfare of children and young people, up to the age of 18 (age 25 for those with learning difficulties and/or disabilities). Following this, the document *Safer Practice, Safer Learning* (NIACE, 2007) was produced to provide guidance in relation to adults in FE. It recommends that safeguarding duties extend to whole-organisation policies, values and ethos, and include all staff and learners. It is everyone's duty to promote the concepts of the safe learner.

Activity

What do you consider a safe and supportive learning environment to mean? Find out what safeguarding procedures are in place at your organisation. Who would you go to if you had any concerns?

The Department of Health (DoH) (2000) document *No Secrets* specifies a definition of vulnerable adults.

> *A vulnerable adult is defined as a person 'who is or may be in need of community care services by reason of mental or other disability, age or illness; and who is or may be unable to take care of him or herself, or unable to protect him or herself against significant harm or exploitation'.*

(Department of Health, 2000, page 8)

A vulnerable adult can be put at risk of harm through a variety of actions, inadequate policies and procedures, and failures of people to act. There are six types of abuse defined by the Department of Health:

- physical
- sexual
- psychological/emotional

- financial or material
- neglect and acts of omission
- discriminatory

A young person or adult could potentially be the victim of abuse. If you suspect this, it is your duty to ensure that you take proper steps to safeguard your learner. If someone discloses abuse to you, take the disclosure seriously and never dismiss any allegation. An allegation of abuse or neglect may lead to a criminal investigation and asking leading questions or attempting to investigate the allegations yourself may cause problems for any subsequent court proceedings.

Don't make promises regarding confidentiality or offer to give support yourself. Explain to your learner at the outset that you will need to report the disclosure and share the information with your organisation's Safeguarding Officer (if there is a designated one) or person responsible for this (you need to find out who this is). They will, where possible, respect the wishes of the individual; however, information will be shared with external agencies, such as the Local Safeguarding Children Boards (LSCB), where it is judged whether a person is at risk of suffering significant harm. You will probably have to partake in safeguarding training at some point to ensure you are knowledgeable regarding the requirements.

Extension Activity

What issues might your learners encounter in the learning environment and how will you overcome them? Explain how you can maintain a safe and supportive learning environment for your learners.

Promoting appropriate behaviour and respect

Behaviour is all about how you and your learners interact with each other in an acceptable way. Respect is about accepting others for what they are, not being rude to them, or lowering their confidence and self-esteem in any way. Depending upon the age range of your learners, the subject and the environment, you might encounter issues which you will need to deal with straight away. However, it is not just about being *reactive* to a situation; you need to be *proactive* and promote appropriate behaviour and respect whenever possible to stop issues arising in the first place. Having ground rules in place should help avoid any issues.

It would be wonderful if you could get through a session without any issues arising. Usually, changes in behaviour or disruptions occur because a learner doesn't follow the ground rules; for example, their mobile phone rings or they do something other than that which you have asked them to do. If this is the case, politely ask them to stop, and remind them of the ground rules and how they are also disrupting their peers' learning. Ground rules are boundaries and rules to help create suitable conditions within which learners (and you yourself) can safely work and learn.

> Establish mutually agreed rules in the first session. Clear boundaries need to be established and expectations regarding behaviour must be made clear.

(Vizard, 2012, page 21)

Agreeing ground rules during the first session will help ensure an appropriate learning atmosphere and help promote a supportive learning environment. You could agree sanctions for when a ground rule is broken, or rewards for regular good behaviour. However, make sure you are consistent regarding how you apply these, and be consistent and fair to everyone. Your learners need to know what is acceptable and what isn't, and why. Disruption sometimes happens because people are bored, they don't understand what you are saying, their attention span is different to the others, or you are not stretching or challenging them enough. If so, you could use an alternative activity to extend their learning, get them involved with other learners as part of an activity, or have a quick one-to-one chat to find out why they are behaving that way.

You may find it useful to maintain a record of the behaviour of your learners during your sessions to help you prepare for future incidents. For example, do some learners become disruptive after a certain time period has elapsed, when seated in particular combinations with others, when asked to carry out a theory task, or when practical activities are taking place? This information can be useful when planning future sessions, for example, the timing of breaks, the use of energiser activities or planning group work. Behaviour patterns could highlight the need for additional support as disruption could be a way of asking for help.

You should lead by example, model good behaviour, be polite, show respect and say *please* and *thank you* to help encourage this behaviour in your learners.

Ways to demonstrate and promote respect include:

- encouraging trust, honesty, politeness and consideration towards others
- ensuring you are non-judgemental
- demonstrating good practice
- listening to others' points of view
- praising good practice
- treating everyone as an individual
- valuing others' opinions and not imposing your own

Whatever the disruption may be, you need to handle it professionally, i.e. by not becoming emotional and keeping to the facts, to minimise any effect it may have on teaching and learning. Don't just ignore the behaviour; address it immediately. However, with experience, you will realise that some things can be ignored providing this does not affect the safety of your learners, for example, if a learner is attention seeking.

Your learners might not be attending voluntarily, or they may be there for social reasons rather than having an interest in achieving something. They may therefore not be as keen as you would like them to be and you will need to keep them continuously interested and motivated. Try to relate your subject to their interests and/or their personal or working life.

Example

Steve was having problems with a group of 14 learners in the computer suite. Some would talk over him, access the internet and use their mobile phones for social networking. He decided to spend a few minutes at the beginning of the next session asking each learner in turn (in front of the rest of the group) to state

(Continued)

(Continued)

a reason for using a computer that they could relate to their personal or working life. He also asked the group to agree some ground rules which included not accessing social networking sites during sessions. This helped the learners see the relevance of having various computer skills, enabling them to be more focused during the sessions.

You can help maintain motivation and promote good behaviour by including all learners in discussions and activities, keeping your sessions active wherever possible and teaching your subject in an interesting and challenging way. Ultimately, you need to find your own way of dealing with situations based upon your experiences. Don't show favouritism, lose your temper or make any threats. Try to have a positive approach, praise performance and good behaviour, and be consistent and fair to everyone. Most learners respond positively to a well-organised programme taught by an enthusiastic person who has a genuine interest in them and the subject.

Activity

What situations might arise with your learners that could lead to issues with behaviour and respect? Explain the importance of promoting appropriate behaviour and respect for others.

Potential needs of learners

It is difficult to help your learners if they don't tell you about any specific issues, needs or concerns they might have. You could ask if there is anything you could do to help make their learning experience a more positive one, which might also benefit other learners. However, anything you do would have to be reasonable, and not be seen as favouritism by others. Encouraging learners to talk to you when you are on your own at an appropriate time would save your learner any embarrassment they might feel when in front of their peers. Needs and concerns also include barriers or challenges such as a lack of finance, transport issues, childcare concerns, cultural issues, learning difficulties and/or English as a second or other language. Hopefully you will ascertain these during the interview or initial assessment process prior to a learner commencing.

If you can be proactive and notice any potential needs before they become issues, you might be able to alleviate your learners' concerns. Otherwise, you will need to be reactive to the issue and deal with it professionally and sensitively. You could create a *risk register* to document any concerns and/or issues with individual learners. You can update it with any occurrences to keep track of progress before anything serious occurs. However, anything you write could be made available for learners to see if they request it. Your learners may trust you and tell you something confidential; however, you may need to pass this information on to more experienced people, particularly if your learner is vulnerable and/or in need of expert help. Please see Chapter 2 for more detailed information regarding meeting the needs of learners.

Points of referral

You should always refer your learners to an appropriate specialist or agency if you can't deal with an issue yourself. Never feel you have to solve any learner problems yourself and don't get personally involved; always remain professional. You will need to find out what is available internally within your organisation or where you could refer them externally if necessary. You may encounter learners with varying degrees of needs; therefore you should remain impartial, but sensitive. You may feel you can deal with some of these yourself; however, it is best to seek advice or refer your learner to someone else who is an expert and can help.

Table 1.2 Examples of potential needs of learners and possible points of referral

Potential needs of learners	Possible point of referral
• access to, or fear of technology	• local library or internet cafe • specialist colleagues and/or training programmes
• alcohol or substance misuse	• telephone helplines • relevant support agencies
• childcare concerns	• childcare agencies
• death in the family	• bereavement support agencies
• learning difficulty	• specialist people and agencies who can provide relevant support
• emotional or psychological problems	• health centres, general practitioners • other professionals or Samaritans
• English as a second or other language	• interpreters, bilingual staff or other specialist colleagues
• financial issues	• banks, building societies • Citizens Advice Bureau • specialist staff with knowledge of funding, grants and loans
• health concerns	• health centres, general practitioners, hospitals
• limited basic skills such as English and maths	• specialist colleagues • online programmes and training centres
• transport problems	• public transport websites and timetables
• unsure which career path to take	• National Careers Service • specialist staff within the organisation

Extension Activity

Why is it important to identify and meet individual learner needs? Describe the points of referral you could use to meet the potential needs of your learners.

Working with other professionals

There will be other professionals with whom you will need to work or liaise at some point during your teaching or training career. These could include:

- administration staff
- assessors
- budget holders
- caretakers
- cleaners
- co-tutors
- counsellors
- customers
- finance staff
- health and safety officers
- human resources staff
- internal and external quality assurers
- learning support staff

- managers
- other teachers and trainers
- other training providers
- probation officers
- reprographics staff
- safeguarding officers
- social workers
- staff development personnel
- supervisors
- support workers
- technicians
- union staff
- work placement co-ordinators

You will need to find out who these people are and how you can contact them. It would also be useful to understand a little about their job role, how they can support you, and how you can support them. However, don't feel you need to support them too much by carrying out aspects of their role, otherwise you might be blurring the boundary between your own professional role and theirs. Even if you don't always get along with other people you work with, you should always be polite and professional and treat them with respect.

> *Establishing a good working relationship with colleagues is important, not just for your own peace of mind at work but for the student, too. We may not approve of the way a colleague does things, but we can still behave towards him or her with the appropriate social skills of politeness and professional co-operation.*

(Wallace, 2011, page 72)

Examples of working with other professionals might include:

- attending team meetings and contributing towards issues under discussion

- contacting companies to purchase or hire equipment and materials

- communicating with administrative staff to ensure that your learners have been registered with the relevant awarding organisation for a qualification

- getting handouts photocopied by the relevant department to ensure they are ready in time

- liaising with an internal quality assurer to enable them to sample your work, and/or an external quality assurer from an awarding organisation

- liaising with learning support staff, teaching assistants and volunteers

- liaising with the caretaker to ensure the room and/or building is open when you start and secure when you leave

- obtaining technical support when using equipment

- team teaching or co-tutoring with other members of staff, i.e. planning who will do what and when

You should never feel you have to resolve a situation on your own; there should be others who can help when necessary. However, you might be delivering a session in a hired venue or a building away from the main premises, in which case it would be useful to know who you could contact and when they are available. In this situation there should be a lone workers policy for staff in your organisation, designed to support you. There should be support staff within your organisation to help you as necessary with any situations you might come across which are outside of your own responsibilities.

Example

Sarah was due to teach a First Aid session and arrived early to set up the room. She found the computer worked but the interactive whiteboard didn't and there was no internet access. She needed to show a video clip which was only available online. Instead of calling the computer technician, she moved the equipment to check the cables. In doing so, she accidentally broke the internet cable. Had she not overstepped the boundary of her role, she would not have caused further problems.

You might need to liaise with people who are external to your organisation. This might include parents and guardians if you are teaching learners under the age of 19, employers and supervisors if you are training in the workplace, auditors and inspectors if you are assessing qualifications, as well as visitors to your organisation. You should always remain professional when in contact with others and not overstep the boundary of your role or discuss anything confidential. If required by your organisation, you will need to inform reception of their arrival time, perhaps organise parking and refreshments, and be accessible as soon as they arrive. They may need to wear a visitors' badge and sign in and out. If you are ever in doubt about the boundaries of your role, or how you should act towards others, always ask someone within your organisation.

You might have other roles to undertake such as attending promotional events, conferences or visiting learners who are in a work placement. If so, always remember you are representing your organisation, and therefore you must uphold its values and act professionally at all times. If you have attended a relevant event, you might be required to pass on information to your colleagues, either in the form of a report, a meeting or by delivering a training session to the team. You will therefore need to remain focused upon the facts and not let any personal opinions get in the way.

Extension Activity

Who might you need to work or liaise with, both internally and externally to your organisation? Make a list of these, along with contact details for future reference.

Legislation, regulatory requirements and codes of practice

Legislation relates to laws passed by Parliament, regulatory requirements are usually specific to certain industries, and codes of practice vary depending upon the organisation within which you will work. It is important for you to keep up to date with these to ensure you are remaining current with your skills, knowledge and understanding, and with any changes or updates that have taken place.

Legislation

Legislation will differ depending upon the context and environment within which you teach. You need to be aware of the requirements of external bodies and regulators such as Ofsted (in England) who inspect provision, along with awarding organisations who will quality assure their qualifications, and funding agencies who will need data and statistics.

The following information was current at the time of writing. However, you are advised to check for any changes or updates, and whether they are applicable outside England.

Children Act (2004) provided the legal underpinning for the *Every Child Matters: Change for Children* programme. *Well-being* is the term used in the Act to define the five Every Child Matters outcomes:

• be healthy

• stay safe

• enjoy and achieve

• make a positive contribution

• achieve economic well-being

Copyright Designs and Patents Act (1988) relates to the copying, adapting and distributing of materials, which includes computer programs and materials found via the internet. Organisations may have a licence that allows the photocopying of small amounts from books or journals. All copies should have the source acknowledged.

Data Protection Act (1998) made provision for the regulation of the processing of information relating to individuals, including the obtaining, holding, use or disclosure of such information. It was amended in 2003 to include electronic data.

Freedom of Information Act (2000) gives learners the opportunity to request to see the information public bodies hold about them.

Health and Safety at Work etc. Act (1974) imposes obligations on all staff within an organisation commensurate with their role and responsibility. Risk assessments should be carried out where necessary. In the event of an accident, particularly one resulting in death or serious injury, an investigation by the Health and Safety Executive may result in the prosecution of individuals found to be negligent as well as the organisation.

Protection of Children Act (POCA) (1999) was designed to protect children. It gives responsibility to local authorities to make enquiries when anyone contacts them with concerns about child abuse.

Safeguarding Vulnerable Groups Act (2006) introduced a vetting and barring scheme to make decisions about who should be barred from working with children and vulnerable adults. Teachers may need to apply to the Disclosure and Barring Service (DBS) to have a criminal records check. The purpose of the DBS is to help employers prevent unsuitable people from working with children and vulnerable adults.

Welsh Language Act (1993) put the Welsh language on an equal footing with the English language in Wales with regard to the public sector.

Activity

Research what legislation will be applicable to your job role and your specialist subject. How will it impact upon teaching, learning and assessment?

Regulatory requirements

Regulations are often called *rules* and they specify mandatory requirements that must be met.

Public bodies, corporations, agencies and organisations create regulatory requirements which must be followed if they are applicable to your job role. For example, in education one of the regulators is Ofqual which regulates qualifications, examinations and assessments in England, and vocational qualifications in Northern Ireland. Ofqual gives formal recognition to awarding organisations and bodies that deliver and award qualifications. There will also be specific regulations which relate to your specialist subject and you will need to find out what these are.

The following information was current at the time of writing. However, you are advised to check for any changes or updates, and whether they are applicable outside England.

Control of Substances Hazardous to Health (COSHH) Regulations (2002) apply if you work with hazardous materials.

Food Hygiene Regulations (2006) apply to aspects of farming, manufacturing, distributing and retailing food.

Health and Safety (Display Screen Equipment) Regulations (1992) apply to using display screen equipment, for example, computers.

Manual Handling Operation Regulations (1992) relate to hazards of manual handling and risks of injury.

Privacy and Electronic Communications (EC Directive) Regulations 2003 apply to all electronic communications such as e-mail and mobile phone messages.

Reporting of Injuries, Diseases and Dangerous Occurrences (RIDDOR) Regulations (1995) require specified workplace incidents to be reported.

Regulatory Reform (Fire Safety) Order (2005) places the responsibility on individuals within an organisation to carry out risk assessments to identify, manage and reduce the risk of fire.

Codes of Practice

Codes of practice are usually produced by organisations, associations and professional bodies. They can be mandatory or voluntary and you will need to find out which are applicable to your job role. If you belong to any professional associations, they will usually have a code of practice for you to follow, for example, the IfL Code of Professional Practice (2008). There are other professional associations such as the Chartered Institute for Educational Assessors (CIEA), the Institute for Leadership and Management (ILM), and the Institute of Training and Occupational Learning (ITOL) to which you could belong.

In addition, your organisation should have documented codes of practice such as:

- acceptable use of information technology
- behaviour
- code of conduct
- conflict of interest
- disciplinary

- dress
- environmental awareness
- sustainability
- timekeeping

Policies and procedures

There will be organisational policies and procedures to follow covering appeals, complaints, misconduct, plagiarism and risk assessments. You will need to find out where they can be located and read the information they contain, whether hard copy or electronic. If you are employed, you should have received a contract of employment and employee handbook which should include your organisation's policies, along with all codes of practice.

If you are a work-based trainer, you may have to design your training and assessment activities around the company's policies and procedures (sometimes called *method statements* or *work instructions*). These will usually have the relevant legislation such as aspects of health and safety built into them.

Sector Skills Councils and Standard Setting Bodies

There will be an employer-led organisation for your specialist subject that gathers information and labour market intelligence to influence the development of qualifications. These organisations are known as Sector Skills Councils (SSC) or Standard Setting Bodies (SSB). Each represents an area of business or industry, for example, construction, finance, hospitality and information technology. All SSCs are members of the Alliance of Sector Skills Councils and are recognised by government throughout the UK as the independent, employer-led organisations which ensure that the skills system is driven by employers' needs. As a result, they have a major impact on the delivery of publicly and privately funded training throughout the UK. They also state what qualifications and experience teachers and assessors must have (or be working towards) to deliver and assess.

Extension Activity

Summarise the key aspects of legislation, regulatory requirements and codes of practice relevant to your role, responsibilities and specialist subject. Find out who the SSC or SSB is for your specialist subject, and read the requirements regarding the qualifications and experience you must hold or be working towards.

Promoting equality and valuing diversity

Equality is about the rights of learners to have access to, attend and participate in their chosen learning experience. This should be regardless of their age, ability and/or circumstances. Any inequality and discrimination should always be challenged to ensure fairness, decency and respect among your learners. Equal opportunity is a concept underpinned by legislation to provide relevant and appropriate access for the participation, development and advancement of all individuals and groups. In the past, equality has often been described as *everyone being the same* or *having the same opportunities*. Nowadays, it can be described as *everyone being different, but having equal rights*.

Diversity is about valuing and respecting the differences in learners, regardless of age, ability and/or circumstances, or any other individual characteristics they may have. If you have two or more learners, you will experience diversity. You may have a mixed group of learners with different past experiences who are aiming to achieve the same qualification but at a different level. You could therefore set different activities and targets for the different assessment criteria.

When teaching and training, you should always ensure you:

- are non-judgemental
- challenge any direct or indirect discrimination, stereotyping, prejudice, harassment, bullying and biased attitudes, by yourself or others
- do not have favourite learners or give some more attention than others
- do not indulge the minority at the expense of the majority
- ensure particular groups are not offended, for example, because of their beliefs or religion
- ensure particular learners are not disadvantaged or overly advantaged
- reflect on your own attitudes, values and beliefs so that you are not imposing these upon your learners

- treat all learners with respect and dignity

- use activities and assessments which are pitched at the right level

- use questions which are worded so as not to cause embarrassment

Activity

How can you promote and develop equality, and value diversity with your learners during your sessions? Are there any naturally occurring opportunities you could use for discussions and activities such as topical news stories and local or national events?

Whenever possible, you should try to embrace, embed and advance all aspects of equality and diversity, and value your learners' contributions. *All students must feel that they are positively and equally valued and accepted, and that their efforts to learn are recognised, and judged without bias. It is not enough that they are tolerated* (Petty, 2009, page 82).

You could use pictures in handouts and presentations which reflect different abilities, ages, cultures, genders and races. You can also help your learners by organising the environment to enable ease of access around any obstacles (including other learners' bags and coats), and around internal and external doors. If you are ever in doubt as to how to help a learner, just ask them.

Incorporating activities based around equality and diversity, and the local community and society within which your learners live and work could help your learners be more understanding and tolerant of each other. You also need to prepare them for the world outside their own living and working environment in case they move elsewhere in the future.

Try and have discussions regarding your subject which are based around areas of learners' interest, cultural topics, popular television programmes and relevant news stories. Place the responsibility on them to choose rather than you. This should get them thinking about the concept of equality and diversity in society, and how to be accepting and tolerant of others.

If you have access to the internet during your session, you could search online for a short equality and diversity video which you could show to help generate discussions. Other activities could involve discussions around perceptions and stereotypes, for example, most fire-fighters are male, most nurses are female, most male footballers are heterosexual and most male hairdressers are gay.

The Equality Act 2010

The Equality Act (2010) replaced all previous anti-discrimination legislation and consolidated it into one Act (for England, Scotland and Wales). It includes rights for people not to be directly discriminated against or harassed because they have an association with a disabled person or because they are wrongly perceived as disabled.

To ensure you comply with the Equality Act (2010), you need to be proactive in all aspects of equality and diversity. You should make sure your behaviour and delivery style, teaching, learning and assessment resources promote and include all learners in respect of the Act's nine *protected characteristics* (known as personal attributes):

- age
- disability
- gender
- gender reassignment
- marriage and civil partnership
- race
- religion and belief
- sexual orientation
- pregnancy and maternity

Finding ways of integrating these characteristics might occur naturally during your sessions.

Example

Marta was teaching the Level 3 Certificate in Hospitality and Catering to a mixed group of learners from various backgrounds and faiths. As Chinese New Year was approaching she decided to use it as a theme and create different menus around it. This opened up a discussion about the Chinese culture, which the group found interesting and meaningful. She decided she would research other cultures, faiths, religions and beliefs to incorporate them during her sessions throughout the year.

Other opportunities could include:

- celebrating local and national events
- creating and using crosswords, word searches, puzzles or quizzes based around aspects of equality and diversity
- discussing issues when they arise during your sessions, such as learners' perceptions of disability, older people, different races
- discussing events in the news such as racist attacks, or an issue in a particular television programme such as disability or ageism
- drawing upon the experiences of learners within your group
- embracing differences
- encouraging research activities which relate to your specialist subject
- mixing different learners during group and paired activities
- using pictures to represent the Equality Act's characteristics in your resources and on publicity and marketing materials

- visiting museums and cultural buildings

- watching short videos and discussing aspects within them which impact on equality and diversity

Try to encourage learners not to make assumptions, for example, *foreigners always take the jobs of British people,* or *mothers always take time off work to look after their children.* If conversations like these occur, take the opportunity to challenge them.

The Act has seven different *types of discrimination:*

- associative discrimination: direct discrimination against someone because they are associated with another person with a protected characteristic

- direct discrimination: discrimination because of a protected characteristic

- indirect discrimination: when a rule or policy which applies to everyone can disadvantage a person with a protected characteristic

- discrimination by perception: direct discrimination against someone because others think they have a protected characteristic

- harassment: behaviour deemed offensive by the recipient

- harassment by a third party: the harassment of staff or others by people not directly employed by an organisation, such as an external consultant or visitor

- victimisation: discrimination against someone because they made or supported a complaint under equality legislation

You should watch for any type of discrimination occurring between your learners, and indeed whether you or a colleague are perhaps discriminating without realising.

Extension Activity

Design an activity you could use with your learners that will enable them to discuss relevant topics relating to equality and diversity. Carry it out and evaluate how effective it was.

Continuing professional development

Continuing professional development (CPD) can be anything that you do that helps you improve your practice. It shows you are a committed professional and it should help improve your skills, knowledge and understanding. CPD should relate to your job role, i.e. as a teacher, as well as your specialist subject. Remember, you are a *dual professional* and therefore need to keep up to date with both aspects. You should reflect on all CPD activities you carry out so that they have a positive impact upon your development and role. There are constant changes in education; therefore it is crucial to keep up to date and embrace them. Examples include changes to the qualifications you will deliver, changes to policies and practices within your organisation, regulatory requirements and government initiatives.

Activity

Think about the last time you did something to improve your specialist subject knowledge and/or your teaching or assessment practice. Write down what you did and why, and then consider how it has helped or improved what you do.

Your organisation might have a strategy for CPD which will prioritise activities they consider are important to improving standards. They may or may not provide any funding for you to undertake them. However, you can partake in lots of activities outside your organisation, which cost very little, such as researching websites, reading journals and reviewing textbooks for use with your learners. CPD can be informal or formal, planned well in advance or opportunistic, but should have a real impact upon your teaching role, leading to an improvement in knowledge and practice.

You will probably participate in an appraisal or performance review system at your organisation. This is a valuable opportunity to discuss your learning, development and any training or support you may need. It is also a chance to reflect upon your achievements and successes. Having the support of your organisation will help you decide what is relevant to your development as a teacher, your job role and your specialist subject. You could share your ideas with your colleagues if it is something everyone could benefit from.

Example

Josh had been teaching his specialist subject of Motor Vehicle Maintenance for three years. He recently had an appraisal with his line manager, Danni, to discuss his performance and progress. Danni identified the fact that Josh would benefit from attending an external event aimed at updating his skills and knowledge. This would enable him to learn about the latest engine diagnostic techniques, as the organisation had received some funding to purchase new equipment. After Josh attended the event, he was able to deliver a training session to the other staff in the department. This ensured everyone was familiar with the new equipment and how to use it. The real impact came when Josh was able to use the equipment with his learners as it ensured they were learning with the latest technology.

The IfL, the voluntary professional body for teachers, trainers and tutors in the Further Education and Skills Sector, states:

> *CPD, in relation to a teacher, means continuing professional development, which is any activity undertaken for the purposes of updating knowledge of the subject taught and developing teaching skills.*

(IfL, 2007, page 2)

Opportunities for professional development include:

- attending events and training programmes
- attending meetings
- e-learning and online activities
- evaluating feedback from peers, learners and others
- formally reflecting on experiences and documenting how it has improved practice
- improving own skills such as English and maths
- membership of professional associations or committees
- observing colleagues
- reading textbooks
- researching developments or changes to your subject and/or relevant legislation
- secondments
- self-reflection
- shadowing colleagues
- standardisation activities
- studying for relevant qualifications
- subscribing to and reading relevant journals and websites
- visiting other organisations
- voluntary work
- work experience placements
- writing or reviewing books and articles

To help you improve and develop your practice, all CPD activities should be reflected upon and documented in some way. This can be via your organisation's systems, or your own manual or electronic records. The template in Table 1.3 could be used or adapted to document your CPD activities. You could give each activity a reference number to link it to any supporting information and documents. The amount of detail you need to write will differ depending upon your organisation's requirements, and any requirements of the professional associations to which you belong. Maintaining your CPD will ensure you are not only competent at your job role, but also up to date with the latest developments regarding your specialist subject, and teaching, learning and assessment approaches. External inspectors and quality assurers may need to see your CPD records at some point. However, don't just partake in and document your activities for the sake of it; CPD must have a real impact upon your knowledge and skills, which should lead to an improvement in practice.

Table 1.3 CPD template

Continuing professional development record				
Name:			Organisation:	
Date	Activity and venue	Time length	Justification towards teaching role and/or subject specialism	Ref no

The following websites are useful to gain up-to-date information regarding developments in the Further Education and Skills Sector. Most of them allow you to register for regular electronic updates.

- Chartered Institute for Educational Assessors – www.ciea.co.uk
- Department for Business, Innovation and Skills – www.bis.gov.uk
- Department for Education – www.education.gov.uk
- Equality and Diversity Forum – www.edf.org.uk
- Education and Training Foundation – www.et-foundation.co.uk
- Government updates: Education and Learning – www.direct.gov.uk/en/EducationAndLearning/index.htm
- Institute for Leadership and Management – www.i-l-m.com
- Institute for Learning – www.ifl.ac.uk
- Institute of Training and Occupational Learning – www.itol.org
- National Institute of Adult Continuing Education – www.niace.org.uk
- Ofqual – www.ofqual.gov.uk
- Ofsted – www.ofsted.gov.uk
- Post Compulsory Education and Training – www.pcet.net
- Times Educational Supplement Online – www.tes.co.uk

You could join free social network sites such as *LinkedIn* which is the professional networking site at www.linkedin.co.uk. Here you will find groups you can join specifically aimed at your specialist subject. You can post questions and answers and join in ongoing discussions online.

Based on your current practice and future needs, you could create a personal development plan to help you focus on what you need to do and when. The template in Table 1.4 could be used or adapted for planning purposes. The plan can be updated at any time and, when an activity has been completed, you can update your CPD record.

Table 1.4 Personal development plan template

| Personal development plan | | | | |
| Name: | | Organisation: | | |
Targets	Aim or activity	Start date	Review date	Completion date (CPD record to be updated)
Short term				
Medium term				
Long term				

Extension Activity

Thinking about the subject you wish to deliver, what do you need to do to ensure you are up to date and current with your skills, knowledge and understanding? Access the websites in the previous bulleted list and subscribe to relevant electronic updates. Search for other appropriate information such as that available on the awarding organisation's website if you are assessing a qualification, or any professional associations to which you belong.

Summary

In this chapter you have learnt about:

- *roles, responsibilities and relationships*
- *maintaining a safe and supportive learning environment*
- *promoting appropriate behaviour and respect*
- *working with other professionals*
- *legislation, regulatory requirements and codes of practice*
- *promoting equality and valuing diversity*
- *continuing professional development*

Cross-referencing grid

This chapter contributes towards the following assessment criteria of the units which form the Certificate in Education and Training, along with aspects of the Professional Standards for Teachers and Trainers in England. Full details of the learning outcomes and assessment criteria of each unit can be found in the appendices.

Certificate units	Assessment criteria
Understanding roles, responsibilities and relationships in education and training	1.1, 1.2, 1.3, 1.4 2.1, 2.2 3.1, 3.2, 3.3
Planning to meet the needs of learners in education and training	2.3
Delivering education and training	1.2, 1.3
Assessing learners in education and training	
Using resources for education and training	

Area	Professional Standards for Teachers and Trainers in England
Professional values and attributes	1, 2, 3, 6
Professional knowledge and understanding	7, 11, 12
Professional skills	19, 20

Theory focus

References and further information

Ayers, H and Gray, F (2006) *An A to Z Practical Guide to Learning Difficulties*. London: David Fulton Publishers.

Berry, J (2010) *Teachers' Legal Rights and Responsibilities: A Guide for Trainee Teachers and Those New to the Profession* (2nd edn). Hertfordshire: University of Hertfordshire Press.

Clark, T (2010) *Mental Health Matters for FE: Teachers Toolkit.* Leicester: NIACE.

Department for Education and Skills (DfES) (2006) *Safeguarding Children and Safer Recruitment in Education.* London: DfES.

Department of Health (2000) *No Secrets.* London: The Stationery Office.

Department of Health, Home Office and Department for Education and Employment (DfEE) (1999) *Working Together to Safeguard Children.* London: The Stationery Office.

Farrell, M (2006) *Dyslexia and Other Learning Difficulties.* London: Routledge.

Gravells, A (2012) *Achieving your TAQA Assessor and Internal Quality Assurer Award.* London: Learning Matters SAGE.

Gravells, A (2013) *The Award in Education and Training.* London: Learning Matters SAGE.

Gravells, A and Simpson, S (2012) *Equality and Diversity in the Lifelong Learning Sector* (2nd edn). London: Learning Matters SAGE.

Gravells, A and Simpson, S (2014) *Passing Assessments for the Certificate in Education and Training.* London: Learning Matters SAGE.

HMI (2004) *Every Child Matters: Change for Children.* London: DfES.

Institute for Learning (2007) *Guidelines for your continuing professional development (CPD).* London: IfL.

Institute for Learning (2010) *Brilliant teaching and training in FE and skills: A guide to effective CPD for teachers, trainers and leaders.* London: Learning and Skills Improvement Service.

IfL (2008) *Code of Professional Practice.* London: Institute for Learning.

LLUK (2006) *New Overarching Professional Standards for Teachers, Tutors and Trainers in the Further Education and Skills Sector.* London: Skills for Business.

LSIS (2009) *Centres for Excellence in Teacher Training: CETT Standard.* Learning and Skills Improvement Service Newsletter issue 1.

National Institute of Adult and Continuing Education (2007) *Safer Practice, Safer Learning.* Ashford: NIACE.

Peart, S and Atkins, L (2011) *Teaching 14–19 Learners in the Lifelong Learning Sector.* London: Learning Matters SAGE.

Petty, G (2009) *Teaching Today* (4th edn). Cheltenham: Nelson Thornes.

Powell, S and Tummons, J (2011) *Inclusive Practice in the Lifelong Learning Sector.* London: Learning Matters SAGE.

Read, H (2011) *The Best Internal Quality Assurer's Guide.* Bideford: Read On Publications Ltd.

Reece, I and Walker, S (2008) *Teaching Training and Learning: A Practical Guide* (6th edn). Tyne & Wear: Business Education Publishers Ltd.

Rogers, A and Horrocks, N (2010) *Teaching Adults* (4th edn). Maidenhead: Open University Press.

Scales et al. (2011) *Continuing Professional Development in the Lifelong Learning Sector.* Maidenhead: OU Press.

Tummons, J (2010) *Becoming a Professional Tutor in the Further Education and Skills Sector* (2nd edn). London: Learning Matters SAGE.

Vizard, D (2012) *How to Manage Behaviour in Further Education.* London: SAGE Publications Ltd.

Wallace, S (2011) *Teaching, Tutoring and Training in the Lifelong Learning Sector* (4th edn). London: Learning Matters SAGE.

Wallace, S (2013) *Managing Behaviour in Further and Adult Education Sector* (3rd edn). London: Learning Matters SAGE.

Wallace, S (2013) *Understanding the Further Education Sector: A Critical Guide to Policies and Practices.* Northwich: Critical Publishing Ltd.

Wilson, C (2012) *Practical Teaching: A Guide to Assessment and Quality Assurance.* Hampshire: Cengage Learning.

Wood, J and Dickinson, J (2011) *Quality Assurance and Evaluation in the Lifelong Learning Sector.* London: Learning Matters SAGE.

Websites

Alliance of Sector Skills Councils – www.sscalliance.org

Behaviour tips – www.pivotaleducation.com

Chartered Institute for Educational Assessors (CIEA) – www.ciea.co.uk

Classroom management free videos – www.bestyearever.net/videos/?goback=.gmr_27003.gde_27003_member_196422762Dealing with behaviour – http://newteachers.tes.co.uk/content/dealing-behaviour-issues-%E2%80%93-guide-new-teachers

Disclosure and Barring Service – www.gov.uk/government/organisations/disclosure-and-barring-service

Equality and Diversity Forum – www.edf.org.uk

Equality and Human Rights Commission – www.equalityhumanrights.com

Government legislation – www.legislation.gov.uk

Health and Safety Executive – www.hse.gov.uk

IfL Code of Professional Practice – www.ifl.ac.uk/membership/professional-standards

Inclusion, Equality, Diversity and Differentiation resources – http://reflect.ifl.ac.uk/viewasset.aspx?oid=3201642&type=webfolio&pageoid=3201743

Institute for Leadership and Management – www.i-l-m.com

Institute for Learning – www.ifl.ac.uk

Institute for Learning: CPD – www.ifl.ac.uk/cpd

Institute of Training and Occupational Learning – www.itol.org

Local Safeguarding Children Boards (LSCB) – www.ofsted.gov.uk/resources/good-practice-local-safeguarding-children-boards

National Institute of Adult Continuing Education – www.niace.org.uk

Ofqual – www.ofqual.gov.uk

Ofsted – www.ofsted.gov.uk

Plagiarism – http://plagiarism.org

Regulatory requirements – www.legislation.gov.uk/

Safeguarding – www.education.gov.uk/search/results?q=safeguarding

Safeguarding Vulnerable Groups Act – www.opsi.gov.uk/Acts/acts2006/pdf/ukpga_20060047_en.pdf

Teaching videos (some good, some not so good) – www.youtube.com/user/lifelonglearninguk and www.youtube.com/user/thetutorpages

2 PLANNING TO MEET THE NEEDS OF LEARNERS

In this chapter you will learn about:

- initial and diagnostic assessment
- negotiating and agreeing individual learning goals
- devising a scheme of work
- designing teaching and learning plans
- challenges when planning
- implementing the minimum core
- evaluating own practice

There are activities and examples to encourage you to reflect on the above which will help you develop and enhance your understanding of how you plan sessions to meet the needs of learners.

At the end of each section within the chapter are extension activities to stretch and challenge your knowledge and understanding. A list of useful references, further information and website links can be found at the end of the chapter in case you would like to research the topics further.

At the end of the chapter is a cross-referencing grid showing how the chapter's contents relate to the units of the Certificate in Education and Training, and the Professional Standards for Teachers and Trainers in England.

Initial and diagnostic assessment

All learning needs to start somewhere. How do you know what your learners know? Do you know what they need to know to achieve the programme or qualification? If you have a learner who already has some knowledge of the subject, they may become bored if you are teaching them what they already know. However, if you have a learner who doesn't know anything about the subject, they will need to learn more. This therefore becomes your starting point for finding out about your learner, and matching what they need to the content of the programme or qualification they will be taking. It is all about the learner and the learning which will take place; it is not about you. However, as you will be facilitating the learning process, you can often choose how you do this, but you must remember to use approaches that meet the needs of your learners, in a way that ensures learning takes place. When you start teaching, you will need to introduce your subject to your learners in a logical and progressive way, building upon their current skills, knowledge and understanding.

Prior to a learner commencing, information, advice and guidance (IAG) should be given to them regarding their programme choice. This should be clear, unambiguous and impartial to ensure it meets their needs and capability. The application process should ensure learners are on the right programme at the right level to help them reach their destination, i.e. the correct qualification for their career path. You should also inform learners of how they will be assessed during the programme, for example, assignments, observations or tests. This will ensure there are no surprises once they have started.

You should find out as much as you possibly can about your learners beforehand. Learners will often decide at the first session whether or not they will return to the next session. First impressions are very important to ensure that your learner has a positive experience and remains with you throughout the programme. If you can get to know something about each of your learners when you first meet them, for example, an interest or hobby they have, you can mention it when you see them next. This will show that you are getting to know them as an individual and not as a statistic. Carrying out an icebreaker during the first session with your learners is a useful method of helping your learners relax. It also helps everyone find out a little about each other and begin to remember everyone's names. Please see Chapter 3 for more information regarding icebreakers.

Initial assessment

The initial assessment process might be the start of your relationship with your learners. For some learners, this will be an opportunity to divulge any concerns or personal (perhaps confidential) information about themselves. Initial assessment takes place at the beginning, but is effective only when seen as part of a wider and ongoing process throughout the programme. It might be your responsibility to carry out the initial assessments, or it might be someone else's. If it is the latter, you will need to liaise with them to obtain and interpret the results.

Using initial assessments will help find out your learners' current skills and knowledge, and identify any particular aspects which might otherwise go unnoticed. If they are carried out prior to the programme commencing, the results can be used to deal with any issues that might arise, or to guide learners to a different, more appropriate programme or level if necessary. It is all about being *proactive* before learning starts, and *active* when learning is taking place, rather than being *reactive* to a situation when it might be too late to do anything. Initial assessment is often referred to as assessment *for* learning, as the results help inform the learning process. Assessment *of* learning is about making decisions regarding progress and achievement. Assessment is an integral part of the teaching and learning process, and should not be in isolation from it.

Programmes aimed at introducing learners to a new subject tend not to require a level of prior knowledge or experience in that subject. For higher level programmes, it is essential to ascertain whether your learner has the appropriate level of experience and knowledge, along with good English, maths, and information and communication technology (ICT) skills. It is important to ensure that your learners are on an appropriate or suitable programme, not only for their own benefit, but for your organisation too. You might have to meet certain retention, achievement and success rate targets set by your organisation. Funding might also be affected if learners commence, but then leave without completing.

You will need to find out what the internal requirements are at your organisation, along with any external requirements imposed by awarding organisations or other bodies.

Initial assessment can:

- allow for differentiation and individual requirements to be met

- ascertain why your learner wants to take the programme along with their capability to achieve

- ensure your learner is applying for the right type of programme and level

- find out the expectations and motivations of your learner

- give your learner the confidence to negotiate and agree individual learning goals

- identify any information which needs to be shared with colleagues

- identify any specific additional support needs or reasonable adjustments which may be required

You will need to keep appropriate records of the results of initial assessments. You might need to discuss these with others who have an involvement with your learners, for example, workplace supervisors. However, some aspects might need to remain confidential and you will need to find out your organisation's requirements for record keeping and confidentiality.

The initial assessment process can include the use of a range of tests, questionnaires and interview techniques. You will need to plan what you want to find out from the process and then choose an appropriate method, for example, an online questionnaire or a face-to-face discussion.

Initial assessment can also take place during a session, for example, the first time you take your learners for your subject, or you change subject or topic. Although you might have obtained some information prior to learners starting, you might need more when you meet them. However, you will need to make sure anything you ask your learners to do during the early stages of the programme is appropriate.

Example

Julie was delivering a session to a group of 14 learners taking an Access to Nursing programme. They consisted of mature learners returning to learning after a career break, many of whom didn't have any formal qualifications. In the first week, as part of their initial assessment, Julie asked them to research recent government legislation on health hygiene in hospitals, and to prepare a written paper which covers the implications for the National Health Service. Julie asked the learners to present their paper at the next session. The following week five learners did not return.

This example demonstrates how important it is to recognise that assessment is a continuous process, starting with a simple initial assessment. If the learners' first experience of assessment terrifies them, they may not return. If any of your learners do not return to your sessions, this may be as a result of an ineffective initial assessment process. Good practice should have ensured the process helps and supports your learners, before they become a *withdrawal statistic,* i.e. a learner who has left the programme without achieving. This could lead to a bad experience for your learner, and cause an impact upon your organisation's targets. You should always try to find out why any learners don't return. Perhaps you can telephone them, or liaise with someone in your organisation who is responsible for the recruitment and retention of learners.

When you change a subject or topic during a session, it is always useful to carry out a quick initial assessment of the knowledge and/or experience your learners have. You can then build upon this during the session and include your learners' experiences in relevant discussions.

Diagnostic assessment

An important aspect of the initial assessment process is diagnostic assessment. This can be used to evaluate a learner's skills, knowledge, strengths and areas for development in a particular subject area. It could be that your learner feels they are capable of achieving at a higher level than the diagnostic assessments determine. The results will give a thorough indication of not only the level at which your learner needs to be placed for their subject, but also which specific aspects they need to improve on. Skills tests can be used for learners to demonstrate what they can do, and knowledge tests can be used for learners to demonstrate their application and understanding.

Diagnostic tests, for example, a manual or online English and maths test, can also be carried out at the time of initial assessment. Some learners may be very nervous about taking tests; therefore it is important that the depth and type of assessments are appropriate for the programme and the learners. Information gained from these tests will help you plan your sessions to meet any individual needs and/or to arrange further training and support if necessary.

You should not accept learners onto a programme just because you need the numbers to make a group viable. The programme may not be suitable for them and they may leave, therefore wasting their time and yours.

Diagnostic assessment can:

- ascertain learning preferences such as visual, aural, read/write and kinaesthetic (VARK)

- enable learners to demonstrate their current level of skills, knowledge and understanding

- ensure learners can access support such as study skills

- identify an appropriate starting point and level for each learner

- identify gaps in skills, knowledge and understanding to highlight areas to work on

- identify previous experience, knowledge, achievements and transferable skills

- identify specific requirements, for example, English, maths and ICT skills

Activity

Find out what initial and diagnostic assessments are currently used at your organisation. Will it be your responsibility to administer these, or is there a specialist person to do this? If it is the latter, introduce yourself to them and find out how you can work together for the benefit of your learners.

Examples of initial and diagnostic assessment activities include:

- application/enrolment forms: completed online or manually

- interview/discussion: asking your learner why they are there, what they want to achieve and discussing their learning history and preferred style of learning

- observations: it may be necessary to observe your learner performing a skill, perhaps in their workplace, before agreeing an appropriate programme and level; observation during initial assessment activities will give you a sense of how your learner performs, which activities they enjoy and which they are least comfortable with

- self-assessment: asking your learner to assess their own skills and knowledge towards the programme outcomes; this is often known as a *skills scan*

- structured activities, for example, role play

- tests, for example, English, maths and ICT; these can be online via the internet or your organisation's intranet

There are many different types of initial and diagnostic skills tests available. Some organisations design and use their own, others purchase and use widely available tests, for example, the system called *Basic Key Skills Builder* (BKSB) to diagnose English, maths and ICT skills.

The results of initial and diagnostic assessments should help you negotiate appropriate individual learning plans (ILPs) with your learners, ensuring they are on the right programme at the right level with the support they need to succeed. An ILP is like a contract with each learner which outlines what they are expected to achieve, and when.

Activity

Ofsted (in England) regularly inspect provision. If your organisation has been inspected by them, have a look at the latest report which can be accessed via their website www.ofsted.gov.uk. Read what was stated regarding initial assessment and ascertain if any changes have been made as a result.

Recognising prior learning

Recognition of prior learning (RPL) and/or achievement (RPA) is about assessing a learner's experiences, learning, and achievements towards the programme or qualification they wish to take. It should save them having to duplicate anything unnecessarily. Depending upon the evidence they can produce in support of their claim, they might not have to repeat some or all of the training or assessment requirements. You would need to compare what they have achieved already against the programme or qualification requirements. You can then agree a plan of action as to how to fill any gaps, for example, by attending further training to gain knowledge, or by being observed.

There are occasions where a learner will not have to repeat anything, particularly if they are taking a qualification which is on the Qualifications and Credit Framework (QCF) and they have been accredited with some units already. Details of qualifications and units achieved on the QCF will be held centrally and your learner will be able to prove this via their electronic learner record or certificate if necessary.

Example

Roberto had achieved the Equality and Diversity unit as part of the Level 4 Certificate in Education and Training which is on the QCF. A year later he decided to take the Level 5 Diploma in Education and Training which is also on the QCF. As the Equality and Diversity unit was also in the Diploma, he did not have to attend the training sessions or be re-assessed.

There might be occasions where a learner will be exempt from a unit. This means the unit they achieved was on the previous National Qualifications Framework (NQF) and is similar to a unit on the current QCF. There is therefore no need for a learner to take the newer version if the older version is still acceptable. Your learner will have a certificate to prove their achievement; however, you should always check the authenticity of these.

The template in Table 2.1 on page 58 could be used or adapted for initial and diagnostic assessment purposes. It should be supported with appropriate skills tests for English, maths and ICT.

Learning support and learner support

If you have a learner requiring support for any reason, there is a difference between *learning support* and *learner support*. *Learning* support relates to the subject, or help with English, maths, ICT and/or study skills. *Learner* support relates to help they might need with any personal issues, and/or general advice and guidance such as financial support, transport or childcare.

Some learners will have needs, barriers or challenges to learning that may affect their attendance, progress and/or achievement. If you can ascertain these prior to your learners commencing, you will hopefully be able to refer them to someone who can help. However, other issues may occur during their time with you which you would need to deal with. You would therefore need to plan a suitable course of action to help your learners, or refer them to an appropriate specialist or agency to alleviate any impact upon their learning.

You should discuss the requirements of the programme or qualification with your learners, along with the range of services and agencies available to assist with any specific needs.

Table 2.1 Initial and diagnostic assessment template

Initial and diagnostic assessment			
Separate skills tests in English, maths and ICT should be taken			
Name:	Date:		
Why have you decided to take this programme/ qualification? (*continue overleaf if necessary*)			
What relevant experience do you have in the subject area?			
What relevant qualifications do you have? *If you have achieved any units on the Qualifications and Credit Framework (QCF), please state them here.*			
Have you completed a learning preference questionnaire? If YES, what is your preferred style of learning? If NO, please complete the questionnaire at www.vark-learn.com and note your results here:	YES/NO Learning preference results: V: A: R: K:		
Do you have any particular learning needs or requirements? If YES, please state here, or talk to your assessor in confidence.	YES/NO		
Are you confident at using a computer? If YES, what experience or qualifications do you have?	YES/ NO	Skills test results: ICT:	
What help would you like with written/spoken English?		Skills test results: English:	
What help would you like with maths?		Skills test results: maths:	

Impartial advice should be available from the National Careers Service regarding job search, preparation for interviews and more.

Some learners may have specific learning difficulties relating to language and skill development. These could include dyslexia and dyspraxia. Others may have a learning difficulty which affects their ability to learn. At some point you might encounter learners with:

- attention deficit hyperactivity disorder (ADHD) – a common behavioural disorder where learners have difficulty controlling their behaviour without medication or behavioural therapy; although not diagnosed as a learning difficulty, its interference with concentration and attention can make it difficult for a learner to perform well

- autistic spectrum disorder/Asperger's syndrome – difficulty with social interaction and with abstract concepts

- dyscalculia – difficulty with calculations or maths

- dysgraphia – difficulty with handwriting

- dyslexia – difficulty with processing written language

- dyspraxia – poor motor co-ordination or clumsiness

Example

Stuart has been diagnosed with Asperger's syndrome and is attending a plumbing apprenticeship course at his local college. He has difficulties in understanding the social and cultural 'rules' that most people take for granted, and so misinterprets intentions, behaviour and the conversation of others. On the surface, Stuart appears to be rude and disruptive and constantly interrupts when others are speaking. His teacher is aware of this, and has asked Stuart if he can inform the other learners of the situation. Stuart is happy about disclosing this and they can all therefore agree ways of dealing with situations as they arise.

It is important that you are aware of any situations in order to support your learners fully, both at the planning stage and throughout their programme of learning. Initial assessment should have identified these; however, sometimes learners may talk to you in confidence about their concerns at other times. If you are unsure how to help, just ask your learners what you can do; they are best able to explain how you can help make their learning experience a positive one.

You will need to consider any particular requirements of your learners, to ensure they can all participate during sessions. Initial assessment would ensure your learners are able to take the subject; however, you (or the organisation) may need to make reasonable adjustments to adapt resources, equipment or the environment to support them (as stated in the Equality Act 2010). If anything is adapted, make sure both you and your learners are familiar with the changes prior to use.

Technological advances have made an enormous difference to learners who have particular needs, enabling them to access suitable learning opportunities. This is particularly true for learners who have physical or sensory impairments, and also for those who are dyslexic or have other learning difficulties. Technology can provide a means of access to learning for those who:

- are blind or partially sighted
- are deaf or have partial hearing
- are dyslexic
- have a degenerative condition which is physically tiring
- have difficulty in speaking
- have difficulty with manipulation and fine motor control

The effective and efficient use of technology relies on carrying out detailed and effective initial and diagnostic assessment, followed up by reviews with learners at appropriate stages in their progress. It also requires human resources in the form of technicians and competent support workers to train teachers and learners to use the technology. The management of such staff is an essential part of planning learning programmes. However, technology is not a universal remedy for all learners and some learners may not wish to use it.

There might be specialist staff in your organisation to assist learners requiring support and they should be consulted when planning ILPs with learners. The provision of learning opportunities is not just a matter for individual teachers but requires a whole-organisation approach to create an appropriate and effective learning environment. This could also include support from other learners.

Learning preferences

Most people learn in different ways, known as *learning preferences*; what suits one person might not suit another. For example, you may like to watch someone perform a task, and then carry it out yourself, or you might just want to try it out for yourself first. What you may tend to do is deliver your sessions in the style in which you learn best – although it will suit you, it might not suit your learners. If you can find out what your learners' preferences are, you can adapt your teaching and learning approaches to suit. There are many different ways that people learn, often known as *learning styles*.

Fleming (2005) states that people can be grouped into four styles of learning: visual, aural, read/write and kinaesthetic, known by the acronym VARK. However, not all learners fall into just one style as they may be *multi-modal*, i.e. a mixture of two or more preferences enabling learning to take place more quickly.

Activity

If you haven't already ascertained the preferences of your learners, ask them to take the short online questionnaire at www.vark-learn.com. See what their results are for each of V, A, R and K. This information will help you differentiate and adapt your activities during sessions to ensure they meet the needs of your learners. You might also wish to complete the questionnaire yourself, as it is interesting to see if you change over time.

It is always useful to get your learners to carry out a learning preferences questionnaire. It can be fun and lead to an interesting discussion, as well as helping you plan your teaching, learning and assessment approaches accordingly. It empowers learners to adapt information in a way that they are comfortable with, for example, using a digital recorder, laptop or tablet rather than hand writing during a session. There are other methods which can be used to ascertain learning preferences; one is by Honey and Mumford (1992) which suggests learners are a mixture of four styles: activist, pragmatist, theorist and reflector. These could be perceived as:

- **Activist** learners like to deal with new problems and experiences, often learning by trial and error. They like lots of activities to keep them busy and enjoy a hands-on approach. They love challenges and are enthusiastic.

- **Pragmatist** learners like to apply what they have learnt to practical situations. They like logical reasons for doing something. They prefer someone to demonstrate a skill first before trying it for themselves.

- **Theorist** learners need time to take in information; they prefer to read lots of material before trying a new activity. They like things that have been tried and tested and prefer reassurance that something will work.

- **Reflector** learners think deeply about what they are learning and the activities they could do to apply this learning. They like to be told about things so that they can think it through. They will also try something, think again about it, and then try it again.

However, there are critics of learning preferences. In 2004, Professor Frank Coffield of The University of London carried out a systematic and critical review of learning preferences and pedagogy in post-16 learning. The report reviewed the literature on learning preferences and examined in detail 13 of the most influential models. The report concludes that it matters which is chosen. The implications for teaching and learning, he states, are serious and should be of concern. Coffield has since written widely on the subject and states: ... *it was not sufficient to pay attention to individual differences in learners; we must take account of the whole teaching–learning environment* (2008, page 31).

Extension Activity

Consider and analyse the role of initial and diagnostic assessment within your organisation. If possible, carry out an initial and diagnostic assessment with a learner. How will you use the results to help plan what your learner will do and when?

Negotiating and agreeing individual learning goals

A learning goal is what the learner wants or needs to achieve from the programme or qualification. They might have different expectations to that stated in the syllabus, often known as a qualification handbook. This will state how your subject should be delivered, assessed and quality assured and will be available from the awarding organisation which accredits the qualification and issues the certificates. It will also give information regarding the professional development and qualifications that staff should have. It will state how the subject should be assessed, and whether assessment activities are provided for you or you need to create your own. It is important that your learners know the content of the programme or qualification, otherwise, if they have different expectations, they may decide to leave.

Alternatively, you might be delivering non-accredited qualifications, which are programmes of learning that do not lead to a formal qualification issued by an awarding organisation. However, a certificate of attendance or achievement might be issued.

Activity

If you are teaching learners who are working towards an accredited qualification, find out who the awarding organisation is for your particular subject (if you don't yet know) and access their website. Locate the qualification handbook and familiarise yourself with the content. If you are delivering a non-accredited qualification, find out from your organisation what topics you need to teach.

You need to know what you are going to teach, and your learners need to know what they are going to learn. These should be formally negotiated and agreed. However, they can be amended at any time if necessary. You should encourage your learners to talk to you and give you feedback on how they are progressing, and how they feel their learning can be supported.

A supportive and respectful relationship between your learners and yourself will ensure that realistic goals and targets are agreed.

Learning goals can be categorised as follows:

- overall goals: long-term goals which encompass the whole programme or qualification; these are often stated as *objectives* or *learning outcomes* and are usually established either by your organisation or the awarding organisation accrediting the qualification

- specific goals: short-term goals which determine changes in your learner's skills, knowledge, understanding and attitudes; the learning process is effective when these goals are clear and match the requirements of the learner

- immediate goals: these break down the specific goals into manageable tasks in order that they can be achieved

- personal goals: these are aspects in addition to the overall goals, for example, to improve communication skills

You need to ensure that your learners have every opportunity to contribute towards the successful outcome of their learning, by actively involving them in making decisions throughout the programme. This is most effective when targets are set, i.e. smaller steps of learning that will help your learners achieve their goals. By the end of the programme the overall goals should have been achieved, but with negotiation from your learners along the way.

When agreeing targets with your learners, these should always be SMART. This is an acronym for:

- **S**pecific – are the targets clearly defined and agreed to meet the required outcomes?

- **M**easurable – can the targets be achieved at the required level?

- **A**chievable – can the targets be met by all learners?

- **R**elevant – are the targets realistic and do they relate to the subject and the learners?

- **T**ime bound – can the agreed target dates and times be met?

Being SMART is all about being clear and precise with what you expect your learners to achieve. SMART targets should always be at the right level for your learners. Knowing your learners and the expected level of achievement will help you plan realistic targets. They should be challenging enough to ensure learning is progressive, yet be inclusive to all learners to ensure they are achievable.

Phenil is agreeing targets with his learners who are taking the Level 3 Diploma in Animal Management. To ensure the targets are SMART, he firstly lists the unit titles on their ILP, followed by how each unit will be assessed, for example, assignment, presentation and observation. Each has an achievable target date for completion. Phenil is therefore ensuring his learners know what they have to do and by when, to achieve the qualification.

Recording individual learning goals

Ideally, you should encourage your learners to take ownership of the process of planning their learning and guide them along the way. To help encourage them to become independent learners you will need to negotiate and agree their goals and targets, and assess their progress and achievement regularly. It is important that all targets are documented, whether they are *hard* targets, i.e. directly based on the qualification, or *soft* targets, i.e. personal goals. If you are teaching a programme which does not lead to a formal qualification, you will still need to record learner progress. This is known as *recognising and recording progress and achievement in non-accredited learning* (RARPA).

There are five processes to RARPA.

1. Aims – these should be appropriate to the individual or group of learners.

2. Initial assessment – this should be used to establish each learner's starting point.

3. Identification of appropriately challenging learning objectives – these should be agreed, renegotiated and revised as necessary after formative assessment, and should be appropriate to each learner.

4. Recognition and recording of progress and achievement during the programme – this should include assessor feedback, learner reflection and reviews of progress.

5. End of programme – this includes summative assessment, learner self-assessment and a review of overall progress and achievement. This should be in relation to the learning objectives and any other outcomes achieved during the programme.

If you use the RARPA system, you will need to check what records must be maintained; there may be standard forms for you to complete or you may need to design your own.

Individual learning plans

All relevant information regarding each learner's goals and targets should be documented in the form of a plan, usually called an ILP or an action plan. The ILP can be updated at any time, and can be used to review ongoing progress towards meeting the planned goals. Table 2.2 is a template which could be used or adapted as an ILP. Signatures might or might not be required on the plan, depending on whether a hard copy or electronic document is used.

Table 2.2 Individual learning plan template

Learner:		Teacher:	
Start date:		Expected achievement date:	
Programme/qualification title & level:			
Programme/qualification aims:			
Results of initial assessments: Results of diagnostic assessments: Learning preferences: Support requirements:			
Targets:			
Learning goals and assessment activities *Including English, maths and ICT*		**Target date**	**Achievement date**
Personal/other goals		**Target date**	**Achievement date**
Reviews/updates to plan			
Date	**Learner comments**		**Teacher comments**

The following is good practice when you are completing an ILP:

- consider how you will embed skills such as English, maths and ICT which are relevant to your learner's needs and to the demands of their programme goals

- ensure there is a clear link between the goals and targets on the ILP, the teaching, learning and assessment approaches, and the qualification aims

- communicate the goals and targets both verbally and in writing, to enable your learners to fully understand the requirements

- involve your learners, encourage them to discuss their learning and any support needs, and to use their knowledge of their strengths and areas for development to set their own relevant learning targets

- make sure the goals and targets are individual to each learner, there is no *one size fits all*

- refer to the results of initial and diagnostic assessments, and learning preference questionnaires as a starting point

- use regular tutorial and review sessions to discuss and update the ILP with your learner

By now you will have realised that the learner is an individual, and at the centre of your teaching role. If learners are taking the right programme at the right level, with the right support, they should achieve their goals and targets.

You might suggest there is too much paperwork involved and the process could be minimised or carried out electronically, or you might want to change the wording on the documents slightly. These changes would help improve the process for both you and your learners.

Devising a scheme of work

Once you know the details of the programme or qualification you will be teaching, and the learners you will have, you should devise a scheme of work. A scheme of work is a document that should be used when you are delivering a sequence of sessions over a period of time as it enables you to structure the learning in a logical and progressive way. It is sometimes referred to as a *learning programme* or *scheme of learning*.

Your programme might have an allocation of *guided learning hours* (GLH) or if it is on the QCF, it will have a mixture of contact and non-contact hours. These are the number of hours within which your learners are expected to achieve a qualification. The hours are sometimes dictated by the awarding organisation and the amount of funding your organisation receives might be based on these. The number of hours you are allocated will help you plan how many sessions you have to deliver and assess the subject.

A scheme of work can be for a whole programme or just a unit of a qualification. You will need to prepare one whether you teach groups or individuals. It will help you plan what you will do and when, along with what resources you will need and when, and give you an idea of what you need to prepare in advance. If you teach the same subject as your colleagues, you could all work together to produce a standardised scheme of work. This will enable all learners to have the same learning experience no matter which teacher they have. Templates or pro formas for schemes of work, and the amount of detail you are expected to include, will vary depending upon the organisation within which you teach. Table 2.3 on page 66 is a template which could be used or adapted to create a scheme of work.

Table 2.3 Scheme of work template

Teacher/trainer		Venue		
Programme/qualification		Group composition		Dates from: to:
Number of sessions		Contact hours Non-contact hours		
Aim of programme				

Dates & session number	Objectives/ learning outcomes *Learners will:*	Teaching and learning activities	Resources	Assessment activities

There might be external situations you will need to consider which could affect the dates of certain sessions such as:

- availability of certain people, resources or rooms

- availability of visiting speakers

- bank and public holidays

- examinations or assessments which can only be held at certain times

Nowadays, not all learners commence and complete at the same time. For example, you might have a group of 16 learners all starting during the first week of a programme, but then another learner commences the week after. You will have to devote time to introduce them to the other learners and update them on what they have missed. You could also buddy them up with another learner so that they don't feel isolated, and involve them in paired or group activities straight away.

It could be that you deliver a *roll on roll off* programme, where learners start and finish at different times. This type of programme is more suited to practical subjects where learners can work at their own pace through various theory and practical activities. For example, a hairdressing programme which is delivered in a training salon can accommodate practical tasks with clients. Theory can be covered in small groups, with the topics being repeated over time. A scheme of work might not be appropriate here as each learner will be following an individual programme of learning. However, you will need to make sure that progress and achievement are documented for each individual.

Group composition and group profile

Groups are composed of individual learners and you will find it useful to state the composition of each group you teach on your scheme of work, for example, 16 learners mainly female, aged 16–65 with little or no experience of the subject. You can then break this down further on your teaching and learning plan. This will contain details regarding each individual learner and their needs, enabling you to give appropriate support as your session progresses. The information should be used to differentiate your activities to suit your learners, and to support any particular needs.

Details to include on a group profile are:

- name, age, ethnicity and gender

- prior skills, knowledge, experience and qualifications

- any particular learning needs and support requirements

- any barriers, challenges, health or personal issues that might affect learning

- attendance, behaviour, and motivation concerns with support strategies

- learning preferences

- initial and diagnostic assessment results

- individual targets and additional targets to stretch and challenge learning further

Producing a detailed group profile is a good way to get to know about your learners as individuals. However, you must make sure you use the information to support your learners, and don't just file it away. You might find it useful to detail your group profile on a separate document, rather than integrate it into your teaching and learning plan, as it might be very detailed. Having your group profile as a separate document will save you repeating the information on each teaching and learning plan if you have the same learners regularly. The information on the group profile should not be shared with other learners. However, you should liaise with any other staff who are also in contact with your learners to pass on any relevant information.

The starting point for devising what you will deliver will come from the awarding organisation's syllabus or qualification handbook. If the qualification is on the QCF, it will state the learning outcomes and assessment criteria which must be taught and assessed. If you are not delivering an accredited qualification, you will still need to devise a programme of learning based around the subject you will teach, and devise your own criteria.

A rationale such as using 'five Ws and one H', *who, what, when, where, why* and *how*, will help you plan your scheme of work, for example:

- who the sessions are for, i.e. the individuals in your groups (who)
- what you want your learners to achieve (what)
- the number of sessions, dates and times (when)
- venue or environment (where)
- the learning outcomes of the programme or qualification (why)
- teaching and learning approaches, resources and assessment methods (how)

In your scheme of work the *what* part of the rationale can be defined as the *aim*. An aim is a clear and concise statement that describes *what you want* your learners to achieve. The aim is then broken down into objectives which are *how your learners* will achieve the aim. Think of what *you* want to achieve as the *aim*, and what your *learners* will achieve as the *objectives*. Objectives are verbs that can be demonstrated by your learners, which will enable you to see that learning has taken place, for example, demonstrate, describe, explain, list, perform, state and use.

If your learners are working towards a qualification, there will be *learning outcomes* for them to achieve, which will be in the syllabus or qualification handbook. You can add the learning outcomes to your scheme of work, or break them down into objectives.

If you are designing your own programme of learning which is not formally accredited, you will need to decide on your own learning outcomes or objectives.

Example

Helga is due to teach a programme for beginners who wish to use the internet. Her overall aim is: to provide an introduction to using the internet.

Helga's objectives are: learners will know all about search engines and understand how they work. These objectives are very vague and Helga's mentor suggests she uses the following which are more specific:

- *Learners will be able to access the internet*
- *Learners will state the names of three search engines*
- *Learners will use a search engine for a specific purpose*

Helga's original objectives were rather vague and did not reflect what her learners will actually do. Words like *know* and *understand* are not specific enough for learners to demonstrate they can do something. *State* and *use* are much better as the learner has to do something and the teacher can assess this has taken place.

If your learners are working towards learning outcomes defined by a particular qualification, you will notice they are often vaguely written. However, there will be *assessment criteria* associated with them which are more specific, and define what each learner can do to achieve the learning outcome. If you have a look at the units of the Certificate in Appendices 1–5, you will see the learning outcomes and assessment criteria which you need to meet.

Aims indicate the general direction in which you want to travel but they are not specific enough to tell you *how* to get there or when you have arrived. It is at this point that you are shifting the focus from what you want to achieve as the teacher (the aim) to what your learners will actually do (the objectives). Aims are teacher centred whereas objectives or learning outcomes are learner centred.

Objectives can be at different levels, for example, if you have a beginner they might *listen* to you explain something first, then *watch* a short video before *performing* a task. This is a logical progression from passively learning something, to actively carrying it out. You need to see that your learners can do something, to confirm that learning has taken place. You might be able to see that they are listening or watching, but you don't know if they are concentrating. Once they can perform a task, it will prove they know what they are doing. However, to prove your learner understands why they are doing something, you will need to ask questions. If they just *know* about something, but don't *understand* it, learning will not be effective.

Example

Greg was teaching a group of adults who were attending an evening class in Wine Tasting. He stated that red wine should always be drunk at room temperature, but did not state why. His learners therefore had the knowledge, but not the understanding.

Table 2.4 on page 70 lists objectives at different levels. You can refer to this when planning what you want your learners to do, to ensure learning is progressive and at the right level for them. The objectives are listed under the headings of skills, knowledge and understanding, and attitudes. Skills are aspects that are usually practical whereas knowledge and understanding are usually theoretical. Attitudes are often the hardest to assess as teachers will often have a subjective view as to whether a person is doing something correctly or not.

Table 2.4 Objectives at different levels (note – some might occur or be repeated at different levels on the QCF)

Level	Skills	Knowledge and understanding	Attitudes
Foundation	Attempt Carry out Learn Listen Read	Answer Match Recall Repeat Show	Adopt Assume Contribute Listen
I	Arrange Switch Help Use Imitate View Obtain Watch	Access Name Know Recap List Recognise Locate State	Adapt Co-operate Familiarise
2	Assist Perform Change Practise Choose Prepare Connect Present Demonstrate Rearrange Draw	Compare Describe Identify Reorder Select Write	Accept Consider Develop Express Question Understand
3	Apply Devise Assemble Estimate Assess Facilitate Build Illustrate Create Make Construct Measure Design Produce	Compose Explain Paraphrase Test	Apply Participate Appreciate Predict Challenge Relate Defend Review Determine Study Discriminate Visualise Enable
4	Calculate Modify Complete Plan Convert Quality Diagnose assure Explore Research Generate Search Maintain Solve	Analyse Invent Contextualise Outline Revise Summarise Verify	Appraise Judge Command Justify Criticise Persuade Debate Rationalise Define Reflect Discuss Influence
5	Accept Interview responsibility Manage Encapsulate Organise Establish Teach	Categorise Classify Contrast Evaluate Interpret	Argue Differentiate Critically Dispute appraise Formulate Define Suggest
6	Operate Utilise	Extrapolate Synthesise Translate	Conclude Hypothesise Justifiably argue
7	Modify	Strategise	Critically differentiate
8	Lead	Redefine	Critically discriminate

You can see that words such as *connect, list, use* and *explain* are SMART and clearly show what your learners will be doing, enabling you as the teacher to check that learning has taken place. It takes a lot of practice to write effective aims, objectives and learning outcomes but you will improve with practice. Be careful not to write these as a list of tasks for *you* to achieve during the session; always consider what your *learner* will achieve.

Although your scheme of work will be created before you begin teaching, it should be flexible enough to be adapted to respond to the needs of your learners. Once you know more about your learners, you may decide to alter the order in which you have planned your sessions. It may be necessary to allocate more time to one particular topic than another depending on your learners' knowledge and experience. Your scheme of work should be a working document and you should be prepared to adapt it throughout your time with your learners.

You might be teaching a programme that is not an accredited qualification or may involve aspects outside of your expertise, but you will still be required to find out if there is an existing qualification handbook, or if you need to design your own content. If it is the latter, there will probably be organisational requirements for you to follow to ensure you teach your subject correctly. If you are planning and designing the programme yourself, you will need to carry out this process before you begin teaching. Never underestimate how much time this takes, particularly if you are teaching a programme for the first time.

You need to find out what information your organisation collects about your learners before they arrive at the first session and use this to help you plan to meet their requirements.

Example

David enrolled for a Creative Arts programme which was to be held in his town's library. When he completed the enrolment form he disclosed that he uses a wheelchair. Unfortunately, when he arrived at the first session, David discovered that the library did not provide access to a disabled toilet.

Sometimes information is not passed on from those who have been responsible within the organisation for recruitment and enrolment. This can lead to problems for learners and may even deter some learners from returning. You should be given the relevant information concerning your learners in advance of your first session or contact with them. This enables you to check that the facilities and resources are suitable. If they are not, you have a chance to contact the learner and discuss any suitable alternatives. If you have been involved in the initial assessment process, you should have all the information you need. However, some learners might not feel confident about disclosing personal details to you until they have attended the first session.

When designing your scheme of work, think about the six key principles of adult learning set out by Knowles (2005). These six key principles for successful adult learning are linked to what adults themselves say about their learning.

1. Adults need to know why, what and how they are learning.

2. Their self-concept is important. They often wish to be autonomous and self-directing.

3. Their prior experience is influential. It can be used as a resource for current learning. It can also shape attitudes to current learning.

4. Readiness to learn is important. Adults usually learn best when something is of immediate value.

5. Adults often focus on solving problems in contexts or situations that are important to them.

6. Motivation to learn tends to be based on the intrinsic value of learning and the personal pay-off.

Adults have built up diverse life experiences and knowledge that may include work-related activities, family responsibilities, and previous education experiences. They need to connect their learning to this knowledge or experience. When designing your scheme of work, allow time early on in the programme to incorporate your learners' experiences and knowledge which are relevant to the topic. Relate theories and concepts to the learners and acknowledge the value of their experience throughout their learning. This will give your learners a sense of achievement and desire for more learning. Include your learners' experiences whenever you can to build on what they already know and can do.

Depending upon how much time you have to deliver your programme, you will need to decide what is essential (the *must*), what is important (the *should*) and what is helpful (the *could*). This is Knowles' *product and process model*. The *product model* ensures all content is delivered within the time, specific only to the qualification requirements. It does not give the option to add value or include other relevant information from which the learner might benefit. You could think of the product model as *teaching to pass a test*. The teacher only delivers the requirements of what will be assessed, for example, in a test. It might enable the learner to gain knowledge, but the knowledge is only recalled when assessed, and not applied to other situations such as in employment.

Knowles' *process model* adds value to the qualification by teaching other relevant beneficial skills and knowledge. This could involve using other professionals with different expertise to speak to learners. This might encourage the learners to think about how they could apply the additional knowledge in different situations. However, you will need to decide, based upon the time you have, what *must* be taught, what *should* be taught, and what *could* be taught. You should always focus on the *must* first, and then add value with the *should* and *could* by encouraging your learners to carry out work in their non-contact time if you don't have time during sessions.

Activity

When planning your next scheme of work, ask yourself the following questions:

What must I include?

What should I include?

What could I include?

If there are lots of topics you could include, but don't have the time, devise some activities for your learners to carry out in their own time.

Bloom (1956) believed that education should focus on the *mastery* of subjects and the promotion of higher forms of thinking, rather than on an approach which simply transfers facts. If you are teaching your learners to quote facts, they might have the knowledge, but not the understanding. Bloom demonstrated decades ago that most teaching tended to be focused on *fact-transfer* and *information recall* (the lowest level of teaching) rather than true meaningful personal development.

Bloom's Taxonomy (1956) model attempts to classify all learning into three parts, or *over-lapping domains*:

* *cognitive domain* (intellectual capability, i.e. *knowledge* or *thinking*)

* *affective domain* (feelings, emotions and behaviour, i.e. *attitudes* or *beliefs*)

* *psychomotor domain* (manual and physical skills, i.e. *skills* or *actions*)

The three domains are summarised as knowledge, attitudes and skills, or *think–feel–do*. Learners should benefit from the development of knowledge and intellect (*cognitive domain*), attitudes and beliefs (*affective domain*), and the ability to put physical and bodily skills into effect (*psychomotor domain*).

In each of the three domains, Bloom's Taxonomy is based on the premise that the categories are ordered in degrees of difficulty. An important premise of Bloom's Taxonomy is that each category (or level) must be mastered before progressing to the next. As such, the categories within each domain are levels of learning development, and these levels increase in difficulty. Effective learning should cover all the levels of each of the domains, where relevant to the subject, situation and the learner.

Extension Activity

Devise a scheme of work which meets the requirements of the programme or qualification you will deliver. You might need to use your organisation's template, or use a similar one to that in Table 2.3 on page 66.

Designing teaching and learning plans

A teaching and learning plan, often referred to as a session plan, contains more detail than your scheme of work, and is devised for each session you will deliver. You will find designing and adapting session plans a very time-consuming activity at first, but this does get easier with practice. It could be that you are using session plans devised by others, and you may not be able to deviate from them. This is often the case for teachers of programmes which are delivered nationally. However, you should still have some control over how you deliver the content to ensure you meet your learners' individual needs.

Your plan should be *fit for purpose* in such a way that the learning taking place is set in a realistic context for the programme and/or qualification, while meeting the individual needs of your learners. Your learners may have divulged information during the initial assessment process which will assist you in your planning. During the first session you could encourage your learners to share information about their interests and hobbies and what their aspirations are. This will help you to get to know your learners, enabling you to individualise learning as necessary. Effective teaching, learning and assessment will only be achieved as a result of careful planning and preparation, and it is your responsibility to ensure that this is completed in plenty of time before having contact with your learners. Table 2.5 on page 75 is a template which could be used or adapted to design a teaching and learning plan.

Your session plan should include details such as:

- the date, time, duration, venue, number of learners

- a clear aim of what you want your learners to achieve

- the context of the session, for example, references to the qualification being delivered

- a group profile, for example, age, prior experience, particular needs, learning preferences, behaviour concerns (see the previous section for more information)

- realistic objectives or learning outcomes at an appropriate level for your learners (you might be required to differentiate these into what you expect all, most and some of your learners to achieve)

- details of how English, maths and ICT will be developed by learners

- details of how equality, diversity and inclusion will be demonstrated throughout the session

- teaching, learning and assessment activities with allocated timings (be prepared to be flexible)

- resources to be used

Activity

Ask a colleague if you can look at some of their teaching and learning plans. See how they have completed them and the level of detail they have included. What would you would change or do differently?

Ideally, you should differentiate your objectives into what you expect *all, most* and *some* of your learners to achieve each session. This will be based upon their ability and enable you to stretch and challenge higher level learners. For example, you should ensure *all* learners achieve the requirements for that session, *most* learners achieve something more if they are capable, and *some* learners are stretched and challenged further. You could do this by using different activities based on the same topic. For example, *all* learners will *demonstrate* a topic, *most* learners will also *evaluate* how they performed, and *some* learners will *analyse* how they will apply their skills and knowledge to different situations.

The teaching, learning and assessment activities you use should be matched against your learners' learning preferences. For example, if you have a group of mainly kinaesthetic learners, you will not be helping them by asking them to read and write for the majority of the session. You should identify how much time you will allocate to each activity during your session, for example, five minutes for the introduction, five minutes for a recap and questions based on the previous session, ten minutes for a group activity and so on.

Table 2.5 Teaching and learning plan template

Teacher		Date		Venue	
Subject/level Qualification reference		Start time Duration		Number of learners	
Aim of session					
How English, maths and ICT will be developed					
How equality, diversity and inclusion will be demonstrated					
Group composition/profile *List details separately if necessary*					
Timing	Objectives/learning outcomes *All learners will:* *Most learners will:* *Some learners will:*	Teacher activities	Learner activities	Resources	Assessment activities

It would be much simpler for you if all your learners were starting from the same point and learnt in the same way. However, you should recognise that each learner on your programme will learn in a different way and at a different pace. You will need to be familiar with the range of support and guidance facilities available within your organisation, or externally, and how to access these if necessary.

You might be required to embed the functional skills of English, maths and ICT during your sessions. This will involve your learners using these skills not as separate subjects in their own right, but as part of the subject of the session. When integrating and embedding the skills during sessions, you need to ensure they are realistic and relevant to enable your learners to engage with real situations in their subject area. You can also encourage your learners to carry out activities in their own time to help them improve their skills. There might be free programmes available which they could attend or access via the internet which learners could take.

Example

Learners taking a programme in plumbing can use communication with customers and writing quotes to demonstrate English, can take measurements of pipes and fittings to demonstrate the use of maths, and can research websites and use e-mail to demonstrate ICT.

When planning your sessions, consider:

- the beginning, middle and end to your session; these should be structured and logical
- learning preferences, for example, VARK
- any individual learning needs and support required
- using practical activities that link to real work experiences, if appropriate
- inviting guest speakers, for example, past learners who have progressed further, or local employers who can bring the subject to life and explain job prospects
- having a contingency plan in case something doesn't work or an activity takes longer or shorter than you had planned
- how you will engage and motivate your learners by varying the activities
- using new technology where possible

Extension Activity

Design a teaching and learning plan for your next session with your learners. It should demonstrate clear planning of your aim and the objectives (or learning outcomes) along with appropriate teaching, learning and assessment activities. Ensure the individual needs of all your learners are identified and can be met. You might need to use your organisation's template, or a similar one to that in Table 2.5 on page 75.

Challenges when planning

You may face many challenges when planning your sessions, for example:

- lack of information

- lack of time for planning and preparation

- limited resources and budgets

It could be there are other staff who have experienced the same challenges as yourself. You will need to find out what support is available, and from whom, to help you during the planning process. If so, talk to them and ask them how they overcame the challenges. There might be specialist support staff within the organisation who can provide you and your learners with the advice and guidance needed at a given point.

Activity

Find out the names of staff in your organisation who are able to offer support and guidance on a range of topics. Introduce yourself to them and ask them what procedures you need to follow if you or your learners need support.

Your learners may also experience challenges which could impact upon their learning based on, for example, their:

- faith, culture and religion

- family and home circumstances and commitments

- fears, for example, about technology, change, not knowing anyone else in the group

- health concerns

- limited basic skills

- previous negative experiences of learning

- transport or childcare arrangements

Example

Rashid wanted to attend a series of evening classes but was apprehensive about joining a group of strangers. He felt the others would all be far more knowledgeable than he was. The teacher who interviewed him reassured him by telling him that most of the others he had interviewed were in the same position. He also said that he paired up all the learners in his groups, so that they had someone to relate to during the first session. This reassured Rashid and he said he would now attend the programme.

Hopefully, you can identify any challenges during the interview or initial assessment process in the hope of addressing them. However, other challenges may occur during the programme and you would need to plan a suitable course of action in an appropriate way. With any challenges that occur, you need to remain in control, be fair and ethical with all your learners and not demonstrate any favouritism towards particular ones, perhaps by giving one more support than others. For example, you might feel it sensible to make a telephone call to a learner who has been absent but making regular calls would be inappropriate.

Extension Activity

Consider the challenges you might face as a teacher when planning your sessions. Make a list of these and then state how you would deal with them.

Implementing the minimum core

The minimum core consists of four elements: literacy, language, numeracy and ICT. As part of your teaching role you should be able to demonstrate these elements to at least level 2. This will enable you to support your learners with English, maths and ICT (known as functional skills). It will also ensure you teach your area of specialism as effectively as possible.

Activity

Look at the four elements of the minimum core in Appendices 6, 7 and 8. Analyse the ways in which you feel you can demonstrate them when planning to meet the needs of your learners. Tick off the ones you can use, and make a note of how you will demonstrate them within your practice.

If possible, obtain a copy of the supporting document: *Addressing literacy, language, numeracy and ICT needs in education and training: Defining the minimum core of teachers' knowledge, understanding and personal skills – A guide for initial teacher education programmes* (LSIS, 2007, revised 2013). Have a look at the content to help you see how you can demonstrate the minimum core elements. The full document is available to download at: http://repository. excellencegateway.org.uk/fedora/objects/import-pdf:93/datastreams/PDF/content

Example: Literacy

- Reading relevant internal and external guidance to ascertain the requirements for initial and diagnostic assessment

- Reading the syllabus or qualification handbook and making notes regarding what will be delivered and assessed

- Completing templates and forms, and checking spelling, grammar and punctuation

Example: Language

- Speaking to learners about their individual needs

- Asking questions to ascertain a learner's prior knowledge and experience and listening to their responses

- Listening to questions and answering them appropriately

Example: Numeracy

- Calculating how long initial and diagnostic assessment activities will take, and the time it will take to ascertain and interpret the results

- Working out how many sessions and hours will be required when devising a scheme of work

- Planning how long various teaching, learning and assessment activities will take during a session

Example: ICT

- Preparing online materials and uploading them to a virtual learning environment (VLE) or other accessible system

- Using a word processor or other application to create handouts and resources

- Using e-mail or social networking to communicate appropriately

- Using new technology to support particular learning needs

Demonstrating your own skills regarding the minimum core should enable you to consider ways of improving the skills in your learners too. Some learners may not have adequate skills in reading, writing, working with numbers and/or using a computer; developing these skills in your learners and embedding them during your sessions can bring positive results.

Example

Owen is a cookery teacher and is due to deliver a session regarding healthy eating. He wants to encourage his learners to use their literacy, language, numeracy and ICT skills. His learners will therefore research and read recipes using cookery magazines, books and the internet, write shopping lists, communicate with others, buy the ingredients, word process a menu and then cook the meal. Owen will ensure his learners use the correct amounts of ingredients required by working these out in both metric and imperial measures. They will also calculate portion sizes and the cost of ingredients, along with the calorie content for each meal cooked. Owen has therefore enabled his learners to employ all these skills as part of the session.

In the above example, everyday aspects of using the skills were based around the subject and embedded into the session. The learners' skills should improve by the application of their knowledge within the subject.

All teachers need to develop a heightened awareness of the literacy, language, numeracy and ICT needs of their learners in order for them to teach their area of specialism as effectively as possible.

(Skills for Business, 2007, page 3)

You can play an important part in providing opportunities to develop your learners' skills in literacy, language, numeracy and ICT. However, it is your responsibility to continually update your own skills in these areas by undertaking professional development.

Extension Activity

The next time you are planning to meet the needs of your learners, try and demonstrate aspects of the four minimum core skills. Did you use the skills without realising, or did you have to consciously plan to use them? Keep a record of the skills you have demonstrated as you may need to prove to your assessor how you used them.

Evaluating own practice

You should always evaluate the effectiveness of your own practice to enable you to develop and improve for the future. The process should take into account the views of your learners and others you come into contact with. Reviewing your practice will also help you identify any problems or concerns, enabling you to do things differently next time. Never assume everything is going well just because you think it is.

Obtaining feedback from learners and others

Obtaining and responding to feedback from learners and others will help you improve your practice. Talking to your learners informally will help you realise how successful the planning process has been. This can be done during tutorial reviews, at break times, or before or after your sessions. Your learners are the best judges of whether they are getting what they feel they need. If given the opportunity, they may give you more feedback in an informal situation. You could give your learners a questionnaire. Always build in time during your session for your learners to complete the questionnaire, otherwise they might take it away and forget to return it. Alternatively, you could create an online survey for learners to access at an appropriate time and place. When issuing questionnaires or using online surveys, decide whether you want the responses to be anonymous, as you might gain more feedback if learners know they can't be identified. Always give a date for their return, otherwise people will take their time and then might forget. The response rate is not usually high when people are left to complete them in their own time. Therefore, if you can allow time during a session for your learners to complete them, you should receive a higher response.

You might decide to use a mixture of open and closed questions when designing your questionnaire. Open questions always require a full response and give you *qualitative* data to work with, i.e. quality feedback. Closed questions obtain only a yes or no answer and give you *quantitative* data, i.e. enabling you to add up the quantity (number) of responses. If you use a closed question, try to follow this up with an open question to enable you to obtain further qualitative information. It might take longer for you to read and analyse the responses, but you will have something more substantial to help with the evaluation process.

Activity

Create a questionnaire or survey (either manual or electronic) to use with your learners after your next session. Think carefully about how you will word your questions based on the information you need to help you improve the planning process with your learners. Analyse the results, write a report of your findings, then, if possible, make any necessary changes. Inform your learners how their feedback has contributed towards the changes.

What works with one learner or group might not work well with others, perhaps due to their individual learning preferences or other influences. However, don't change something for the sake of it; if it works, hopefully it will continue to work.

When evaluating the planning process, ask yourself the following questions.

Did I ...?

- ☐ carry out an initial and diagnostic assessment with my learners
- ☐ obtain details regarding any specific requirements or needs my learners have
- ☐ ascertain anything about my learners that could affect my teaching or their learning
- ☐ use a learning preference questionnaire, and differentiate my session plan accordingly
- ☐ agree an ILP with each learner
- ☐ obtain the syllabus or qualification handbook to ascertain all the requirements
- ☐ create a scheme of work which showed a logical progression of learning
- ☐ create a teaching and learning plan which met individual needs
- ☐ create a group profile of individual learner details
- ☐ have a clear aim and SMART objectives
- ☐ know in advance where I would be teaching, to how many learners and for how long
- ☐ plan to use appropriate teaching, learning and assessment activities
- ☐ devise resources and check availability of equipment

After evaluating your practice, you should be able to make any necessary changes. Don't forget to ask for feedback from your learners as they are best able to inform you how effective the planning process was.

Reflection

Reflection is about becoming more self-aware, which should give you increased confidence and improve the links between the theory and practice of teaching, learning and assessment.

Self-reflection should become a part of your everyday activities, enabling you to analyse and focus on things in greater detail. All reflection should lead to an improvement in practice; however, there may be events you would not want to change or improve as you felt they went well. If this is the case, reflect as to why they went well and use these methods in future sessions. As you become more experienced at reflective practice, you will see how you can improve and develop further.

Brookfield (1995) identified the importance of being critical when reflecting. Being critical is all about questioning what you have read, and not just agreeing with it because it has been published. Being critical also means looking for reasons why you should not agree with something, and arguing against it with your own ideas or those of others.

Brookfield advocated four points of view when looking at your practice which he called *critical lenses*. These lenses are from the point of view of:

- the teacher
- the learner
- colleagues
- theories and literature

Using these points makes the reflection critical, by looking at it firstly from your own point of view; secondly, from how your learner perceived your actions and what they liked and disliked; thirdly, from the view of colleagues, for example, your mentor or another teacher. Fourthly, you should link your reflections to theories and literature, comparing your own findings and ideas with those of others. All this enables you to have a critical viewpoint about your actions which might highlight things you hadn't originally considered.

Example

Pauline had been teaching for many years and felt she was quite experienced at identifying and supporting the individual needs of learners. However, when one of her learners, Jim, was struggling to carry out a practical activity, Pauline wondered if he had dyspraxia. She therefore had a quiet word with him, and he confided that he did but had been embarrassed to say. Pauline asked Jim how she could support him during sessions and he was very forthcoming. She later asked a colleague who also taught Jim how they supported him in other sessions. Pauline then researched how other teachers supported learners who have dyspraxia. This way, she was looking at the points of view of others as well as her own.

Martin (1996) developed six aspects to critical incident analysis. A critical incident is something that has occurred which is important or significant to you. The six aspects are as follows.

1. Choose a critical incident: this would be something that stands out for you, for example, a learner being disruptive.

2. Describe the incident to include: when and where it happened (time of day, location and context); what actually happened (who said or did what); what you were thinking and feeling at the time and just after the incident.

3. Interrogate your description to include: Why did this incident stand out? What was going on? Did you have a personal bias or a particular mindset regarding the event?

4. Find a friend or colleague to: share your account of the incident; discuss your interpretation to see what you can learn from the incident and reach a resolution; modify your analysis, where necessary, in the light of peer feedback to interpret the incident differently from another point of view.

5. Compare your analysis with the views of other key people involved in the incident (learners, colleagues, etc. where appropriate).

6. Write a report of the incident, maintaining confidentiality.

Following Martin's six aspects will help you reflect upon a critical incident, with a view to learning from the experience.

There may be aspects of your practice that will need time for changes or improvements to take effect. You might need to attend training, or devise something new before you can try out these changes.

Activity

Think of a critical incident that has happened lately during the planning process. Work through Brookfield's or Martin's theory to reflect upon it and see if you can reach an alternative solution.

Reviewing your progress will help you learn about yourself and what you could improve, for example, how you react to different situations or learners, how patient you are and what skills you may need to develop. You might also decide you need further training or support to improve your teaching skills, subject knowledge and/or English, maths and ICT skills.

Extension Activity

Based on your evaluation of how you plan the learning process, what areas have you identified as needing improvement? How can you act on what you have identified and what will you do differently as a result? Do you need any further training and/or support? If so, how will you go about obtaining it?

Summary

In this chapter you have learnt about:

- *initial and diagnostic assessment*
- *negotiating and agreeing individual learning goals*
- *devising a scheme of work*
- *designing teaching and learning plans*
- *challenges when planning*
- *implementing the minimum core*
- *evaluating own practice*

Cross-referencing grid

This chapter contributes towards the following assessment criteria of the units which form the Certificate in Education and Training, along with aspects of the Professional Standards for Teachers and Trainers in England. Full details of the learning outcomes and assessment criteria of each unit can be found in the appendices.

Certificate units	Assessment criteria
Understanding roles, responsibilities and relationships in education and training	1.1, 1.4
Planning to meet the needs of learners in education and training	1.1, 1.2, 1.3 2.1, 2.2, 2.3, 2.4, 2.5 3.1, 3.2 4.1, 4.2
Delivering education and training	1.3
Assessing learners in education and training	1.1, 1.2, 1.3 2.1, 2.3, 2.4, 2.5
Using resources for education and training	1.2, 1.3

Area	Professional Standards for Teachers and Trainers in England
Professional values and attributes	1, 2, 3, 4, 5, 6
Professional knowledge and understanding	7, 9, 10, 11, 12
Professional skills	13, 14, 15, 16, 17, 18, 19, 20

Theory focus

References and further information

Ayers, H (2006) *An A–Z Practical Guide to Learning Difficulties*. London: David Fulton Publishers.

Bloom, BS (1956) *Taxonomy of Educational Objectives: The Classification of Educational Goals*. New York: McKay.

Brookfield, S (1995) *Becoming a Critically Reflective Teacher.* San Francisco: Jossey-Bass.

Coffield, F (2004) *Learning Preferences and Pedagogy in Post-16 Learning.* London: Learning & Skills Research Centre.

Coffield, F (2008) *Just Suppose Teaching and Learning Became the First Priority.* London: Learning and Skills Network.

Farrell, M *The Effective Teacher's Guide to Dyslexia and other Learning Difficulties (Learning Disabilities) Practical Strategies* (2nd edn). Abingdon: Routledge.

Fleming, N (2005) *Teaching and Learning Preferences: VARK strategies.* Honolulu: Honolulu Community College.

Gravells, A and Simpson, S (2014) *Passing Assessments for the Certificate in Education and Training.* London: Learning Matters SAGE.

Hargreaves, S (2012) *Study Skills for Students with Dyslexia.* London: SAGE Publications Ltd.

Honey, P and Mumford, A (1992) *The Manual of Learning Preferences* (3rd edn). Maidenhead: Peter Honey Associates.

Honey, P and Mumford, A (2000) *The Learning Preferences Helper's Guide.* Coventry: Peter Honey Publications.

Knowles, M, Holten III, E and Swanson, R (2005) *The Adult Learner* (6th edn). Oxford: Butterworth-Heinemann.

LSIS (2007, revised 2013) *Addressing literacy, language, numeracy and ICT needs in education and training: Defining the minimum core of teachers' knowledge, understanding and personal skills – A guide for initial teacher education programmes.* Coventry: LSIS.

Martin, K (1996) Critical Incidents in Teaching and Learning. *Issues of Teaching and Learning*, 2(8).

Read, H (2013) *The Best Initial Assessment Guide.* Bideford: Read On Publications.

Roffey-Barentsen, J and Malthouse, R (2013) *Reflective Practice in Education and Training* (2nd edn). London: Learning Matters SAGE.

Rushton, I and Suter, M (2012) *Reflective Practice for Teaching in Lifelong Learning.* Maidenhead: OU Press.

Schön, D (1983) *The Reflective Practitioner: How Professionals Think in Action.* USA: Basic Books Inc.

Skills for Business (2007) *Inclusive Learning approaches for literacy, language, numeracy and ICT: Companion Guide to the Minimum Core.* Nottingham: DfES Publications.

Wood, J and Dickinson, J (2011) *Evaluating Learning in the Further Education and Skills Sector.* London: Learning Matters SAGE.

Website list

Basic Key Skills Builder – www.bksb.co.uk

Citizens Advice Bureau – www.citizensadvice.org.uk

Database of self-help groups – www.self-help.org.uk

Dyslexia Association – www.dyslexia.uk.net

Dyspraxia Foundation – www.dyspraxiafoundation.org.uk/

Equality Act (2010) – www.legislation.gov.uk/ukpga/2010/15/contents

Equality and Diversity Forum – www.edf.org.uk

Initial and diagnostic assessment – http://archive.excellencegateway.org.uk/page.aspx?o=BSFAlearning difficulty%2Finitialassess

Initial Assessment Tools – http://archive.excellencegateway.org.uk/page.aspx?o=toolslibrary

Learning preference questionnaire – www.vark-learn.com

National Careers Service – https://nationalcareersservice.direct.gov.uk/Pages/Home.aspx

NIACE report on Prior Learning within the Qualifications and Credit Framework –

www.niace.org.uk/sites/default/files/project-docs/niace_rpl_report_v0_2_formatted.pdf

QCF shortcut – http://tinyurl.com/2944r8h

RARPA – www.learningcurve.org.uk/courses/ladder4learning/resources/rarpatoolkit

Videos by Ann Gravells on various topics – www.youtube.com/channel/ UCEQQRbP7x4L7NAy4wsQi7jA

3 DELIVERING EDUCATION AND TRAINING

In this chapter you will learn about:

- the teaching and learning environment
- teaching and learning theories
- teaching and learning approaches
- communication methods
- using information and communication technology (ICT)
- implementing the minimum core
- evaluating own practice

There are activities and examples to encourage you to reflect on the above which will help you develop and enhance your understanding of how to deliver education and training.

At the end of each section within the chapter are extension activities to stretch and challenge your knowledge and understanding. A list of useful references, further information and website links can be found at the end of the chapter in case you would like to research the topics further.

At the end of the chapter is a cross-referencing grid showing how the chapter's contents relate to the units of the Certificate in Education and Training, and the Professional Standards for Teachers and Trainers in England.

The teaching and learning environment

The teaching and learning environment includes not only the venue, equipment and resources used, but also aspects such as your attitude, the way you act with your learners and the support you give them. Having a positive attitude can help create the right atmosphere for learning to occur. Learning can take place in a variety of contexts, for example, classrooms, the workplace, training rooms, workshops, prisons, outdoors and online. While learning can take place almost anywhere, not all environments will be totally suitable; however, it is *how* you teach that will lead to effective learning. If you can convey passion and enthusiasm for your subject you will help motivate your learners to want to learn more. Creating a good first impression, being organised and acting in a professional way should help your learners feel they are receiving a quality service.

If you are teaching a practical subject, you will need a suitable environment so that you can demonstrate and your learners can practise, for example, a workshop or a laboratory. If you are teaching a theoretical subject, you may be fine in a room with tables and chairs, but you may need a computer, data projector and/or an interactive whiteboard. You might be delivering a seminar or event in a venue you have never visited before. If this is the case, it would be useful to telephone or visit in advance to check what facilities are available.

You might be restricted by the availability of particular rooms or resources; therefore you need to be imaginative with what is available to you. Your learners don't need to know about any problems, as your professionalism should enable you to deliver and assess your subject effectively. However, you do need to take into account any health and safety issues and let your organisation know of any concerns. You need to establish an environment where your learners feel safe, secure, confident and valued.

The venue, toilets and refreshment areas should be accessible and appropriate for every-one. Advanced knowledge of your learners will help you check that everything is suitable. If your session includes a break, make sure you tell your learners what time this will be and for how long. If you don't, learners might not be concentrating on their learning but think-ing about when they can go to the toilet or get a drink.

You need to ensure the environment is suitable not only for learning, but for social interac-tion too. If possible, aim for 70 per cent of the time for learner involvement and practical activities, and 30 per cent of the time for teaching activities. This will of course depend upon the subject, the environment and your learners. However, using activities, projects, discussions, paired and group work for your learners to carry out should aid the learning process by keeping them active, included, interested, involved and motivated.

According to Fawbert:

> There are many things that you can do to reassure them, [your learners] whatever their needs are, that you and the environment you have created, will be positively responsive. Try simple things, such as [among others]:
>
> * minimise authoritarian notices or instructions, use humorous, interesting displays
>
> * smile, reassure, explain, use their names as soon as possible
>
> * encourage questioning and respond sincerely as a facilitator
>
> * find something about each of them to like

(2008, page 140)

The learning environment has three aspects: physical, social and learning. See Table 3.1 for examples of each. All three aspects should be appropriate, relevant and safe, and each will have an impact upon the other. Some aspects will interact and overlap to ensure teaching, learning and assessment can be effective for everyone.

Activity

Look at the following table and add at least one more aspect to each column. Choose one aspect from each and state how you will ensure it can happen.

Table 3.1 Examples of physical, social and learning aspects

Physical	Social	Learning
Ensure adequate heating, lighting and ventilation	Use a suitable icebreaker to put learners at ease and create a rapport	Have clear aims and objectives/learning outcomes of what will be covered and plan what will take place during each session
Ensure ease of access to all learning areas	Agree ground rules to help promote appropriate behaviour and respect	Engage and motivate learners; give support and encouragement
Ensure the layout of the room is suitable or adjust if possible (e.g. to ensure all learners can see and hear)	Communicate effectively (speaking, listening, body language, eye contact)	Make the session interesting and relevant; summarise and recap regularly
Ensure toilets and refreshment facilities are accessible	Use paired and group activities; draw on learners' skills, knowledge and experiences	Use a variety of suitable teaching, learning and assessment approaches
Ensure safe use of equipment, materials and resources	Encourage learners to listen to you and each other	Differentiate for individual needs; refer learners elsewhere if necessary
Carry out risk assessments and minimise hazards; know who the first aider is	Use learner names and eye contact; include all learners in activities and when communicating	Assess progress and achievement on an ongoing basis (formally and informally)
Know where fire extinguishers and emergency exits are	Give adequate breaks at appropriate times	Provide ongoing constructive feedback
Make sure the room is tidy before and after use	Challenge inappropriate behaviour	Keep records of what has been taught, and the progress of all learners

Another aspect to consider regarding the environment is the room layout. You might not be able to change this, for example, if tables or desks are in fixed positions. However, you need to ensure your learners can all see and hear you, and can communicate with each other. The seating arrangements can also have a big impact on learning. People like their comfort zones and you may find that learners will sit in the same place each time they are with you. This is often the place where they sat during the first session. This is useful as it can help you remember learners' names; you can sketch a seating plan and make notes. Using names will show respect, and encourage your learners to talk to you in confidence if they have any concerns. Moving learners around or getting them to work with others can either help or hinder their learning depending upon the group dynamics and learner maturity. Learners' ages can also have an impact upon what happens in the environment. Younger learners might need more discipline and motivation, whereas older learners might not. Getting to know your learners and the environment in advance of any sessions will help ensure you are prepared and organised.

If possible, arrive early to set up the room as you may find it hasn't been left in a suitable condition by the previous user. You should always leave the room tidy at the end, for example, cleaning a white board if used, and asking your learners to put any rubbish in the bin. Starting and finishing your sessions on time will help convey a sense of order and routine.

Extension Activity

Make a list of the different environments or rooms within which you will teach. What are the positive and negative aspects of using them for teaching and learning? How can you overcome any negative aspects to create an inclusive teaching and learning environment for all?

Teaching and learning theories

There are many different theories regarding the way people learn. This section will very briefly explore some of them (in alphabetical order), which you might like to research further and try out with your own learners. However, don't get too concerned thinking you must teach in a certain way because a theorist says so. What works with one group or individual learner might not work with another. You might find at first you are teaching the way you were taught at school, college or university. It might have suited you at the time, or it might have had a detrimental effect. Don't be afraid to try something different and step out of your comfort zone. You will need to find out through experience what works and what doesn't work with your own learners.

Behaviourism

Behaviourism assumes a learner is essentially passive, and will be shaped through positive or negative reinforcement. Learning is therefore defined as a change in behaviour. Skinner (1974) believed that behaviour is a function of its consequences, i.e. learners will repeat the desired behaviour if positive reinforcement is given. The behaviour should not be repeated if negative feedback is given. Giving immediate feedback, whether positive or negative, should enable your learners to behave in a certain way. Positive reinforcement or rewards can include verbal feedback such as *That's great, you've produced that document without any errors* or *You're certainly getting on well with that task,* through to more tangible rewards such as a certificate at the end of the programme, or a promotion or pay rise at work.

Cognitivism

Cognitivism focuses on what happens in the mind such as thinking and problem-solving. New knowledge is built upon prior knowledge and learners need active participation in order to learn. Changes in behaviour are observed, but only as an indication of what is taking place in the learner's mind. Cognitivism uses the metaphor of the mind as a computer: information comes in, is processed, and learning takes place.

Constructivism

Constructivism is about learning being an active, contextualised process of constructing knowledge rather than acquiring it. The learner brings past experiences and cultural factors to a current situation and each person has a different interpretation and construction of the knowledge process.

Vygotsky's (1978) theory is one of the foundations of constructivism. It asserts three major themes.

1. Social interaction plays a fundamental role in the process of cognitive development. Vygotsky felt social learning precedes development and stated: *Every function in the child's cultural development appears twice: first, on the social level, and later, on the individual level; first, between people (interpsychological) and then inside the child (intrapsychological)* (Vygotsky, 1978 page 57).

2. The More Knowledgeable Other (MKO). The MKO refers to anyone who has a better understanding or a higher ability level than the learner, with respect to a particular task, process, or concept. The MKO is normally the teacher, or an older adult, but the MKO could also be a peer, a younger person, or even information from the internet.

3. The Zone of Proximal Development (ZPD). The ZPD is the distance between a learner's ability to perform a task under adult guidance and/or with peer collaboration and their ability to solve the problem independently. According to Vygotsky, learning occurred in this zone.

Think of these themes as:

1. what the learner can do

2. what the learner can do with help from others

3. what the learner can't yet do but will attempt to do

Experiential learning

Experiential learning is about the learner experiencing things for themselves and learning from them. Kolb (1984) proposed a four stage model known as the experiential learning cycle. It is a way by which people can understand their experiences and, as a result, modify their behaviour. It is based on the idea that the more often a learner reflects on a task, the more often they have the opportunity to modify and refine their efforts. The process of learning can begin at any stage and is continuous, i.e. there is no limit to the number of cycles which can be made in a learning situation. This theory suggests that without reflection, people would continue to repeat their mistakes.

- Concrete experience is about experiencing or immersing yourself in the task and is the first stage in which a person simply carries out the task assigned. This is the *doing* stage.

- Observation and reflection involve stepping back from the task and reviewing what has been done and experienced. Your values, attitudes and beliefs can influence your thinking at this stage. This is the stage of *thinking* about what you have done.

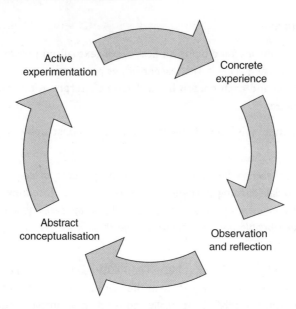

Figure 3.1 Kolb's (1984) experiential learning cycle

- Abstract conceptualisation involves interpreting the events that have been carried out and making sense of them. This is the stage of *planning* how you will do it differently.

- Active experimentation enables you to take the new learning and predict what is likely to happen next or what actions should be taken to refine the way the task is done again. This is the *redoing* stage based upon experience and reflection.

Humanism

Humanism is an approach that believes learning is seen as a personal act to fulfil potential. Humanists believe that it is necessary to study a person as a whole, particularly as they grow and develop over their lifetime. Rogers (1983) and others developed the theory of facilitative learning based on a belief that people have a natural human eagerness to learn and that learning involves changing your own concept of yourself. This theory suggests that learning will take place if the person delivering it acts as a facilitator. The facilitator should establish an atmosphere in which their learners feel comfortable, are able to discuss new ideas and learn by their mistakes, as long as they are not threatened by external factors.

Pedagogy and andragogy

Formal teaching is known as *pedagogy*, where the teacher directs all the learning. Informal teaching is known as *andragogy*, where the learner is the focus, for example, via group work and discussions. Pedagogy does not always allow for individual knowledge to be taken into account and often focuses on teaching the same topic at the same time to all learners. Knowles et al. (2005) initially defined andragogy as the art and science of helping adults learn. An andragogical approach places more emphasis on what the learner is doing. You can include your learners' experiences and knowledge by involving them whenever possible, and building upon what they already know and what interests them. Learners can also learn from their peers' knowledge and experiences, as well as from you.

Pragmatism

John Dewey (1859–1952) believed that formal schooling was falling short of its potential. He emphasised facilitating learning through promoting various activities rather than by using a traditional teacher-focused method. He believed that learners learnt more from guided experience than from authoritarian instruction. He subscribed to a *pragmatist* theory which placed the learner as the focus rather than the teacher. Dewey argued that *learning is life*, not just *preparation for life*. Using different delivery approaches, combined with practical activities, will help reach the different learning preferences of the individuals you are teaching.

Sensory theory

Laird (1985) suggests that learning occurs when the senses of sight, hearing, touch, smell and taste are stimulated. This is easy if you are teaching a practical session, but not so if you are teaching a theoretical subject. However, if you are willing to try something different, you can make your sessions really interesting and memorable. Whenever possible, link theory to practice, and use practical activities based around the subject and the areas of interest of your learners. If you can make your session fun and interesting, relating to all the senses, it will help your learners remember the topics better. Don't forget two other senses you can use as a teacher: a sense of humour and common sense.

Extension Activity

Research the theories explained here and compare and contrast them. Find out what other relevant theories there are. Use textbooks and journals, or key in the words 'learning theories' into an internet search engine.

Teaching and learning approaches

Teaching and learning approaches are the methods you use to facilitate the learning process. Think of these as the techniques which focus on your learners being *actively engaged* during the session and not just *passively listening* to you. The approaches you use will depend upon the subject and level you are teaching, the context and environment you are teaching in, the length of each session and any particular learner needs. Will you be teaching formally, for example, giving a lecture, or informally, for example, facilitating group discussions with learners? It is not about *what you will teach*, but *how they will learn*. Approaches should always be fit for purpose, i.e. to enable learning to take place, and not just used for the sake of it, or because you like to do things in a certain way. You should always take into account any prior knowledge and experience your learners might have. To give you some ideas, see Table 3.2 at the end of this chapter. The table lists several teaching and learning approaches and activities along with their strengths and limitations.

Teaching and learning should not be in isolation from the assessment process. You can assess that learning is taking place each time you are with your learners. This can simply be by observing their actions or asking questions. If your learners are taking a qualification, there will be formal methods of assessment such as an assignment, or an observation in the workplace. However, you can devise informal methods to use with your learners to check their progress. For more information regarding assessment please see Chapter 4.

Induction

When you begin teaching a new group or an individual, there will be lots of information you must explain regarding your organisation, the facilities available and the programme content. This is known as an *induction* and will usually take place during the first meeting with your learners.

An induction should include aspects such as:

- introducing yourself and giving a little information about your experience and knowledge regarding the subject

- facilitating an icebreaker to introduce learners to each other

- explaining the dates and times of attendance, break times and refreshment facilities

- checking your learners have received relevant information, advice and guidance

- explaining the programme/qualification content and assessment requirements

- giving a tour of the site (if applicable) including the location of study areas, toilets, catering venues, parking and smoking areas

- explaining organisational policies such as health and safety, equality and diversity, safeguarding, appeals and complaints

- explaining procedures such as for fire and accidents

- negotiating and agreeing ground rules

If you are delivering a short event, you might carry out certain housekeeping aspects rather than a detailed induction. This might include stating the times of breaks, where certain facilities are such as toilets and refreshments, and information regarding safety procedures.

You could use an induction checklist to ensure all aspects are covered, and give your learner a copy, or make it available electronically. This will act as a reminder of what was covered. Often, so much information is given out during the first session that learners can easily forget some important points. During inspections, when learners have been asked if they took part in an induction process they have often said 'no'. This has mainly been due to the fact they did not understand what the word induction meant. You could keep a signed copy as a record that the induction process has taken place.

There may be some administrative aspects to be completed during the first meeting with your learners, such as filling in relevant forms. Don't let this take over – your learners will want to leave their first session having learnt something interesting about the subject. If you have any learners who commence late, make sure you spend time with them to cover what they have missed, and introduce them to the others so that they don't feel isolated.

Icebreakers

Carrying out an icebreaker is a good way of everyone getting to know each other's name, and encouraging communication to take place. Some learners may already know each other, or have carried out an icebreaker with another teacher or trainer they currently have. Knowing this beforehand will help you decide upon an appropriate and suitable icebreaker to carry out, and saves repetition. You could carry out the icebreaker before covering the induction requirements as this will encourage your learners to relax, and give them confidence to speak or ask questions in front of others. Always introduce yourself first otherwise learners may be wondering what your name is, or whether you are just someone facilitating the first session. First impressions count; therefore you need to portray that you are a professional, knowledgeable person who is competent and approachable.

Icebreakers can also be used during an established session, perhaps after a break to help learners refocus. These are called *energisers* and can be subject specific such as a quiz or a fun activity or game which gets learners moving about. Always have a contingency plan in case anything you planned to use isn't available, or if some learners finish before others, or don't wish to take part.

Whichever way you use an icebreaker or an energiser, it should be designed to be an inclusive, fun and light-hearted activity to:

- build confidence
- create a suitable learning environment
- enable learners to talk confidently in front of their peers
- encourage communication, motivation, interaction, teamwork and inclusion
- establish trust and respect
- get the programme off to a good start
- help learners relax
- introduce learners to each other
- minimise barriers
- reduce apprehension and nervousness
- reduce intimidation

Ground rules

Negotiating and agreeing a few ground rules will help establish the boundaries for an effective learning environment. Giving the learners ownership of these should help to ensure that they are maintained, and minimise any disruption. Keeping them on display throughout each session will act as a visual reminder.

Ground rules should be agreed by the whole group rather than imposed by you. By showing an interest in their decisions, you are communicating with your learners that they are valued as individuals, who bring useful skills and knowledge to the session.

Activity

You have a group of ten learners who are feeling relaxed and comfortable after their icebreaker. You now want them to discuss and agree some ground rules, which they will then negotiate with you. How will you facilitate the activity and what do you think they might suggest?

You might think that they will agree to arrive on time and switch off their electronic devices. However, it might be useful to get them to think about dividing their ground rules into rights and responsibilities, for example:

- We have a right to:
  - be treated with respect
  - be listened to
  - be assured of confidentiality
- We have a responsibility to:
  - be on time for all sessions
  - not disrupt the session
  - switch off electronic devices

It is important to encourage all your learners to express their opinions in the group, providing these are valid. However, some learners may take longer to express themselves than others. The group will need to know that decisions made regarding ground rules at the start of the programme may need to be renegotiated or evaluated at a later stage. This renegotiation process may give those learners who preferred to stay quiet at the start an opportunity to participate. You, or your learners, could write the ground rules on flipchart paper or create a poster to display each session to act as a reminder. Alternatively, they could be uploaded electronically to an online area which all learners can access, or be e-mailed to each learner.

Your organisation might have its own learning contract/agreement with written commitments that you, your learners and your organisation will agree to. The negotiated ground rules can be seen as an extension of this to include aspects which may affect the group as a whole. Involving your learners in making decisions about their programme increases their interest, commitment, motivation and learning.

Delivering sessions

When delivering a session, you should be organised and professional, and follow all relevant policies, procedures and codes of practice. Careful planning and preparation will lead to an effectively delivered session, with all learners having been included and learning what was intended. It is useful to prepare a teaching and learning plan (also known as a session plan) in advance, as this will detail all the activities and resources you will use, as well as approximate timings. Please see Chapter 2 for further information.

You can probably recall attending a session in the past, perhaps at school or college, where the teacher was really enthusiastic about the subject, and made the session interesting, enabling you to enjoy and learn in a comfortable atmosphere. Equally so, you have probably attended a session delivered by a teacher who was badly organised or lacked confidence, causing you to lose interest. You therefore need to be enthusiastic and make your sessions interesting and memorable. Wherever possible, recognise the individual differences and experiences of your learners, encourage interaction between them and empower them; if they are mature enough, give them responsibility for their own learning. Having positive expectations of your learners and encouraging them to accomplish tasks, even if this is in small stages, will help them to see their progress and achievement.

Sessions should include a logical and progressive introduction to the subject and topics, and have a beginning, middle and ending section.

The beginning

When commencing a session, if you are unsure what to say to gather your learners' attention, start with *Welcome to the session, today we will ...* in a louder than normal but assertive voice. To settle your learners and focus their attention towards learning, you could facilitate a *warm up* or *starter activity*. This could be a quiz to test knowledge gained so far, a discussion to open up thinking about the current topic, or an energiser activity focusing upon the subject. If any learners are late, they will only have missed the starter activity and not any important aspects of the session.

Example

Zarek teaches British Sign Language one evening a week to learners who are at work during the day. The programme is due to start at 6.00 p.m. Due to work commitments, some learners often arrive at various times during the first ten minutes of the session. Zarek uses a starter activity based on the previous week's topic which enables learners to put into practice the signs they have learnt. Once everyone has arrived, he formally commences the session.

This management of time to meet the needs of individual learners can have a positive impact on their progress. Learners will make an effort to arrive as soon as possible if they feel that there is a benefit in doing so. Do consider carefully what to deliver in the first part of the session; you need to make an impact to gain and maintain your learners' attention.

The beginning section of a session should include:

- a starter or warm up activity

- an introduction to the session aims and objectives

- a recap of the previous session and link to the current session

- time for questions from learners

- ascertaining what prior skills and/or knowledge learners have of the topic to be covered

The middle

The middle section is where teaching and learning take place using a variety of approaches and activities. This is where new facts, knowledge, concepts and skills are taught. Your learners will discover the why and how of what they are expected to be able to know or do. Your overall aim (what you are planning your learners will achieve) will then be broken down into objectives (how the learners will achieve the aim). You should allocate timings to the various activities you plan to use throughout your session. When planning these activities consider the three domains of learning, i.e. cognitive, affective and psychomotor, and how you will meet all learning preferences.

It is during the delivery of the main content section of your session that you might adapt your teaching and learning plan; you need to be flexible to accommodate any changes. During the session, you may find some activities take longer than you planned, and some will take less time. You might be facilitating a group discussion that you feel is contributing more to learning than you anticipated. You will therefore need to amend your timings of the other activities to enable this one to continue.

What really matters during the session is what is being learnt. Assessment to check this should be ongoing, for example, observing actions and asking questions. You need to decide how you are going to check that learning has taken place, and how you will give feedback to your learners. It is good practice to reinforce learning regularly by linking activities together and asking open questions.

When using activities, you need to ensure that they are inclusive, and that they differentiate for any individual needs. You should refer to your group profile to help you. Make sure your learners are aware of why they are carrying out the activities and don't overcomplicate your sessions with too much too soon, or too many confusing activities which are not linked together. Experimenting with new or different approaches and activities should make your sessions interesting and reach all learning preferences.

If you are passionate about your subject, this should help engage, enthuse and motivate your learners. Any subject can be made interesting to your learners; it is all about the way you choose to deliver it. A session is boring to the learners only if the teacher delivers it in a boring way. If you are not interested, or don't prepare your materials adequately, your learners may lose confidence in you, begin to lack motivation, and the result might be disruption and behaviour issues. Keep your sessions active, involve your learners and build their self-esteem; ask relevant questions, use eye contact, use their names and give positive praise and feedback. You may have to repeat things several times to your learners before they understand it. Remember this is the first time they have heard it so try to say it enthusiastically each time.

You might need to embed aspects such as English, maths, and ICT within your session to help your learners improve these skills.

As you progress, allow time for questioning, repeating and summarising important points. Incorporate the knowledge and experience of your learners and if you can, give relevant anecdotes to bring the subject to life. Ensure your session flows progressively, i.e. is delivered in a logical order and assesses progress before moving on to the next topic. When changing topics, try to link them together somehow or summarise one before moving onto the other.

Never lose your temper, embarrass your learners in front of their peers, or make disparaging comments about other learners, colleagues or the organisation within which you work; this is very unprofessional. Your learners need to feel good about their teacher, about themselves and their learning, and you can help this with the environment you create and the experiences you give your learners. You want your learners to return to your sessions keen to learn and to participate. Penalising bad behaviour, for example, by disallowing a break, asking a learner to stay behind, moving a learner to another seating position or issuing extra homework, may be effective with younger learners, but it is harder to challenge an adult, particularly if they are older than you. You need to get to know your learners. If they are being disruptive try to find out the cause of the problem, instead of generating further bad feeling. It is better to create order in a proactive way within the group, by finding strategies that work for you all, than to impose order in a reactive way.

If you finish any activities earlier than planned, make sure you have some extra ones you could use, for example, worksheets or a quiz. If particular learners finish tasks earlier than others, you could give them an extension activity to stretch and challenge their learning further. You should also plan what *all, most* and *some* learners will do to differentiate for abilities, i.e. all learners will complete all activities, most learners will complete an extension activity and some learners will complete an additional activity. It is always useful to carry a few spare activities around with you, or to have access to them electronically.

If you feel you are overrunning on your timings, don't be afraid to carry something over to the next session, cut it out altogether or give it as homework. Alternatively, you can adjust the timings of the activities to reduce or increase them as necessary. Don't feel you must keep to the number of minutes you have written on your plan. It is more important to ensure learning is taking place, than keeping to your timings.

The middle section of a session should include:

- a variety of teaching and learning approaches
- activities which actively promote learning at an appropriate level
- assessment to check progress and achievement
- appropriate class management
- the use of relevant resources
- embedding English, maths, and ICT skills
- embedding equality and diversity
- support and guidance to meet any individual needs
- extension activities to stretch and challenge learners further

The ending

At the end of your sessions, ensure that you recap the aims and objectives. You can also summarise all the relevant points which have been learnt. However, don't introduce anything new at this point as this might confuse your learners. Ensure that your learners are aware of how to apply their newly acquired skills and knowledge and how these are transferable to different contexts.

You could facilitate a *finishing activity* based on the topic of the session by asking individual questions or holding a group quiz to check knowledge. You could give points for successful answers that can be added up throughout the programme, and give a prize at the end to the learner or group with the most points. Some learners are motivated by friendly competition and this can be a fun way to end each session. You could ask each team to decide upon a team name for a bit of fun.

Introduce the topic of the next session (if applicable), to give the learners something to look forward to and set any homework or further activities. Qualifications on the Qualifications and Credit Framework (QCF) require learners to study in their own time, known as *non-contact time*. You will need to plan various activities for learners to carry out as homework, i.e. reading, research and assignments. Always follow up or check on what they have done, otherwise they might see it as meaningless.

If you have spare time at the end of a session, ask each learner in turn to state one thing they have learnt during the session. This is a good time filler if necessary and helps you see what they have learnt.

If you are unsure what to say to formally end your session, simply say *Thank you, I've enjoyed my session with you today.* If you are due to see your learners again for another session, you could say *Thank you, I look forward to seeing you all again on ...* Plan time at the end for clearing up; you don't want to be rushed, particularly if you have another session to go to.

As soon as possible after the session, you should carry out a self-evaluation and reflect on how it went and why. Make notes of any changes you would make that would help you if you were to deliver this same session again. Also consider whether or not you need to address any gaps in your own skills and knowledge and make sure you do something about it.

The ending section of a session should include:

- a recap of the session aims and objectives

- a summary of the main points of the session

- time for questions from learners

- a finishing activity

- the setting of homework or other activities

- an introduction to the next session

- time for clearing up

Attention spans

An attention span is the amount of time that a learner can concentrate without being distracted. This will vary according to the age of your learners; often younger learners will concentrate less as they are easily distracted. Being able to focus without being distracted is crucial for learning to take place. There are two types of attention, *focused* and *sustained*.

- Focused attention is a short-term response to something that attracts awareness and is very brief, for example, the ring of a telephone or an unexpected occurrence. After a few seconds, it is likely that the person will return to what they were originally doing or think about something else.

- Sustained attention is a longer-term response which will enable the achievement of something over a period of time. For example, if the task is to take a few photos, choose the best three and upload them to a website, then the person showing sustained attention will stay on task and achieve it fully. A person who loses attention might take a few photos but move on to doing something else before choosing and uploading the best three.

Most healthy teenagers and adults are able to sustain attention on one thing for about 20 minutes (Cornish and Dukette, 2009, page 73). They can then choose to refocus on the same thing for another 20 minutes. This ability to renew concentration enables people to stay on task for as long as necessary. However, there are other factors to take into consideration, such as self-motivation, ability, tiredness, thirst and hunger. If a learner is hungry their concentration may lapse as a result. If you find your learners losing focus, ask them if there is anything distracting them as you might be able to resolve it, for example, opening a window if it is too warm.

When planning to deliver your sessions, try to use several short tasks to enable your learners to stay focused. If you do need to use longer tasks, try to break these down into 20 minutes for each, with a chance for a discussion or something different in between. If you teach longer sessions, for example, over an hour, try to include a break to enable your learners to experience a change of scenery, obtain refreshments and visit the toilet if necessary.

Activity

Plan an activity to carry out with your learners which will take 20 minutes. Carry out the activity and observe how many learners stay on task or get easily distracted. If they are distracted, ask them why this was and then use their responses to improve the activity for the future.

You might find that attention spans are decreasing due to the use of modern technology. For example, learners who are regularly searching the internet, changing television channels and using electronic devices and mobile phones might have a reduced concentration time. If you have learners who use a lot of electronic devices, they may need to move on to other tasks more frequently. If applicable, you could incorporate the use of ICT, for example, learners could research relevant topics online and create a presentation regarding their findings.

Inclusive learning

Inclusive learning is about recognising that each of your learners is different from other learners in many ways, and therefore should not be excluded from any activities for any legitimate reason. You should plan your sessions to enable all of your learners to take part, and achieve their learning goals by the end of the programme.

To effectively promote the inclusion of all learners, there is a need to bring equality, diversity and rights issues into the mainstream, to ensure they are no longer viewed as something affecting only minority groups. Those affected by stereotyping, prejudice and discrimination are not always in the minority and you should be careful not to indulge the minority at the expense of the majority. When teaching, you may have a group of learners from different backgrounds and cultures, and/or with different needs and abilities. You can add value to your teaching by recognising the many differences your learners have, and incorporating their diverse experiences into your sessions. By combating discrimination, valuing diversity and promoting equality, you should be able to create a positive and equal learning environment. If you have a learner with a disability, don't label them as *disabled* but consider them as an individual with a variation in ability. These variations are what make your learners unique, and they shouldn't be excluded from the learning process as a result.

To help inclusivity, when planning your sessions, you should:

- create, design and/or select appropriate resources and activities

- organise specialist help when needed

- encourage social, cultural and recreational activities relevant to the programme (if possible)

- provide opportunities for comments, feedback and suggestions

- give honest information about the programme and how it will be organised, delivered and assessed

- signpost and offer guidance towards other learning opportunities and/or access to additional support

If you ever feel unsure as to whether you, or other learners and colleagues, are valuing equality and diversity, just ask yourself *Is this fair?* or, *How would I feel in this situation?* or *Would I want to be treated in this way?* If your answer is a negative one, then make sure you do something about it.

Always include your learners in relevant activities and give them access to the full learning process, rather than excluding anyone for any reason. The best way to ensure you are effectively including all learners and treating them equally is to ask them if there is anything you can do to help, or that can be done differently for them. To value and promote equality and diversity among your learners, you need to embrace their differences, and encourage interaction and support, challenging any negative actions or beliefs.

Inclusive learning should ensure a match between each individual's requirements and the provision that is made for them. Your organisation may have a *learner entitlement statement* which will reflect learners' individual circumstances and needs. The statement should take into account the needs of particular groups, such as those with learning difficulties or disabilities, a visual or hearing impairment, those whose first language is not English and/or those who require support with their literacy, language, numeracy and/or ICT skills. It should therefore encourage equality of opportunity for all learners.

The way in which guidance is given to learners will vary and could be hard copies or electronic. It should be possible to incorporate some aspects of learners' entitlements and responsibilities in documents such as:

- assessment plans

- brochures and leaflets

- existing written statements, for example, learning agreements/contracts

- individual learning plans (ILPs) and action plans

- induction or enrolment documents

- learner charters

- learner handbooks

- prospectuses

You need to work in partnership with your learners to ensure that learning is effective. Partnerships always work best when both sides know where they stand. If your learners understand what is required of them and what they can expect from you, they are more likely to make the necessary commitment to learning and to be successful in achieving their goals.

It is part of your role to ensure that you provide an inclusive learning environment and equality of opportunity in all aspects of the learning experience.

Differentiation

Differentiation is about using a range of different approaches and resources to meet the needs of individuals. It is very rare to have a group of learners who are all at the same level of ability, with the same prior knowledge and experience, and with the same needs. You don't have to individualise everything you do; you just need to take individual needs into account. However, this relies on your knowing what these needs are. Hopefully, you will have obtained the appropriate information during the initial assessment process, or you will have found out more by getting to know your learners during your time with them. Keeping your group profile up to date should help you remember the different needs of your learners.

Small group work and paired activities are a good way to use differentiation. Depending upon what you want your learners to achieve, you could group them by their:

- current knowledge

- learning preference

- level of ability

- level of qualification aim

- past experiences

Your teaching and learning plan should show the different activities you plan to use during your session. These can be further broken down into what *all* your learners are capable of achieving, as well as what *most* or *some* can achieve according to their level and ability. This shows that you have planned what all your learners will achieve according to the programme or qualification requirements. It also shows you are differentiating to stretch and challenge more able learners further. However, planned activities might change as the session proceeds depending upon the progress being made by each learner.

Petty gives a summary of key differentiation strategies as:

> ... *differentiation by:*
>
> - *task*
>
> - *outcome*
>
> - *time allowed*
>
> - *accommodating different learning styles and support needs*
>
> - *setting individual tasks and targets*

(2009, pages 587–88)

Differentiated questioning can also help support learners; for example, learners for whom English is a second language may need longer to process information or might need questions to be rephrased. A learner who has dyslexia may prefer to work with more images, have handouts printed on pastel coloured paper, wish to make an audio recording of the session to listen to afterwards, or key in notes directly to a laptop or tablet. An older learner might shy away from using new technology whereas younger learners may expect to access and use it.

Differentiating your teaching, learning and assessment approaches should lead to more confident learners who feel included, are motivated to learn and are able to achieve. While it may take longer to plan and prepare your sessions to differentiate effectively, you will find your learners are more engaged and motivated rather than being bored and uninterested.

Activity

What do you know about each of your learners to enable differentiation to take place during your next session? Based on this, what activities could you create and/or adapt for them to ensure they are included during the session?

Working with groups

When teaching a group, you need to realise that this is a collection of individuals, each with different needs and wants, and it is up to you to address these while keeping focused on the subject or topic of learning. Make sure you include everyone, either during activities or when asking questions. Your learners will probably be from different backgrounds and different age groups, have different skills, knowledge and experiences, but will all expect to learn something from you. Having some prior knowledge of these, gained from initial assessment or by talking to your learners, is a good foundation on which to start.

Individuals often behave differently in a group situation from when they are with other people. Group dynamics can change, for example, when new learners commence, when the venue or seating arrangements alter, or if there are personality clashes. You will need to make new learners welcome, perhaps buddying them with another learner, or challenging behaviour and changing seating positions if disruption occurs.

Activity

Imagine you are due to facilitate a three-hour session with 16 learners whom you have never met before. You plan to use two different group activities of 20 minutes each during the session. How would you manage the process of grouping the learners and keeping them on task? All you know is their names.

Ideally, you need to find out a little about your learners in advance, perhaps their prior knowledge and experience, to enable you to relate the activities to their interests and/or job roles. If you can't obtain this information, ask the learners at the beginning of the session. Knowing their learning preferences can also help. If you have a mixture of each preference in each group, they should keep on task as they will complement each other.

When facilitating group activities, make sure you give very clear instructions and a time limit. If the activity is to be carried out in small groups, knowledge of your learners will help you decide if they have the maturity to group themselves or whether you need to do it. Consider which learners will work together in case learners with strong personalities dominate and change the group dynamics. Equally, make sure quiet learners don't get left out and are able to participate. You might like to decide who will work with whom, or decide according to their learning preferences, levels of ability/experience, random names, or pairs. If you are carrying out several activities, you could mix your learners each time to give them the opportunity to work with everyone.

Don't be afraid of trying something different, for example, giving your learners responsibility for part of a session. Always remain in control and consider what you will be doing while your learners are working, for example, going around each group, listening to them working, giving advice and encouragement, and reminding them of the time left for completion of the activity.

Individual personalities and the roles learners take on when part of a group may impede the achievement of the task. Make sure you supervise group work carefully to keep all individuals focused.

Some issues which might occur with groups include:

- higher level learners not being stretched and challenged enough
- interruptions and behaviour issues
- learners finishing activities before others
- learners being excluded by others during group activities
- lower level learners falling behind
- peer pressure
- personality clashes

It takes practice to control a group and deal with any situations which might occur. You might like to arrange to observe an experienced teacher or trainer to see how they manage their group.

Belbin's (2010) team roles

Belbin (2010) defined team roles as: *a tendency to behave, contribute and interrelate with others in a particular way* (page 24). Belbin's research identified three group roles, each with three team roles. Each team role has a combination of strengths they contribute to the group, and allowable weaknesses. It is important to accept that people have weaknesses; therefore if you can focus on their strengths you will be able to help manage their weaknesses.

The group roles are *action, people* and *cerebral*, each have three team roles:

- action-oriented roles: Shaper, Implementer and Completer Finisher
- people-oriented roles: Co-ordinator, Teamworker and Resource Investigator
- cerebral roles: Plant, Monitor Evaluator and Specialist

Sometimes groups or teams become problematic, not because their members don't know their subject, but because they have problems accepting, adjusting and communicating with each other as they take on different roles. Knowing that individuals within teams take on these different roles will help you manage group work more effectively, for example, by grouping a mixture of the *action, people* and *cerebral* roles within each group.

Coverdale's (1977) task, team and individual needs

Coverdale (1977) states the essence of team working is that individuals have their own preferred ways of achieving a task, but that in a team, they need to decide on one way of achieving this. In a team, three overlapping and interacting circles of needs have to be focused upon at all times. The *task needs*, the *team needs* and the *individual needs*.

When setting tasks or activities for learners to carry out in groups, consider the following.

To achieve the task ensure:

- a SMART objective or target is stated
- responsibilities are defined
- working conditions are suitable
- supervision is available

To build and maintain the team ensure:

- the size of the team is suitable for the task

- health and safety factors are considered

- consultation takes place

- discipline and order are maintained

To develop the individual ensure:

- responsibilities are defined

- grievances are dealt with

- praise is given

- learners feel safe and secure

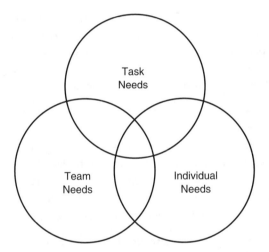

Figure 3.2 Task, team and individual needs

Tuckman's (1965 and 1975) group formation theory

When working with groups, you could consider Tuckman's (1965, in Egolf, 2001, page 102) group formation theory of forming, storming, norming, performing and adjourning. This relates to how a group bonds and works on a task, either short term or long term.

Forming This is the *getting to know you* and *what shall we do?* stage. Individuals may be anxious and need to know the boundaries and code of conduct within which to work.

Storming This is the *it can't be done* stage. It is where conflict can arise, rebellion against the leader can happen and disagreements may take place.

Norming This is the *it can be done* stage. This is where group cohesion takes place and the norms are established. Mutual support is offered, views are exchanged and the group co-operates.

Performing This is the we are *doing it* stage. Individuals feel safe enough to express opinions and there is energy and enthusiasm towards completing the task.

Adjourning This is the we *will do it again* stage. The task is complete and the group separates. Members often leave the group with the desire to meet again or keep in touch.

Working with individuals

Working with an individual on a one-to-one basis may sound like the ideal approach, but if your learner is not committed to their learning you will need to motivate them. You will still need to set clear aims, objectives and targets, and you must remain professional at all times and not get personally involved. It could be that you are training a staff member in a workshop or working environment; therefore you are carrying out your own job role as well as supporting their learning. They may feel they can come to you at inappropriate times and you would need to set clear boundaries of what you expect from each other.

Individuals often act differently depending upon the situation and the other people they are with at the time. How you act towards your learner might also be different depending upon the context, environment or circumstances you are in. Different issues will arise when teaching or training an individual, as opposed to a group. It takes practice to remain focused upon the topic while giving the individual an appropriate amount of attention and not feeling you want to do things for them. It is still useful to agree ground rules with an individual to ensure the learning process remains professional.

Usually, individual learners have the opportunity to work at their own pace and have their training geared towards particular outcomes, for example, learning a new skill to support their job role, or gaining new knowledge to pass a test. You still need a plan of what you want to achieve, often referred to as an ILP or action plan. These are very similar to a teaching and learning plan, but are geared towards one person rather than groups. You can easily adapt your teaching or training approaches to fit in with your learner's requirements, change dates and times to suit, and address any barriers or challenges to learning.

One-to-one teaching or training can also occur as part of the coaching and mentoring process. It could be that you are responsible for coaching and/or mentoring a staff member as opposed to formally training them. It is important you find out what your role involves, and the time you can allocate to it, otherwise your own job role might begin to suffer as a result.

Other one-to-one training, coaching and mentoring opportunities might occur during:

- appraisals
- meetings
- online learning programs
- tutorial reviews
- workplace discussions

Whichever approach you take with individuals, remember to remain professional throughout and resist the temptation to get too personal. You will be spending quite a lot of time with the individual and although this will enable you both to get to know each other well, you mustn't blur the boundaries of your role.

Motivation

When using different teaching and learning approaches, it is crucial you motivate your learners to create a desire to learn. If you are enthusiastic and passionate about your subject you should be able to inspire, stimulate and challenge your learners. They may already be motivated for personal reasons and be enthusiastic and keen to learn. This *wanting* to learn for its own sake comes from within, known as *intrinsic motivation*. However, learners may be motivated to learn for other reasons, such as to gain a qualification, a promotion or a pay rise at work, or to attend because they need to in order to receive funding. This is known as *extrinsic motivation*, which addresses an external *need* to learn. If you can recognise the difference between your learners' *wants* and *needs*, you can see why they are motivated, and can ensure that you make their learning meaningful and relevant. Learners who don't have intrinsic motivation may require more encouragement to learn. They must have a *need* to learn as well as *want* to learn, and you may have to promote this desire within them by creating a climate of learning that is relevant, interesting, inclusive and exciting.

Whatever type of motivation your learners bring to the sessions, it will be transformed, for better or worse, by what happens during their learning experience with you. Some learners may need more attention than others, but take care not to neglect those who are progressing well; they still need encouragement and feedback to know they are on the right track. You also need a positive attitude towards the subject and the learning environment. You may not be able to change the type of environment you are teaching in, or the resources you are using. However, remaining professional and making the best of what you have will help encourage learning to take place.

Learners may already have some knowledge or experience of the subject. In that case, you could incorporate time within your sessions to encourage discussions, paired or group work to enhance their learning experience. Learners do like to talk about their own experiences, and others in the group may gain from these. You also need to acknowledge any limitations in your own knowledge and experience. You can improve or update this by taking part in professional development.

You should encourage and motivate your learners to reach their maximum potential. If you set tasks that are too hard, learners may struggle and become frustrated and anxious. If tasks are too easy, learners may become bored. Knowing your learners and differentiating for their needs with a variety of activities will help keep them motivated.

Your learners may already have a desire to learn for their own fulfilment or benefit, but still need motivating during your sessions, perhaps to pay attention, focus on tasks or take part in activities. Some learners may be attending your sessions as a requirement of training or employment, and may not really want to be there. If you can make the learning experience relevant to each learner by making it reflect, as closely as possible, real-life scenarios, this should help them pay attention and remain motivated to learn. Creating a *What's in it for me?* culture, where learners create their own desire to learn, supported by your desire to teach them, will help their motivation.

Example

Sahib was having problems with a group of 14 learners in the computer room. Some would talk over him, use applications which were not relevant to the session and use their mobile phones. He decided to spend a few minutes at the beginning of the next session asking each learner in turn (in front of the rest of the group) to state a reason for using a computer, that they could relate to in their personal or working life. He also asked the group to agree some ground rules which included switching off their mobile phones. This helped the learners see the relevance of various computer skills, enabling them to be more focused during the sessions.

Try to create an environment of respect, between learners and towards you. Whenever possible, give learners responsibility for making decisions regarding their own learning needs. If you have learners who are quite motivated already, keep this motivation alive with regular challenges and constructive and positive feedback.

Maslow's (1987) Hierarchy of Needs

Maslow (1987) introduced *a Hierarchy of Needs* in 1954 after rejecting the idea that human behaviour was determined by childhood events. He felt that obstacles should be removed that prevent a person from achieving their goals. He argued there are five needs which represent different levels of motivation which must be met. The highest level was labelled *self-actualisation,* meaning people are fully functional, possess a healthy personality, and take responsibility for themselves and their actions. He also believed that people should be able to move through these needs to the highest level provided they are given an education that promotes growth. Figure 3.3 shows the needs expressed as they might relate to learning, starting at the base of the pyramid.

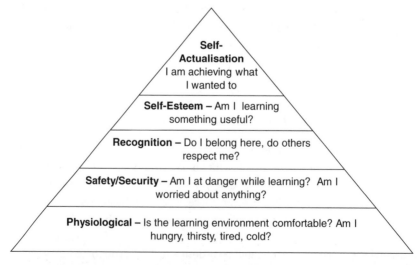

Figure 3.3 Maslow's (1987) Hierarchy of Needs expressed in educational terms

When learners satisfy their needs at one level, they should be able to progress to the next level. Something may set them back a level, but they should feel the need to keep striving upwards. It is the fulfilment of these needs that motivates learning to take place. However, some people may not want to progress through the levels, and may be quite content where they are at that moment in their life.

To help your learners' motivation, always ensure that the environment you create meets your learners' first-level needs. This will enable them to feel comfortable and secure enough to learn and progress to the higher levels. You will need to appreciate that some learners may not have these lower needs met in their home lives, making it difficult for them to move on to the higher levels.

Always try to establish a purposeful environment where your learners can feel safe, secure, confident and valued.

Example

Caroline was due to teach a session from 5 p.m. to 7 p.m. She arrived early and noticed the room was hot and stuffy so opened the windows. She also realised that most of her learners might not have had a chance to eat something prior to the session. When they arrived she told them they could have an early break to enable them to get refreshments. After the break, she kept one window open to let some fresh air in the room and allowed her learners to have bottled water if they wished. This ensured her learners' first-level needs were met, enabling concentration and learning to take place.

Keller's (1987) ARCS model of motivation

Keller (1987) combined existing research on psychological motivation and created the ARCS model: **A**ttention, **R**elevance, **C**onfidence, and **S**atisfaction.

Attention is the first and most important aspect of the ARCS model and is about gaining and maintaining your learners' attention. Keller's strategies for attention include stimulating the senses (ensuring you reach all learning preferences), inquiry arousal (using thought-provoking questions and challenges), and variability (using various delivery approaches and media).

Relevance is the second aspect. To ensure motivation is retained, the learner has to believe the session content is relevant to them. It is the *What's in it for me?* question being addressed. Benefits should be clearly stated to the learner to enable their needs to be met.

Confidence is the third aspect to help learners put effort into their learning and to think they are capable of achieving. Learners should always be given constructive and developmental feedback to help maintain motivation. Clear targets and deadlines need to be stated and agreed.

Satisfaction is the final aspect. Learners must obtain some type of satisfaction or reward from their learning experience. This can be in the form of a sense of achievement or of gaining a qualification. Satisfaction could also come from external rewards, for example, praise from others, a pay rise, more responsibility or a promotion. Ultimately, the best way for learners to achieve satisfaction is for them to put their new skills and knowledge to immediate use.

Activity

Using the ARCS model, consider a topic you are going to deliver and plan how to gain your learners' attention for each aspect. How will you make this relevant to each learner, ensuring they feel confident about learning and are satisfied in some way?

Herzberg's (1991) hygiene needs and motivation needs

Herzberg (1991) created a two-level theory with *hygiene* needs and *motivation* needs. Hygiene needs (also known as maintenance needs), in Herzberg's view, do not provide positive motivation, but their absence causes dissatisfaction, in the same way that hygiene prevents disease rather than increasing well-being. Motivation needs lead to satisfaction.

Hygiene needs include: environmental factors such as salary, interpersonal relationships, working conditions, style of leadership and types of supervision, security, type of work, working hours and status. They are called hygiene needs as they work like preventative medicine. They can help stop an illness but do not do anything to promote good health. In a teaching context this means that hygiene factors don't motivate learners to do their very best but they are needed to stop them becoming dissatisfied with their learning experience.

Motivation needs include factors which allow for: achievement, responsibility, recognition, advancement and challenge. Herzberg suggests that these factors are the ones which encourage people to strive to do well, and motivate them to do their best.

Herzberg believed that hygiene and motivation needs were equally important for satisfaction; however, they worked in different ways. If the hygiene needs are inadequate, learners will quickly become dissatisfied. However, as these needs are satisfied, trying to motivate them by adding more hygiene needs is an inefficient and short-term solution. A better way would be to appeal to the learners' motivation needs by giving them more responsibility or giving them greater challenges. In this way they are satisfied and motivated.

Example

Sharron is progressing well towards a Level 2 Diploma in Beauty Therapy. When she receives compliments from her teacher for keeping her working area clean and tidy, she feels good. However, she doesn't expect compliments every day and isn't demotivated as a result (her hygiene needs are met). The following week Sharron is given the chance to supervise a new learner and enjoys the challenge (meeting her motivation needs).

Try to differentiate between learners' hygiene needs and motivation needs but ensure they can both be met. Creating a motivated learning environment can lead to improved communication and enable successful learning to take place.

Extension Activity

Plan a session based upon your specialist subject, which combines several teaching, learning and assessment approaches. Refer to Table 3.3 for some ideas and create a teaching and learning plan. Think carefully about what activities and resources you will use to ensure all your learners are included, and plan appropriate timings. Deliver your session and use your imagination to bring your subject to life, thereby making your session memorable and keeping your learners motivated. Decide what could be removed if you run out of time or what you could add if you have spare time.

Communication methods

Communication is a means of passing on information from one person to another; it can be verbal, non-verbal or written.

One of the skills of communicating effectively is projecting *confidence*. You may not feel confident when meeting a new group for the first time; you might even feel quite nervous. Imagine though that you are an actor playing a role, and try to keep relaxed, calm, composed and focused. Your knowledge of, and passion for, your subject should help your confidence. You also need to be organised and plan what you want to communicate and how you are going to do this. Your learners don't know what you know, that's why they want to learn. Keep things simple and don't try to achieve too much too soon; it takes time for your learners to assimilate new skills and knowledge.

Your main communication will be with your learners; therefore you need to ensure that what you are communicating is accurate, not ambiguous or biased and is expressed in a professional manner. Show your professionalism, not only in what you say, but also in the way you say it, and in your attitude, your body language and the way you dress. A warm and confident smile, a positive attitude, self-assurance and the use of eye contact and names will put both you and your learners at ease. Remember, you never get a second chance to make a first impression.

Empathy and *sympathy* are also skills of communication. You can express empathy when you have personally experienced something your learner has gone through. You can only sympathise when you haven't. However, don't be too keen to reveal to your learners any personal information about yourself. You may feel you are gaining their confidence but you might also lose their respect. Don't get too friendly with your learners and keep the relationship professional at all times. Learners may tell you things that need to remain confidential, or they may discuss things with you that you cannot deal with; therefore you may need to liaise with others if necessary.

Example

Marilyn had just finished her session with a group of 16–18 year olds taking a Level 3 Diploma in Retail Skills. One of her learners, Jenna, asked to talk to her in confidence. She confided that she was pregnant and didn't know how to tell her parents. Marilyn listened to what she said and could empathise as she had been in the same situation at that age. However, she did not reveal this to Jenna as it was personal. With Jenna's agreement, Marilyn arranged a meeting with the college counsellor who was more qualified to help.

You may also need to communicate with others, for example, colleagues, managers, awarding organisation staff and external inspectors. The way you do this will also help to form other people's impressions of you. You may have to attend meetings or video conferences. Wherever you are with other people, they might make assumptions about you based upon what they see and hear. You may have to write reports, and the way you express yourself when writing is as important as when you are speaking. Always remain professional and leave any personal issues behind, otherwise these might impact upon your job role.

When you communicate with other professionals you should do so at an appropriate time and not when you are with your learners. It is important that you have an organised and formal approach to communications with others when the discussions involve your learners. If you are going to have regular contact with others, you should agree what the protocols are. You should always document the details of the communication, i.e. who, what, when, where, why and how. There should also be a record of any actions agreed and who is responsible for carrying them out. You could create a contacts sheet for this purpose if your organisation doesn't already have one. This is a list of all the professionals you will need to communicate with, along with their contact details.

Examples of verbal, non-verbal and written communication include the following.

Verbal:

- face-to-face, for example, small group discussions

- live online voice and video calls or video e-mails, for example, a one-to-one tutorial with a learner or a conference with colleagues

- telephone, for example, exchanging information

Non-verbal:

- body language, for example, a warm, confident smile

- eye contact, for example, giving reassurance

- listening, for example, conscious listening with a purpose

Written:

- documents, for example, planning and feedback

- media, for example, websites, videos, VLE

- online, for example, e-mails, uploaded documents

- resources, for example, handouts, presentations

Activity

Consider the different communication methods and media you will use for your next session. Analyse the benefits and limitations of their use in relation to meeting individual learner needs.

You need to communicate effectively and that involves planning appropriate ways. For example, you might plan to introduce a complex topic to your learners, which could be misinterpreted if not conveyed in a logical order. Poor body language, poor voice projection and/or handouts with too much text or jargon, or which contain spelling errors, will lead to confusion. Speaking too quickly or giving too much factual information too fast will not allow learners time to assimilate their new knowledge.

Your learners may have preoccupations which lead to lapses in concentration, or they may not understand the terminology you are using or your accent. They may have had previous educational experiences which were not good, or have cultural differences which may have an impact upon their literacy and language learning. Initial assessment may help with your understanding of their needs. Once you are aware of any issues – yours or your learners' – you can work on them and communicate in a way that enables your learners to interpret what you are conveying, in the way you intended.

Activity

Ask a colleague or your mentor to observe one of your sessions, with a particular focus on how you communicate with your learners. Alternatively, make a visual recording of your session (with your learners' permission), and watch this afterwards. You may be surprised at what you see: perhaps mannerisms you weren't aware of when communicating, such as waving your hands about or repeatedly saying 'erm'. Did you experience any barriers to effective communication? If so, how could you overcome them?

Active listening

What someone says and what you hear can be very different. Often, personal assumptions and beliefs can distort what is heard. Try to use active listening, which includes repeating back or summarising what was said, to ensure that you have understood. If you are unsure what someone has said, ask them to repeat it or say, *Have I understood you correctly? Did you mean ...?* Feedback is a verbal communication skill that clearly demonstrates that you are actively listening, and confirms the communication between you and your learners.

Listening is also an important communication skill. You may be able to convey your message to your learners effectively, but if you can't listen to what they say, or answer their questions satisfactorily, communication will break down; it should be a two-way process. Alternatively, you may be distracted by external noises and may not be able to concentrate on what is being said at the time. If a learner asks a question, repeat it to enable the full group to hear it, and to show that you have heard it correctly. Listening to what is said is different from hearing what is going on in the background. You may need to pay more attention and to keep focused on what your learners are saying. Active listening involves listening with a purpose; that is, to hear what you want to hear and yet remain able to listen to all that is being said without letting other things distract you. If you find it hard to remember what is being said, repeat key words or make notes to help you. This is a skill you can encourage your learners to develop too.

Understanding a little about your own personal communication style will help you create a lasting impression upon your learners and enable you to become a better listener. If you are aware of how others see and hear you, you should be able to adapt accordingly.

Activity

There are several theories regarding communication such as Mehrabian's (1981) Communication theory and Berne's (1973) Transactional Analysis theory. Research these or other relevant theories via textbooks, journals or the internet, and compare and contrast them. Consider how they influence the way you communicate with your learners. What might you change as a result of your research?

Managing disruption

Disruption might occur if your learners are not self-motivated, challenged or stimulated to learn. You can help to create a climate which will encourage learning to take place. However, if disruptive situations arise, you will have to deal with them promptly, otherwise they could lead to further disruption which will hinder effective learning. Unfortunately, there isn't room within this book to cover all the information you might need throughout your teaching career. However, there are many relevant textbooks available on the subject. Please see the end of the chapter for details.

Vizard states: *Students who are challenging will try to blame everyone else for their poor behaviour ... Explain to them that they own their behaviour and they can change the consequences of it by choosing to modify their behaviour* (2012, page 47).

If you are teaching post-compulsory learners, they will probably be self-motivated and have a good attitude towards their learning. This in turn can be rewarding for you. However, adults can still be disruptive if they are not challenged enough or don't feel their learning is relevant. If you are teaching learners of school age, they may have issues or problems which they bring to your sessions. They may be immature, causing them to arrive late, talk among themselves, send text messages or just appear uninterested. Sadly, it is a rare privilege to teach a group of motivated, interested learners and it falls upon you to manage and control the situation you are presented with, however exasperating, otherwise it might get out of hand. Finding suitable ways of dealing with disruption as it occurs should lead to an effective learning environment. This will come mainly from experiencing various situations and finding your own way of dealing with them. Observing experienced teachers will enable you to witness a variety of situations and see how others manage them.

If you are delivering a one-off session, you could ask the group what they hope to learn from the session. You may find that your learners' expectations are different from what you had planned. Knowing what your learners are hoping for will enable you to address their needs, or at least explain why you won't be covering certain aspects. Your learners will then know what to expect, and will be less likely to be disruptive or leave your session feeling disappointed or let down.

Extension Activity

After each session you deliver, note down any aspects of disruption that occurred and how you dealt with them. Consider how you felt at the time and what else was happening. If similar kinds of disruption are happening repeatedly, consider different ways of responding to them and ask colleagues for advice.

Using information and communication technology

ICT includes all the uses of digital media, equipment, tools and online sources that are currently available, and which will enhance the teaching, learning and assessment process. The term *digital literacy* is used to denote the effective use of ICT by both teachers and learners. If you don't feel very confident about using digital media, you could invite someone who is familiar with it to deliver an awareness session to your learners, perhaps as part of the induction process. This would also help increase your own skills and knowledge.

Technology is only as good as the person using it; therefore both you and your learners would need to know how to use it effectively. It should always be used in a way that educates and informs, for example to illustrate a point, to promote a discussion, and to further skills, knowledge and understanding. It should not be relied on as a means to entertain learners or used to fill in time during a session.

Wherever possible, you should try to involve your learners with ICT during and after their sessions with you. An example of involving your learners during a session is to give them responsibility for researching a topic online. They can then collaborate to produce a presentation using various applications, and deliver it using technology such as an interactive whiteboard. Learners could then give feedback via an online survey or questionnaire that they have devised beforehand. Documents, presentations, pictures and videos could be uploaded to a web-based storage area, where everyone can access, collaborate, share and view them. There are many free applications available for this – just search the internet for *free online storage*. These applications are often known as *cloud computing* as the documents are stored online and can be accessed from any device at any time by anyone with an internet connection.

A way of involving learners after the session could be to continue working on something they started during the session. This is ideal if learners are working on a project together but cannot physically meet. It can enable learners to collaborate on documents from different locations, at different times. The term *flipped* learning is increasingly being used. This flips the work normally carried out *during* a session, to *away* from the session. Examples include learners using multimedia, i.e. watching videos, listening to podcasts and collaborating with their peers away from the session, then discussing the content during the next session. This gives the teacher the opportunity to use a more personalised and interactive approach during the session. The teacher becomes more of a facilitator of learning, guiding and supporting learners to find things out for themselves.

Your organisation should have a fair use policy regarding access to computers and internet devices. You should therefore ensure your learners are aware of the policy, and that both they, and you, adhere to it. You should also be aware of learners using social media or checking e-mails during sessions, and keep an eye out for any instances of cyber bullying. Cyber bullying is where an individual or a group of individuals carry out behaviours and actions that are deliberate, repeated and hostile towards others. These behaviours and actions are intended to upset and cause harm. You could incorporate these aspects as part of the ground rules you agree with your learners at the beginning of the programme. You can always revisit the ground rules at any time to add to, or amend them in the light of situations which have occurred.

ICT can encompass a wide variety of methods, media and resources, for example, using:

- applications (apps)
- audio, video, digital and online clips (creating or viewing, recorded or live)
- blogs
- calculators
- chat rooms
- cloud computing applications
- computer programs
- digital cameras, camcorders and video recorders
- discussion boards
- distance/online/open learning
- e-assessments
- electronic brain games
- e-mail (text and video, with or without attachments)
- e-portfolios and e-assessment
- e-readers
- file sharing websites
- graphic organisers
- interactive and online programs and educational games
- interactive whiteboards linked to the internet
- internet/intranet access
- laptops, netbooks and tablets

- mobile phones and smart phones
- online discussions
- online voting
- podcasts
- presentation packages
- scanners
- smartboards
- social media (if appropriate)

- three-dimensional printers
- video conferencing and video e-mail
- VLEs
- webcasts, weblogs, short messages
- webinars
- websites which are interactive for creating and using surveys, polls and questionnaires
- wikis

Prior to using any technology with your learners, you will need to ensure they are familiar with how to use it. You might need some training yourself beforehand; it is fine to admit you don't know something as technology is advancing so rapidly. You might have some learners who are very experienced in some areas; therefore they could demonstrate to the other learners and you could watch and learn too. Often, learners are happy to share their knowledge and experience. You would just need to make sure they weren't doing anything inappropriate or dominating a session.

When using ICT, remember to vary your methods to address individual needs. Differentiating by using aspects of technology can help some learners overcome barriers to learning, for example, pairing an experienced learner with an inexperienced learner so that someone who hasn't used ICT before doesn't feel alone.

Some learners may be quite concerned about using ICT; for example, a learner with epilepsy may need regular breaks from a computer screen. You could let your learners bring their own laptops, tablets, smart phones and e-readers to use for reading downloaded texts and/or writing notes rather than using hard copy textbooks, pen and paper. Learners could use these during sessions to carry out research or for other activities. This is now known by the acronym BYOD which stands for *bring your own device*.

E-learning

E-learning, short for *electronic learning*, includes the use of electronic learning technologies, for example, data projectors, interactive whiteboards, VLEs and the teaching, learning and assessment methods that they encompass. If someone is learning in a way that uses any information and communication technologies – for example, computers and other equipment, software and online applications – they are using e-learning.

You need to establish what technology is available for your own and your learners' use in your organisation, and what support is available. You may be teaching in an environment which has access to all types of technology and technical support, for example, wi-fi enabled computers, tablets and smart phones. However, do you know if support would be available at all times, for example, at 8.30 p.m. on a Thursday for those delivering evening classes? You may, however, be teaching in a community building with restrictions to the systems and no internet connection. You will need to take account of this when deciding which resources you will use and whether they will work or not.

There might be a learning resource centre (LRC) or library within your organisation, or that is accessible locally. They are no longer places which just contain books, but many have computers connected to the internet, and other resources such as journals, magazines, newspapers and periodicals.

E-journals and books can be easily accessed at any time, are cost-effective, require less paper and can be easy to file and locate ... It is a good idea to encourage students to access these to enhance knowledge and understanding before and after taught sessions (Armitage et al., 2012, page 153).

If there is an LRC or library at your organisation, you could give your learners a short tour, showing them what is available to encourage them to access the resources. You could also spend time in there with your learners during a session, for example, while they research a topic.

If you have computer and internet facilities in your teaching environment, do make use of them whenever possible. However, never make assumptions about technology. Always check the equipment personally and in the context in which you are planning to use it. Have a contingency plan in case of technical failure at the time you are teaching. If it is at all possible, request that assistance from technical support staff be on hand if you are using a piece of technology for the first time. There may be staff called *E-Guide Co-ordinators* or *ICT Champions* whose job it is to help teachers integrate ICT into their specialist subject area. You need to find out who these people are and ask for a training session if you are not fully confident yourself. They should be able to demonstrate examples of e-learning in your specialist area.

Some learners may prefer or need to learn when and where it is convenient for them. This could include a *blended* learning approach which mixes online learning with attended sessions. Alternatively, learners could partake in online learning either from home, a suitable location such as a library or anywhere where they have access to a device with internet access.

Activity

List the different technologies and media you could use for your specialist subject. Analyse the benefits and limitations of each in relation to meeting individual learner needs.

Synchronous and asynchronous learning

Synchronous learning is carried out by people at the same time, whereas asynchronous means it is carried out by people at different times.

Synchronous learning enables learners to study via a virtual classroom and duplicates the capabilities found in a real classroom. The teacher and learners log on at set times. This provides:

- a place to meet: teachers and learners use their computers to go to a virtual meeting place instead of a classroom

- an attendance register: a record is made of learners logging on

- facilitation of learning: teachers can choose from a variety of synchronous technologies including:

  - slide presentations
  - audio and video conferencing
  - application sharing
  - shared whiteboard

- interaction with learners: learners can indicate when they want to speak by virtually raising their hand; teachers can enable learners to speak through audio and video conferencing; teachers and learners can use instant messaging and chat rooms

- quizzes: teachers can present questions to learners which are automatically assessed

- breakout sessions: learners can work together in groups

- assessment: feedback and records are maintained

Asynchronous learning happens anywhere and at any time. Learners are able to interact with resource materials, and with their teachers and each other at a time of their choosing. Learners across different time zones and different continents can participate in the same programmes. Content can be explored and discussed in great depth – allowing learners the time to reflect and formulate thoughtful responses. A discussion thread is an example of asynchronous learning. One learner can post a question, and hours (or days) later, another learner can post a response. Asynchronous tools like e-mail and discussion forums have transformed the way learners communicate and share knowledge.

Asynchronous learning gives e-learning much of its appeal. Traditionally, learners needed to be physically present to engage with teachers and other learners. Now, learners can engage with each other when it is most convenient, and a *knowledge thread* or trail of their postings is left.

Social media

Social media focuses on building networks or social relationships among people who share interests and/or activities. A social network service consists of a profile for each user (name, interests, etc.), their social links, and a variety of additional services. Most social network services are web based and provide a means for users to interact via the internet, such as messaging and talking to others who are accepted and trusted by the user. Social media is software that allows learners to communicate based around an idea or topic of interest. Popular tools are Facebook, Twitter and LinkedIn, which are used worldwide.

Activity

Access the internet and have a look at various social media sites such as Facebook, Twitter and LinkedIn. You could join them and use them for professional networking and communication. Be careful of revealing anything

(Continued)

(Continued)

personal about yourself as it will remain accessible for a very long time. You could also look at using cloud-based storage sites such as Dropbox, Pinterest and YouTube. These sites are ideal to upload materials for your learners to access in their own time.

You could use these sites to encourage your learners to communicate and engage in discussions, and to support each other outside the learning environment. Learning should reflect the world and society of today, which includes working in virtual social environments. You will need to teach your learners how to be effective collaborators, how to interact with people around them, how to be engaged and informed, and how to stay safe in the virtual world.

Example

Sadiq created accounts for his learners using a social network site, which lets them store, organise and share information. His learners then shared useful web links they discovered, and communicated with each other regularly to discuss the current topics. Sadiq uploaded the qualification resources, reading list and links to useful videos. Sadiq could browse to see what his learners were discussing and then incorporate their topics into the next session. His learners could also collaborate on various projects online. The site therefore became a way of communicating and learning using social media.

Learners need to be aware of the powerful ways in which social media can change how they look at education, not just their social lives. You need to promote the incredible power of social-networking technology which can be used for academic benefits. It could be called *academic networking* rather than *social networking*. Anyone with a computer and an internet connection can set up and use the facility.

Extension Activity

Create a new resource for your subject, using ICT. This could be an activity for learners to collaborate on via cloud computing, a computerised presentation, or a video or podcast. Choose something that makes you feel excited about using it and consider how it will inspire and motivate your learners. Use the activity with your learners and then evaluate how effective it was.

Implementing the minimum core

The minimum core consists of four elements: literacy, language, numeracy and ICT. As part of your teaching role you should be able to demonstrate these elements to at least level 2.

This will enable you to support your learners with English, maths and ICT (known as functional skills). It will also ensure you teach your area of specialism as effectively as possible.

Extension Activity

Look at the four elements of the minimum core in Appendices 6, 7 and 8. Analyse the ways in which you feel you can demonstrate them when delivering sessions. Tick off the ones you can use, and make a note of how you will demonstrate them within your practice.

If possible, obtain a copy of the supporting document: *Addressing literacy, language, numeracy and ICT needs in education and training: Defining the minimum core of teachers' knowledge, understanding and personal skills – A guide for initial teacher education programmes* (LSIS, 2007, revised 2013). Have a look at the content to help you see how you can demonstrate the minimum core elements.

The full document is available to download at: http://repository.excellencegateway.org.uk/fedora/objects/import-pdf:93/datastreams/PDF/content

Example: Literacy

- Reading policies and procedures, qualification guidance and supporting materials for the delivery of your subject

- Creating handouts, teaching and learning materials and checking spelling, grammar and punctuation

Example: Language

- Communicating clearly and effectively with learners during sessions, as well as other professionals

- Asking questions and listening to responses. Listening to learners' questions and answering them appropriately

Example: Numeracy

- Calculating how long various activities will take

- Interpreting how long learners are actually taking to carry out an activity, and what time they have left to complete

Example: ICT

- Preparing teaching and learning materials using various applications, media and technology

- Using e-mail or social media to communicate appropriately with others

- Using digital media for visual/audio recording and playback of activities and presentations

Demonstrating your own skills regarding the minimum core should enable you to consider ways of improving the skills in your learners too. Ways of improving your learners' skills in these areas could include encouraging them to demonstrate skills similar to those you have used. You can also correct any mistakes, for example, in speech and written work.

You can play an important part in providing opportunities to develop your learners' skills in literacy, language, numeracy and ICT. However, it is your responsibility to continually update your own skills in these areas by undertaking professional development.

Extension Activity

The next time you are delivering a session, try and demonstrate aspects of the four minimum core skills. Did you use the skills without realising, or did you have to consciously plan to use them? Keep a record of the skills you have demonstrated as you may need to prove to your assessor how you used them.

Evaluating own practice

You should always evaluate the effectiveness of your own teaching practice to enable you to develop and improve for the future. The process should take into account the views of your learners and others you come into contact with. Reviewing your practice will also help you identify any problems or concerns, enabling you to do things differently next time. Never assume everything is going well just because you think it is. Please see Chapter 2 for further information regarding evaluating your practice and obtaining feedback.

Activity

The next time you deliver a session with your learners, review how effective the process was. Ask your learners how they felt it went, along with anyone else who has been involved in the process.

What works with one learner or group might not work well with others, perhaps due to their learning preferences or other influences. However, don't change something for the sake of it; if it works, hopefully it will continue to work.

When evaluating the delivery process, ask yourself the following.

Did I ...?

☐ ensure the environment was suitable, e.g. heating, lighting, ventilation, seating arrangements, resources and access

☐ complete any necessary administrative requirements, e.g. register or record of attendance

☐ have a teaching and learning plan with a structured and logical approach

☐ introduce the session aim and objectives

☐ stipulate the times of breaks (if applicable)

- ☐ use an icebreaker, energiser or starter activity
- ☐ recap the previous session (if applicable)
- ☐ check the prior skills, knowledge and understanding of learners
- ☐ engage and motivate learners
- ☐ allow time for learners' questions
- ☐ ask open questions (ones beginning with *who, what, when, where, why* and *how*)
- ☐ dress and act appropriately
- ☐ establish and maintain a rapport, putting learners at ease
- ☐ follow all relevant regulations and codes of practice
- ☐ use a variety of teaching and learning approaches, activities and resources to include, involve and differentiate for all learners, taking into account equality and diversity
- ☐ differentiate the activities for all, most and some learners
- ☐ embed English, maths and ICT as necessary
- ☐ use appropriate body language and non-verbal communication skills
- ☐ use eye contact with all learners
- ☐ use formative assessment activities and give individual constructive feedback
- ☐ use the group profile to good effect
- ☐ integrate appropriate use of digital media and technology
- ☐ keep learners interested and suitably challenged and motivated
- ☐ leave personal problems behind and act professionally at all times
- ☐ limit the use of jargon and/or acronyms
- ☐ link topics to the aim as well as to practical situations (i.e. theory to practice)
- ☐ listen actively
- ☐ manage behaviour and disruption as it occurred
- ☐ ensure ground rules were followed
- ☐ project energy, enthusiasm and passion for the subject
- ☐ recap points regularly
- ☐ use learners' names
- ☐ speak and communicate clearly and confidently
- ☐ take any additional learner needs into consideration and support learners as necessary, referring to the group profile
- ☐ provide opportunities for learner feedback
- ☐ summarise the session and recap the aim and objectives

☐ link to the next session (if applicable)

☐ achieve the planned topic aim, enabling the learners to achieve their objectives

☐ maintain all relevant records

☐ leave the venue tidy

☐ enjoy the session; if not, why not

☐ reflect on the session content, along with the teaching, learning and assessment process to make improvements for the future

After evaluating your practice, you should be able to make any necessary changes. Don't forget to ask for feedback from your learners as they are best able to inform you how effective the delivery of the session was.

One way of obtaining feedback to help you improve the programme in the future is by using a questionnaire or online survey. Table 3.3 is an example of a template which could be used or adapted to obtain feedback from a learner when they have completed their programme or qualification. If the choices are limited to four (1, 2, 3, 4), this takes away a middle choice if offered (such as 1, 2, 3, 4, 5) and stops a learner taking the easy option. It can make the feedback more positive or negative.

Obtaining feedback anonymously might enable you to gain more information than if a learner has to give their name.

Reflection

Ecclestone (1995) states there is a danger of reflective practice becoming nothing more than a *mantra*, a comforting and familiar wrap as opposed to a professional tool for exploration:

> ... *people might also want – or need – reflection because they seek interest, inspiration, cultural breadth, critical analysis and reasoning, social insight and awareness, challenge and critique, or to create new knowledge.*

(Ecclestone, 1995, page 150)

Reflective practice therefore implies a flexibility and willingness to adapt, putting theory into practice.

Reflection can encompass:

- *a way of applying Kolb's learning cycle to reflect on and solve practical problems in the classroom;*

- *a focus for evaluating professional practice against external criteria;*

- *an in-depth and rigorous inquiry into professional practice, with a view to implementing change;*

- *a rare and much-needed chance to compare practice and problems through structured and supportive discussion with peers;*

- *an opportunity for disempowered complaining and negativity;*

- *an exchange of practical teaching hints.*

(Ecclestone, 1995, page 150)

Table 3.2 Programme evaluation template

Programme title:	Dates of programme:				
Teacher:	Venue:				
	Please circle from 1–4 *(1 is low/no, 4 is high/yes)*				
Did you receive thorough information, advice and guidance before starting your programme?		1	2	3	4
Was the programme content as you expected?		1	2	3	4
Were the resources and activities helpful?		1	2	3	4
Were the delivery methods suitable?		1	2	3	4
Were the assessment methods suitable?		1	2	3	4
Were your questions dealt with adequately?		1	2	3	4
Was the teacher helpful and supportive?		1	2	3	4
Did the venue meet your expectations?		1	2	3	4
Did the facilities meet your expectations?		1	2	3	4
Did the programme meet your requirements?		1	2	3	4
Do you feel you have benefited from the programme?		1	2	3	4
Did you have access to expert advice and guidance on progression opportunities at the end of your programme?		1	2	3	4
Was there sufficient access to staff and materials outside the programme time?		1	2	3	4
What changes would you recommend?					
Further comments:					

You may be familiar with the term *critical incident analysis*. A critical incident is something you interpret as a problem or a challenge in a particular context, rather than a routine occurrence, for example, if learners repeatedly arrive late for a session. Critical incident analysis is a way of dealing with these challenges and exploring incidents that occur, to understand them better and find alternative ways of reacting and responding to them.

Often, a critical incident is personal to an individual. Incidents only become critical, that is, problematic, if the individual sees them in this way. It is after the event that it is defined as critical. Carrying out a critical incident analysis can help you question your own practice and enable you to develop and improve it.

Example

Pablo has a group of 25 learners, eight of whom always arrived five minutes late to his session. Pablo asked them why and ascertained they finished another class at the same time as this one was due to start. They therefore did not have enough time to move from one room to another without being late. Pablo agreed with everyone in the group to start and finish the session slightly later. This enabled the group to be together at the beginning, minimising the disruption.

Tripp stated: *When something goes wrong, we need to ask what happened and what caused it to happen* (1993, page 54). The guiding principle is to change the incident into a question. Therefore *learners repeatedly arrive late to my session* changes to *why do learners repeatedly arrive late to my session?* In this way, critical incidents can become major turning points. Asking *why* enables you to work on finding a solution.

Activity

Think of a critical incident that has happened lately during a session. Work through Ecclestone's or Tripp's theory to reflect upon it and see if you can reach an alternative solution.

Reviewing your progress will help you learn about yourself and what you could improve, for example, how you react to different situations or learners, how patient you are and what skills you may need to develop. You might also decide you need further training or support to improve your subject knowledge, teaching skills and/or English, maths and ICT skills.

Extension Activity

Based on your evaluation of delivering education and training with your learners, what areas have you identified as needing improvement? How can you act on what you have identified and what will you do differently as a result? Do you need any further training and/or support? If so, how will you go about obtaining it?

Summary

In this chapter you have learnt about:

- the teaching and learning environment

- teaching and learning theories

- teaching and learning approaches

- communication methods

- using ICT

- implementing the minimum core

- evaluating own practice

Cross-referencing grid

This chapter contributes towards the following assessment criteria of the units which form the Certificate in Education and Training, along with aspects of the Professional Standards for Teachers and Trainers in England. Full details of the learning outcomes and assessment criteria of each unit can be found in the appendices.

Certificate units	Assessment criteria
Understanding roles, responsibilities and relationships in education and training	1.1, 1.4 2.1, 2.2
Planning to meet the needs of learners in education and training	1.2 2.3, 2.4, 2.5
Delivering education and training	1.1, 1.2, 1.3 2.1, 2.2, 2.3 3.1, 3.2 4.1, 4.2 5.1, 5.2
Assessing learners in education and training	1.3, 1.5
Using resources for education and training	1.2, 1.3

Area	Professional Standards for Teachers and Trainers in England
Professional values and attributes	1, 2, 3, 4, 5, 6
Professional knowledge and understanding	7, 8, 9, 10, 11, 12
Professional skills	13, 14, 15, 16, 17, 18, 19, 20

Theory focus

References and further information

Appleyard, N and Appleyard, K (2010) *Communicating with Learners in the Lifelong Learning Sector.* London: Learning Matters SAGE.

Armitage, A, Evershed, J, Hayes, D, Hudson, A, Kent, J, Lawes, S, Poma, S and Renwick, M (2012) *Teaching and Training in Lifelong Learning.* Maidenhead: OU Press.

Belbin, M (1993, 1996, 2010) *Team Roles at Work.* Oxford: Elsevier Science & Technology.

Berne, E (1973) *Games People Play: The Psychology of Human Relationships.* London: Penguin Books Ltd.

Commission on Adult Vocational Teaching and Learning (2013) *It's about work ... Excellent adult vocational teaching and learning.* London: Learning and Skills Improvement Service.

Cornish, D and Dukette, D (2009) *The Essential 20: Twenty Components of an Excellent Health Care Team.* Pittsburgh: RoseDog Books.

Coverdale, R (1977) *Risk Thinking.* Bradford: The Coverdale Organisation.

Curzon, LB and Tummons, J (2013) *Teaching in Further Education: An Outline of Principles and Practice.* London: Bloomsbury.

Dennick, R and Exley, K (2004) *Small Group Teaching: Tutorials, Seminars and Beyond.* Abingdon: Routledge.

Ecclestone, K (1995) The Reflective Practitioner: Mantra or Model for Emancipation *Studies in the Education of Adults,* 28(2): 150.

Egolf, D (2001) *Forming Storming Norming Performing Successful Communication in Groups and Teams.* Lincoln USA: Writers Club Press.

Faraday, S, Overton, C and Cooper, S (2011) *Effective Teaching and Learning in Vocational Education.* London: LSN.

Fawbert, F (2008) *Teaching in Post-Compulsory Education.* London: Continuum Publishing Ltd.

Gould, J (2012) *Learning Theory and Classroom Practice in the Lifelong Learning Sector.* London: SAGE Publications Ltd.

Gravells, A and Simpson, S (2014) *Passing Assessments for the Certificate in Education and Training.* London: Learning Matters SAGE.

Haythornthwaite, C and Andrews, R (2011) *E-learning Theory and Practice.* London: Learning Matters SAGE.

Herzberg, F (1991) *Herzberg on Motivation.* New York: Penton Media Inc.

Hill, C (2008) *Teaching with E-learning in the Further Education and Skills Sector* (2nd edn). London: Learning Matters SAGE.

Holmes, B and Gardner, J (2006) *e-learning Concepts and Practice.* London: SAGE Publications Ltd.

Ingle, S and Duckworth, V (2013) *Enhancing Learning through Technology in Lifelong Learning Fresh Ideas: Innovative Strategies.* Maidenhead: OU Press.

Ingle, S and Duckworth, V (2013) *Teaching and Training Vocational Learners.* London: Learning Matters SAGE.

Keller, JM (1987) Strategies for Stimulating the Motivation to Learn. *Performance & Instruction*, 26(8): 1–7.

Kidd, W and Czerniawski, G (2010) *Successful Teaching 14–19.* London: SAGE Publications Ltd.

Knowles, M, Holten III, E and Swanson, R (2005) *The Adult Learner* (6th edn). Oxford: Butterworth-Heinemann.

Kolb, DA (1984) *Experiential Learning: Experience as the Source of Learning and Development.* New Jersey: Prentice-Hall.

Laird, D (1985) *Approaches to Training and Development.* Harlow: Addison Wesley.

LSIS (2007, revised 2013) *Addressing literacy, language, numeracy and ICT needs in education and training: Defining the minimum core of teachers' knowledge, understanding and personal skills – A guide for initial teacher education programmes.* Coventry: LSIS.

Maslow, AH (1987) (edited by Frager, R) *Motivation and Personality* (3rd revised edn). New York: Pearson Education Ltd.

Mehrabian, A (1981) *Silent Messages: Implicit Communication of Emotions and Attitudes.* Belmont, CA: Wadsworth.

Peart, S and Atkins, L (2011) *Teaching 14–19 Learners in the Lifelong Learning Sector.* Exeter: Learning Matters.

Petty, G (2009) *Teaching Today: A Practical Guide.* Cheltenham: Nelson Thornes.

Roffey-Barentsen, J and Malthouse, R (2013) *Reflective Practice in Education and Training* (2nd edn). London: Learning Matters SAGE.

Rogers, A and Horrocks, N (2010) *Teaching Adults* (4th edn). Maidenhead: OU Press.

Rogers, CR (1983) *Freedom to Learn for the 80s*. Columbus, OH: Charles Merrill.

Rushton, I and Suter, M (2012) *Reflective Practice for Teaching in Lifelong Learning*. Maidenhead: OU Press.

Skills for Business (2007) *Inclusive learning approaches for literacy, language, numeracy and ICT: Companion Guide to the Minimum Core*. Nottingham: DfES Publications.

Skinner, BF (1974) *About Behaviourism*. San Francisco, CA: Knopf.

Stewart, I and Joines, V (1987) *TA Today: A new introduction to Transactional Analysis*. Kegworth: Lifespace Publishing.

Tripp, D (1993) *Critical Incidents in Teaching: Developing Professional Judgement*. London: Routledge.

Vizard, D (2012) *How to Manage Behaviour in Further Education* (2nd edn). London: Sage Publications Ltd.

Vygotsky, LS (1978) *Mind and Society: The Development of Higher Mental Processes*. Cambridge, MA: Harvard University Press.

Wallace, S (2007) *Getting the Buggers Motivated in FE* (2nd edn). London: Continuum.

Wallace, S (2013) *Managing Behaviour in the Further Education Sector*. London: Learning Matters SAGE.

Wood, J and Dickinson, J (2011) *Evaluating Learning in the Further Education and Skills Sector*. London: Learning Matters SAGE.

Younie, S and Leask, M (2013) *Teaching with Technologies: The Essential Guide*. Berkshire: McGraw Hill.

Website list

Ann Gravells: videos to support teaching, learning and assessment – www.youtube.com/channel/UCEQQRbP7x4L7NAy4wsQi7jA

Classroom management free resources – www.pivotaleducation.com/free-resources/

Classroom management free videos – www.bestyearever.net/videos/?goback=.gmr_27003.gde_27003_member_196422762

Cloud computing storage – www.dropbox.com/

Cyber bullying – http://stopcyberbullying.org/

Dewey – www.infed.org/thinkers/et-dewey.htm

Dropbox – www.dropbox.com

Facebook – www.facebook.com

Further Education Guide to using learning technology – http://feweek.co.uk/2013/02/22/guide-to-fe-learning-tech/?goback=.gde_4139923_member_217969739

ICT free support – www.learnmyway.com/get-started/online-basics

Learning preference questionnaire – www.vark-learn.com

Learning theories – www.learning-theories.com

LinkedIn – www.linkedin.com

Mind mapping software – www.xmind.net

Ofsted – ofsted.gov.uk

Online presentations – www.prezi.com

Pinterest – www.pinterest.com

Puzzle software – www.crossword-compiler.com

www.educational-software-directory.net/game/puzzle

http://hotpot.uvic.ca

www.mathsnet.net

Teacher training videos for using ICT – www.teachertrainingvideos.com/latest.html

Teaching and learning theories –http://classweb.gmu.edu/ndabbagh/Resources/IDKB/models_theories.
htm

Teaching groups – www.faculty.londondeanery.ac.uk/e-learning/small-group-teaching

Team roles – www.belbin.com/

Theories of learning – www.learningandteaching.info/learning/

Tips for teaching adults – www.helium.com/knowledge/61278-tips-for-teaching-adult-learners-
instead-of-younger-learners

Tuckman – www.infed.org/thinkers/tuckman.htm

Twitter – www.twitter.com

Using computers and technology: free guides – http://digitalunite.com/

Using ICT – www.reading.ac.uk/internal/its/training/its-training-index.aspx

Using VLEs – www.ofsted.gov.uk/resources/virtual-learning-environments-e-portfolio

Video e-mail – http://mailvu.com/

Table 3.3 Teaching and learning approaches and activities: strengths and limitations

Approach/ activity	Description	Strengths	Limitations
Activities	Tasks carried out by pairs, a group or individual, relevant to the topic being taught	Learners are active Develops group interaction	Not all learners may want to participate Clear objectives should be set; activity must be clearly explained Time limit required Time needed for feedback or debrief
Assignments	A longer-term activity based around the qualification or topic, which provides evidence of learning Can be practical or theoretical	Can be created by the teacher to challenge a learner's potential or consolidate learning Can be formative or summative	If set by an awarding organisation, ensure all aspects of the syllabus have been taught beforehand Must be individually assessed and written feedback given which can develop learning further
Blended learning	Using more than one method of teaching, usually including technology For example, a teaching session can be supported with learning materials and resources available via the organisation's website, with e-support/ assessment from teachers as required	Several methods of learning can be combined, enabling all learning preferences to be met Formal teaching can be supported with informal learning	Not all learners may have access to the technology
Brainstorming	A list of suggestions or ideas regarding a particular theme, topic or problem without judgements or criticisms The list can then be refined and used as a basis for other activities; usually written on flip chart paper or a board so all learners can see	Quickly stimulates thoughts and ideas Involves everyone Builds on current knowledge and experience Can be teacher led or group led	Some learners may not contribute or might be judgemental and overpowering Ideas may be given too quickly to write down Time limits need to be set

(Continued)

Table 3.3 (Continued)

Approach/ activity	Description	Strengths	Limitations
Buzz groups	Short topics to be discussed in small groups	Can break up a more formal session Allows interaction of learners and focuses ideas Checks understanding Doesn't require formal feedback	Learners may digress Specific points could be lost Checking individual learning has taken place may be difficult
Case studies	Can be a hypothetical situation, a description of an actual event or an incomplete event, enabling learners to write how they would deal with it	Can make topics more realistic, enhancing motivation and interest Can be carried out individually or in a group situation Builds on current knowledge and experience	Time limits must be set If carried out as a group activity, roles should be defined Must have clear outcomes Allow time for a debrief to include a group discussion
Coaching	A one-to-one, or small group activity which can occur spontaneously	Ideal for on-the-job training Ongoing advice and guidance can be given Takes account of individual needs	Not suitable for large groups Can be time-consuming Suitable environment needed
Debates	Learners or guests present a case to others, with subsequent arguments, questions and discussions	Learner centred Allows freedom of viewpoints and demonstrates understanding	Some learners may not get involved, others may take over – teacher needs to manage this carefully Can be time consuming Learners may need to research a topic in advance Can generate inappropriate behaviour
Demonstration	A practical way of showing how something works	Can be supported with handouts and activities to cover all learning preferences Can increase attention and confidence	Equipment may not be available or in working order Larger groups may not be able to see the demonstration or have enough resources Individuals may not pay attention or may get bored

Approach/ activity	Description	Strengths	Limitations
Dictation	Reading notes out loud for learners to write down	Gives emphasis to key points – should be used in moderation Can be followed up with learners carrying out research regarding what was dictated, i.e. via the internet	Learners write down what is said, but may not understand it Some learners may get behind with their writing and miss points Does not allow for clarification or questions
Discussion	Learners talk about a topic or the teacher can introduce a topic for the group to discuss	All learners can participate and share knowledge and experiences	Some learners may be shy or not want to be involved Easy to digress Teacher needs to keep the group focused and set a time limit Some learners might dominate
Distance learning or open learning	Learning which takes place away from the organisation offering the programme/qualification Work can be posted (online or manually) to learners and returned for assessment	Learning can occur at a time and place to suit the learner Can be combined with other learning methods, e.g. blended learning	Could be a long gap between submitting work for assessment and receiving feedback Self-discipline is needed Targets must be clearly agreed Learner may never meet teacher/assessor
Drawing	Illustrations to show how something works	Good for visual learners	Needs explaining carefully
e-learning (see also online learning)	Electronic learning – learning which is supported or enhanced using ICT	Learning can take place anywhere a computer is available Learning can be flexible Ongoing support is given	Learners need access to a computer and need to be computer literate Self-discipline is needed, along with clear targets Authenticity of learner's work may need validating Technical support may be required

(Continued)

Table 3.3 (Continued)

Approach/activity	Description	Strengths	Limitations
Essays	A formal piece of written or word-processed text, produced by the learner, for a specific topic	Useful for higher level subjects Can check a learner's English and maths skills Can confirm knowledge and understanding, along with application to practice	Not suitable for lower level learners Requires clear assessment grading criteria Marking can be time-consuming Plagiarism can be an issue
Experiential/discovery	Practical tasks enabling learners to act out or experience an event	Good for group work and to put theory into practice Learners find out things for themselves	Not all learners may want to participate Some learners may lack confidence or not want to embarrass themselves in front of their peers Can be time-consuming
Extension activity	A task to stretch and challenge learners	Can be used when learners finish a task earlier than others Can be used to extend a learner's thinking about a subject	Some learners might feel pressured to complete them when they are not able to, i.e. peer pressure
Flexible learning	Learning that can take place at a time and place to suit the learner and/or using different delivery approaches within a session to meet particular challenges	Suits learners who cannot attend formal sessions	Ongoing support and monitoring of achievement is required Not all learners are motivated by this style of learning
Games	A fun way of learning in pairs or groups to enable problem-solving and decision-making to take place	Board or card games can be designed to make learning enjoyable Assesses skills, knowledge, understanding and/or attitudes Encourages interaction and healthy competition Physical games put theory into practice Online games develop computer skills	Need to be well prepared in advance Learners need to remain focused Objectives need to be clear A pilot should take place first to make sure it works Careful supervision is needed Rules must be followed

Approach/ activity	Description	Strengths	Limitations
Gapped handout	Blank spaces within a handout for learners to fill in missing words in sentences	Different versions for different levels of learners could be devised Useful to fill in time during a session	Some learners might find it too easy
Group work	Enables learners to carry out a specific activity, for example, problem-solving Can be practical or theoretical	Allows interaction between learners Learners learn from each other's experiences and knowledge Encourages participation and variety Rotating group members enables all learners to work with each other	Careful management by the teacher is required regarding time limits, progress, and ensuring all group members are clear about the requirements Potential for personality clashes One person may dominate Learners might get left out or be too shy to contribute Ground rules might be needed to keep the group on track Time is needed for a thorough debrief and feedback
Handouts	Written information/drawings, etc. to promote and support learning	Useful for learners to refer to after a session Can incorporate questions for learners to answer as a homework activity Can be differentiated for levels of learners	Should be used in conjunction with other activities Needs to be adapted for any special learner requirements Should be produced well in advance Spelling, grammar, punctuation and syntax must be accurate
Homework	Activities carried out between sessions, for example, further reading, answering questions Learning doesn't have to stop just because the session has	Learners can complete at a time and place that suits them Maintains interest between sessions Encourages learners to stretch themselves further	Clear time limits must be set Learners might not do it Must be discussed, or marked/assessed and individual feedback given

(Continued)

Table 3.3 (Continued)

Approach/ activity	Description	Strengths	Limitations
Icebreakers/ energisers/ team building exercises	A fun and light-hearted way of introducing learners and topics	A good way of learners getting to know each other, and for teachers to observe skills and attitudes Can revitalise a flagging session	Not all learners may want to take part Some learners may see these as insignificant – careful explanations are needed to link the experience to the topic
Instruction	Formal method of teaching learners, whereby the teacher tells or shows the learner what to do, to achieve a particular skill, the learner then performs this	If one-to-one, a good method of pacing learning to suit the individual Learners can hear and/or see what they should do, and try this out immediately	If to a group, some learners may get left behind or forget what to do Needs supporting with a handout or further information/activities Appropriate positioning is required, e.g. for left-handed learners of right-handed teachers
Interactive whiteboard	Teachers and learners can use various functions including linking to the internet	Useful for group work and presentations	Not all learners can use it at the same time
Journal or diary	Learners keep a record of their progress, their reflections and thoughts	Develops self-assessment skills Relates theory to practice (if learners are having work experience) Helps the teacher assess English skills	Should be specific to the learning taking place and be analytical rather than descriptive Learners need to be guided as to how to write in a particular way to meet the programme criteria Contents need to remain confidential Can be time-consuming to read
Lecture	Traditional teacher-centred technique of delivering information	Useful for teaching theoretical subjects Key points can be prepared in advance on postcards as prompts Ideal for large groups Can be supported with visual images	Learners are passive and may not listen to what is being said Learners may not feel they can interrupt or ask questions to clarify points Learners need good listening and note-taking skills Good voice projection and clarity of speech required

Approach/ activity	Description	Strengths	Limitations
Mentoring	One-to-one guidance and support by someone other than the teacher, who is usually experienced in the subject	Expertise and knowledge can be passed on through ongoing support Times can be arranged to suit both parties	Can be time-consuming Mentor and mentee might not get along
Micro teaching	A simulated teaching session taught by the learner, usually in front of their peer group	Enables learners to practise in a safe environment Can be recorded to aid self-evaluation Peer feedback can be given by the other learners	Not all learners enjoy the experience Recording equipment, if used, can be difficult to manage while observing learners Some learners might not give constructive feedback
Mind maps/ spidergrams	A visual way of organising information and making plans; learners draw a circle with a key point and branch from this with subheadings to explore and develop points further – can be done manually or electronically	Learners are active Topics can be explored in a fun and meaningful way Links between ideas are easy to see New information can easily be added	Not all learners may want to contribute or understand what to do One learner may dominate Needs careful supervision Large paper or a board and marker pens required
Mnemonics	Remembering things by associating the first letters of words with something else, e.g. Richard Of York Gave Battle In Vain (ROYGBIV) is Red, Orange, Yellow, Green, Blue, Indigo, Violet for the colours of the rainbow	A quick way of remembering facts	Demonstrates knowledge but not understanding Some learners might get the letters mixed up
Models	Useful where the real object cannot be seen Life models, for example, in art classes or machinery models in engineering	Learners have a chance to see how something looks and/or works, and ask questions	Must be clearly explained and demonstrated May be an additional cost Needs careful planning and preparation Should be supported with a handout

(Continued)

Table 3.3 (Continued)

Approach/ activity	Description	Strengths	Limitations
Online learning (see also e-learning)	Learning that takes place in a virtual learning environment (VLE) via a computer connected to an intranet or the internet *Asynchronous learning* does not need to be accessed at fixed times *Synchronous learning* takes place in an environment where the teacher and learner are simultaneously present, perhaps at different locations, but communicating with each other in real time	Learning can take place anywhere a computer with internet access is available Learning can be flexible Ongoing support is given	Learners need access to a computer with internet connection Learners need to be computer literate Self-discipline is needed, along with clear targets Authenticity of learner's work may need validating Technical support may be required Reliable internet connection needed
Paired work	Enables learners to carry out a specific activity with their peer, for example, problem solving Can be practical or theoretical	Allows interaction between learners Learners learn from each other Encourages participation and variety Pairs can then link up as fours and so on to share experiences and knowledge	Careful management by the teacher is required regarding time limits, progress, and ensuring each pair is clear with the requirements Potential for personality clashes Difficult to assess individual contributions Time is needed for feedback from each pair
Peer learning Peer assessment Peer feedback	Learners gaining skills and/or knowledge from their peers	Enables learners to work together in an informal way to learn from each other's experiences and knowledge Learners support each other throughout the session or programme Learners give feedback to each other	There may be personality clashes resulting in subjective feedback Not all information given may be correct

Approach/ activity	Description	Strengths	Limitations
Podcast	A digital, audio or video file of the session uploaded to the internet	Useful if learners cannot attend a session Can listen or watch the session again	Some learners might not be able to access them May encourage non-attendance
Pose, pause, pick questioning	Ask a question, pause for a few seconds so that all learners are thinking about a response, then pick a learner to answer the question, stating their name as you look at them	Enables all learners to consider the answer rather than thinking they might be asked	Chosen learner might not know the answer
Practical work	A task that individuals can carry out, while the teacher observes progress; usually follows a demonstration or presentation	Actively involves the learners Help and advice can be given as needed	Some learners may not respond well to practical activities Can be time-consuming
Presentations	Similar to a lecture, with greater use of audio-visual aids	Interaction can take place between the teacher and learners Visual and aural learning preferences can be reached Effective use of media can make presentations stimulating, motivating and inspiring A good activity can be for learners to carry out research and then present their findings to others	Kinaesthetic learning preferences might not be included Some learners may not pay attention Too many slides can switch off learners' attention

(Continued)

Table 3.3 (Continued)

Approach/ activity	Description	Strengths	Limitations
Projects	A longer-term activity enabling learners to provide evidence of, or consolidate their learning and experiences	Can be interesting and motivating Can be individual or group led Learners could choose a relevant topic to cover the learning outcomes, leading to autonomous learning	Clear outcomes must be set, along with a time limit; must be relevant, realistic and achievable Progress should be checked regularly If a group is carrying out the project, be aware of each individual's input Thorough feedback should be given
Questions	A key technique for checking understanding and stimulating thinking	Can be written or oral Enables the learner to think about what they are learning Can challenge a learner's potential An effective way of testing knowledge when open questions are used	Closed questions only give a yes or no response which doesn't demonstrate knowledge Questions must be unambiguous Learners might struggle to answer oral questions in front of their peers Written questions might be misinterpreted Time constraints might be necessary
Quizzes	Fun activities to test skills, knowledge and/or attitudes through the use of crosswords, panel games, online activities, etc.	Learners are actively involved Useful backup activity if spare time available	Can seem trivial to mature learners Dominant learners might take over Shy learners might not get involved
Reading	Learners work from relevant texts, books, journals, etc.	Good for read/write learning preferences Encourages further learning	Reading and note-taking skills required Learners can get bored or easily distracted May need to have differentiated texts to account for a range of levels in the group
Repetition or rote learning	Learners repeat aspects such as the times tables (1×6 is 6, 2×6 is 12, etc.)	A good way of remembering useful facts	Only demonstrates the learner can remember and repeat; doesn't demonstrate understanding

Approach/activity	Description	Strengths	Limitations
Reports	Learners produce a document to inform, recommend and/or make suggestions based on a given topic	Useful for higher level learners Encourages the use of research techniques	Good writing skills and the use of referencing might be required Learners need to interpret and evaluate their reading to demonstrate their understanding
Research	An in-depth way of finding out answers or more information regarding a topic	Learners can use the internet, texts, journals, etc. in their own time	Learners need to know how to research Learners might not know how to apply their research to real situations
Rhyme and Rap	Repeating phrases or songs to aid memory, for example, 30 days have September, April, June and November	Learners can create their own phrases or songs Can be fun	Can seem trivial to mature learners Does not test knowledge and understanding, only the ability to recite or recall
Role plays	A practical activity to demonstrate skills, knowledge and understanding of a particular topic Acting out a hypothetical situation or scenario	Can see learners' behaviour and actions Encourages participation in a safe environment A fun method of learning Can lead to debates Links theory to practice Gives learners the opportunity to demonstrate communication skills Learners can observe and give peer feedback	Can be time-consuming Clear roles must be defined Not all learners may want or be able to participate Time limit should be set Some learners may get too dramatic Time is needed for a thorough debrief Some learners might be excluded
Self-assessment	Learners decide how they have met the assessment criteria, or are progressing at a given time	Promotes ownership, learner involvement and personal autonomy Encourages learners to check their own work before handing in Encourages reflection	Some learners may feel they are doing better or worse than they actually are Assessor needs to discuss progress and achievements with each learner to confirm their decisions

(Continued)

Table 3.3 (Continued)

Approach/ activity	Description	Strengths	Limitations
Self-assessment (continued)		Promotes individual thinking regarding progress and achievements	Learners need to be specific about what they have achieved and what they need to do to complete any gaps Difficult to be objective when making a decision
Seminars	A presentation of ideas, followed by questions and a discussion – usually by the learners	Allows learners to research topics and gain confidence at speaking to a group Can lead to worthwhile discussions	Agree topics well in advance along with a running order of who will present first Learners need specific objectives and a time limit Other learners may not pay attention
Simulation	An imitation activity carried out when the real activity would be too dangerous, for example, the evacuation of a building when the fire alarm goes off; there's no need to set fire to the building for a simulated evacuation	Enables learners to demonstrate skills Learners may realise things about themselves they were not aware of	Careful planning is needed Can be time-consuming Specialist equipment may be needed Ground rules must be agreed Not all learners may be able to participate fully May not be taken seriously Thorough debrief needed
Starter activity	A short activity at the beginning of a session to settle learners and focus their attention on learning (also known as a welcome activity) It could be a quiz to test knowledge gained so far, a discussion to open up thinking about the current subject, or an energiser activity focusing upon the session topic	If a learner arrives late, they only miss the starter activity not the introduction to the session	Some learners might feel it is trivial or wasting time

Approach/ activity	Description	Strengths	Limitations
Surveys	Learners gather information from others regarding a particular topic	Active task, learners can work individually, in pairs or groups Learners can meet other people enhancing their experience	Permission may be required Ethical approach and confidentiality required Quality of question content is important Confidentiality should be maintained Time-consuming to analyse
Teaching/ training/ tutoring	Educating learners in a subject, furthering their skills, knowledge, understanding and/or attitudes using formal and informal approaches	A variety of approaches can be used depending upon the subject If planned well, can reach all learning preferences, motivate learners and encourage development and progression	Some learners do not respond well to formal teaching Not all learning preferences reached all of the time
Team teaching or co-training	Facilitating a session with a colleague	Enables learners to see different styles of delivery	Staff involved need to plan carefully who is doing what and when
Technology-based learning	Using relevant equipment and materials, for example, videos, CD ROMs, DVDs, the internet, etc.	Generates discussions and leads to further learning and questions Brings real events to learners	Can be time-consuming Learners need to pay attention Learners should not be left unsupervised
Tests	Written questions (open, closed, multiple choice) to test knowledge and understanding Practical activities to assess skills	Learners are active Can be used to fill in time towards the end of a session or to extend learning Useful for individual learners who like to be challenged further	Needs to be carried out in supervised conditions Time limits required Can be stressful to learners Feedback may not be immediate If set by an awarding organisation, ensure all aspects of the syllabus have been taught before issuing the test

(Continued)

Table 3.3 (Continued)

Approach/activity	Description	Strengths	Limitations
Tutorial reviews	A one-to-one or group discussion between the teacher and the learner/s, with an agreed purpose, for example, discussing progress so far	A good way of informally assessing a learner's progress and/or giving feedback An opportunity for learners to discuss issues or for informal tuition to take place	Needs to be in a comfortable, safe and quiet environment as confidential issues may be discussed Time may overrun Records should be maintained and action points followed up
Undoing	Learners can undo or take apart an object, to learn how it was put together. An example is taking a plug apart to see how it was originally wired	Great for kinaesthetic learners and for developing practical skills Needs to be demonstrated by the teacher first Useful in practical sessions; needs to be supported with a handout, further information and careful guidance	Not so good for theoretical learners Objects/resources need to be available for all learners
Video/TV/DVD/webinar and online recordings	Watching a recording or a live programme via various media including the internet	Good for visual learners Promotes discussions	Not interactive Doesn't suit all learning preferences
Virtual learning environment (VLE)	An online platform for teachers to upload learning materials and interact with learners	Enables learners to access materials outside the sessions Can be used for online learning instead of attending sessions Allows online interaction between other learners and the teacher Assignments can be accessed by learners and uploaded once complete; teachers can give feedback via the VLE and records are automatically maintained	Not all learners might be computer literate Not all learners have internet access

Approach/activity	Description	Strengths	Limitations
Visiting speakers	An expert in the subject area speaks to the group	Can give variety and expertise to a topic, with a different perspective	Must be arranged well in advance Some speakers may charge a fee Allow time for questions and discussions
Visits/field trips	Learners visit a venue relevant to the programme or qualification	Fact finding, active, interesting and stimulating Makes the subject real Puts theory into practice Can be discussed in subsequent sessions Can link with projects and assignments	Needs careful planning; organisational and health and safety procedures must be followed Needs finance Group needs to be well briefed and prepared; ground rules must be set Supervision usually required Debrief needed
Webcast	Videos and information uploaded to the internet Similar to podcasts	A useful way of distributing additional information to support current teaching	No interaction between learners Not all learners have internet access
Worksheets	Handouts to read and complete to check knowledge and understanding (can also be electronic) Blank spaces can be used for learners to complete sentences Words can be circled, phrases completed, lists put in order	Fun informal activity can be done individually, in pairs or groups Useful for lower level learners or homework Can be created at different degrees of difficulty to address differentiation	Mature learners may consider them inappropriate Too many worksheets can be boring; learners might not be challenged enough
Workshops	An opportunity to share practice, use activities and develop knowledge and understanding in a real or simulated working environment (RWE/SWE)	Enables learners to work at their own pace Learners can support each other and learn from each other's experiences	Individual support is required Suitable workpacks need producing or resource packs need purchasing to enable learners to progress at their own pace

(Continued)

4 ASSESSING LEARNERS

In this chapter you will learn about:

- assessment in education and training
- assessment types and methods
- peer and self-assessment
- making decisions and giving feedback
- maintaining records
- implementing the minimum core
- evaluating own practice

There are activities and examples to encourage you to reflect on the above which will help you develop and enhance your understanding of how to assess learning in education and training contexts.

At the end of each section within the chapter are extension activities to stretch and challenge your knowledge and understanding. A list of useful references, further information and website links can be found at the end of the chapter in case you would like to research the topics further.

At the end of the chapter is a cross-referencing grid showing how the chapter's contents relate to the units of the Certificate in Education and Training, and the Professional Standards for Teachers and Trainers in England.

Assessment in education and training

Assessment is a way of finding out if learning has taken place. It enables you to ascertain if your learner has gained the required skills, knowledge, understanding and/or attitudes needed at a given point in time, towards their programme of learning. It also provides your learners with an opportunity to demonstrate what progress they have made and what they have learnt so far. If you don't plan for and carry out any assessment with your learners, you will not know how well, or what they have learnt.

Assessment should not be in isolation from the teaching and learning process. You can assess that learning is taking place each time you are with your learners. This can simply be by watching what they are doing to assess a skill and/or asking questions to assess knowledge. If your learners are taking a qualification, there will be formal methods of assessment you will need to use such as an assignment, or a workplace observation. However, you can devise informal methods to use with your learners to check their progress at any time, such as a quiz or role play activity. There are some assessors who don't also teach or train, but will just assess, make decisions and give feedback. This could be where competent staff are demonstrating their skills, knowledge and understanding towards their job role, or an aspect of a qualification in their workplace.

Assessment should focus on improving and reinforcing learning as well as measuring achievements. It should help your learners realise how they are progressing and what they need to do to improve and/or develop further. Assessment should be a regular and continual process; it might not always be formalised, but you will be watching what your learners are doing, asking them questions, and reviewing their progress whenever you are in contact with them. If you also teach or train, your learners will be demonstrating their skills, knowledge and understanding regularly, for example, through tasks, discussions and regular working activities. Try to avoid teaching purely to pass a test, i.e. only teaching what will be asked in the test. This will not maximise your learners' potential as they will only be competent at passing the test and might not be able to apply their learning elsewhere.

It is good practice to give your learners feedback when assessing them informally to help them see what progress they are making. If they haven't reached a certain standard, you should still give feedback on what they have done well so far, and how they can develop and improve.

As the assessor, you are responsible for deciding whether or not your learners have achieved the relevant standards (Read, 2011, page 17). If you make a decision to pass a learner, and they have not fully met the requirements, you are not doing them any favours. They might feel they can do something which they can't, and this could impact upon their future career.

You are therefore constantly making judgements and you should be aware of the impact that your comments and grades can have on your learners' confidence, and on their future. Comments which specifically focus on the activity or work produced, rather than the individual, will be more helpful and motivating to your learners. Assessment should not become a personal subjective judgement, but should be objective and relate only to the activity or criteria being assessed.

Assessment can help your learners by:

- acknowledging what progress has been made
- addressing issues where there are gaps in learning
- confirming achievements
- diagnosing any areas of concern to enable support to be arranged
- encouraging discussions and questions
- ensuring they are on the right programme at the right level
- identifying areas for development
- identifying what is yet to be learnt and achieved
- maintaining motivation
- seeing any inaccuracies, for example, spelling errors in a written task or mistakes during a practical task

Assessment is not another term for evaluation; assessment is *of the learners* whereas evaluation is *of the programme*. Assessment is specific towards a learner's progress and achievement and how they can improve and develop. Evaluation includes feedback from your learners and others to help you improve your own practice and the overall learner experience.

Assessments are usually:

- internally set – produced by you, or your organisation, for example, case studies, questions, projects and role play activities, which will also be assessed by you

- externally set – usually produced by an awarding organisation, for example, an assignment, examination, observation checklist or test, which might be assessed internally or externally

Example

Harry has a group of 15 learners taking a Level 2 Diploma in Customer Service. All the learners will be undertaking a work placement; therefore Harry has designed a role play activity regarding awkward situations which can be carried out in class beforehand (internally set). When he visits each learner at their work placement, he will use an observation checklist to document how they deal with real awkward situations with customers (externally set).

There will be internal and external requirements and procedures to follow regarding the assessment of learning programmes. Internal relate to those within your organisation, such as checking a learner's work for plagiarism and ensuring it is authentic. External relate to those from other organisations such as the time limit within which learners must be registered with an awarding organisation. Procedures are the ways in which you perform what is required. For example, if you suspect plagiarism, you must follow your organisation's policy. This might require you to talk to your learner first and establish the facts, before taking it further.

There will be several policies and procedures which you must follow. These might include:

- access and fair assessment

- appeals

- authenticity

- complaints

- confidentiality of information

- copyright and data protection

- equality and diversity

- health and safety

- quality assurance

- plagiarism

- safeguarding

There may be other requirements such as a dress code, acceptable use of computer equipment, a behaviour code, and regulations such as the Control of Substances Hazardous to Health (COSHH) that you will need to follow. If you are assessing a qualification which is regulated in England, you will also need to follow requirements relating to the Qualifications and Credit Framework (QCF), those imposed by Ofqual who are the examinations regulators, and Ofsted who inspect provision.

Activity

What internal and external requirements and procedures will you need to follow regarding the assessment of your learners for your subject?

Principles of assessment

Principles are *how* the assessment process is put into practice, for example, being:

- ethical by ensuring the assessment process is honest and moral, and takes into account confidentiality, integrity, safety and security

- fair by ensuring the assessment activities are fit for purpose, at the right level, differentiate for any individual needs, and that planning, decisions and feedback are justifiable

- safe by ensuring there is little chance of plagiarism, the work can be confirmed as authentic, confidentiality has been taken into account, learning and assessment have not been compromised in any way, nor have the learner's experience or potential to achieve (safe in this context does not relate to health and safety but to the assessment types and methods used)

Two important principles are known by the acronyms VACSR and SMART. Following these will help ensure all the assessment requirements can be met by your learners, providing they have acquired the necessary skills, knowledge and understanding at the time of assessment.

VACSR

All work assessed should be valid, authentic, current, sufficient and reliable. Using VACSR will help you plan and assess in a way that should meet the expected requirements.

Valid – the assessment process and work produced by the learner is appropriate and relevant.

Authentic – the work has been produced solely by the learner.

Current – the work is still relevant at the time of assessment.

Sufficient – the work covers all the assessment requirements.

Reliable – the work is consistent and at the required level, i.e. if the assessment was carried out again with similar learners, similar results would be achieved.

SMART

Being SMART is all about being clear and precise with what you expect your learners to achieve. SMART stands for:

Specific – the activity relates only to what is being assessed and is clearly stated.

Measurable – the activity can be measured against the assessment requirements, allowing any gaps to be identified.

Achievable – the activity can be achieved at the right level by the learner.

Relevant – the activity is realistic and will give consistent, valid and reliable results.

Time bound – target dates and times can be achieved.

Another important principle is that of ensuring you are assessing at the correct level. Please see Table 2.4 in Chapter 2 for examples of objectives that could be used at different levels. For example, to assess your learner by asking them to *explain* something could be at level 3, whereas asking them to *analyse* could be at level 4.

You also need to consider the environment in which you are assessing, i.e. ensuring that it is suitable, accessible and does not create any unnecessary barriers. Any resources you use should be relevant and effective. Always make sure you are assessing only what is necessary and relevant at the time.

Planning for assessment

Assessment planning should be a two-way process between you and your learners; you need to plan what you are going to do, and they need to know what is expected of them. Unless all your learners are taking an examination or test on the same day at the same time, assessment should be planned for and carried out on an individual basis. Failing to plan how you are going to assess your learners may result in your learners failing the assessment activity. If your learners are all working towards the same assignment, you will still need to agree target dates for completion and discuss any specific requirements your learners may have. If your learners are to be assessed in their place of work, you will need to agree how, along with relevant target dates. You might need to complete an assessment plan or action plan with your learners to formally document what they are aiming to achieve. This record is like a written contract between you and your learner towards their achievement. However, it can be reviewed, amended and updated at any time. Your organisation should be able to provide you with the relevant documentation to use. Table 4.1 is an example of a template which could be used to plan assessment activities and also to give feedback to your learners. If the document is completed electronically, you might not require signatures. You will need to take into account any aspects of equality and diversity when planning to assess your learners. Please see Chapter 2 for further details.

Table 4.1 Assessment plan and feedback template

Assessment plan			
Learner: Assessor: Qualification/unit: Level:			
Aspects to be assessed		**Methods of assessment**	**Target date**
Learner signature and date:		**Assessor signature and date:**	
Feedback record			
Date	**Aspects assessed**	**Feedback**	**Action required**	**Target date**

Communicating with others

At some point, you might need to liaise with other people who are involved in the assessment process of your learners, for example, to inform them of any particular learner requirements to ensure consistency of support. You might need to liaise with a representative from the awarding organisation if you want to change an assessment activity, for example, if you have a learner who would benefit from oral questions instead of written questions. You could have a learner who would prefer to be assessed bilingually, and you would therefore need to liaise with another member of staff who could help. Examples of other professional people and the roles they might have include:

- administration staff – to register learners with an awarding organisation
- awarding organisation personnel – to ensure compliance with their regulations
- assessors – to provide information on progress and achievement
- co-tutors – to provide information on progress
- finance staff – to help with funding, grants and loans
- internal quality assurers – to ensure the assessment process is fair
- learning support staff – to provide support to learners as necessary
- managers – to ensure organisational procedures are followed
- other teachers and trainers – to communicate information regarding learner progress
- safeguarding officers – to help ensure the well-being of learners
- support workers – to provide help and support when needed

- workplace supervisors – to provide information regarding progress

- work placement co-ordinators – to arrange and monitor suitable work experience placements

You will need to know what information can be available to help support the assessment process for your learners and the others who are involved, for example, information such as the standards or units to be assessed, progress and achievement records, assessment plans and feedback documentation, and resources such as textbooks, internet websites and journals that will prove useful. Workplace supervisors, mentors and witnesses will need details of your learners' progress and achievements. Support staff will need relevant information regarding your learners to provide any necessary help and guidance. Communicating regularly will ensure everyone who is involved with your learners knows of their progress and achievement, and what else might be required.

It could be that you have learners who are taking a programme or a qualification in conjunction with an employer, for example, a learner taking an apprenticeship programme who is undertaking a substantial amount of work experience. You will therefore need to communicate with their supervisor regarding the progress they are making. You will also need to explain the areas they need to cover at work to demonstrate achievement of the qualification requirements. It could be that their supervisor might carry out some form of assessment, for example, by giving a witness statement of what has been achieved. However, if you are responsible for assessing the learner, all decisions regarding achievement will rest with you.

It is important that you communicate with all concerned to ensure the learning and assessment process is effective. You should also ensure that aspects are not unnecessarily duplicated or assessed more than necessary.

If you are liaising with external contacts, you should remain professional at all times as you are representing your organisation. People might not always remember your name; however, you will be known as *that person from XYZ organisation*. You therefore need to create a good and lasting impression of yourself and your organisation. You should also remember aspects of confidentiality and data protection, and keep notes of all activities in case you need to refer to them again.

Activity

What assessment information will you need to communicate to other professionals who have an interest in your learners' achievement and why?

The role of information and communication technology in assessment

Information and communication technology (ICT) is constantly evolving and new resources are frequently becoming available. It is crucial to keep up to date with new developments and you should try to incorporate these within the assessment process when possible. It is not only about you using technology to help assess your learners, but also about your learners using it to complete their assessment activities. Encouraging your learners to use technology will help increase their skills in this area. If your learners are based at different locations to you, they could send digital recordings or live transmissions of their activities. Technology can be combined with traditional methods of assessment; for example, learners can complete a written assignment by word-processing their response, and submitting it by e-mail or uploading it to a virtual learning environment (VLE). You can then give feedback via e-mail or the VLE system. Combining methods also promotes differentiation and inclusivity; for example, learners could access assessment materials via the VLE outside the normal learning environment to support their learning.

Technologies in common use include:

- blogs, chat rooms, social networking sites, webinars and online discussion forums to help learners communicate with each other

- computer programs and applications for learners to produce their assignments and save documents and pictures

- cloud storage facilities that learners and assessors can use to upload and access materials from various devices

- digital media for visual/audio recording and playback

- electronic portfolios for learners to store their work

- e-mail for electronic submission of assessments, communication and informal feedback on progress

- interactive whiteboards for learners to use for presentations and to display their work

- internet access for research to support assignments or presentations

- mobile phones and tablets for taking pictures, video and audio clips, and communicating with others

- networked systems to allow access to applications and documents from any computer linked to the system

- online and on-demand tests which can give instant results, for example, diagnostic, learning preferences and multiple-choice tests

- online discussion forums which allow asynchronous (taking place at different times) and synchronous (taking place at the same time) discussions

- scanners for copying and transferring documents to a computer

- web cameras or video conferencing if you can't be in the same place as your learners and you need to see and talk to them

- VLEs to access and upload learning materials and assessment activities

E-learning and e-assessment processes are constantly advancing. Unfortunately, there isn't room in this book to explain these in great detail. Please refer to other appropriate texts such as those listed at the end of this chapter.

Meeting individual needs

If you have learners with any particular needs or requirements, you should consider how you can help meet these. Always check with your organisation regarding what you can and can't do as you may need approval to make any reasonable adjustments.

Some examples of meeting your learners' needs include:

- adapting or providing resources and equipment for a learner who is partially sighted

- adapting the environment for a learner who is physically disabled

- allowing extra time for a learner with dyslexia or dyscalculia

- arranging to use another language such as British Sign Language with a learner who is partially deaf

- changing a date and/or time for a learner who works shifts

- liaising with others who could offer advice regarding financial concerns

- providing specialist support staff to improve English and maths skills

- providing the assessment information in an alternative format such as spoken instead of written for a learner who has impaired vision

- using a different location which is more accessible to learners who have to travel far

- using different assessment activities to suit individual learning preferences

- using new and emerging technologies to help improve confidence with ICT skills

- using larger print, Braille, or other alternative support mechanisms for learners with particular needs

If you need to adapt anything, make sure you check with your awarding organisation to ensure you are following their regulations and requirements before making any changes.

Extension Activity

How can you ensure that your learners can produce assessment evidence that is valid, authentic, current, sufficient and reliable (VACSR)?

Assessment types and methods

Assessment types include initial (at the beginning), formative (ongoing) summative (at the end) and holistic (assessing several aspects at the same time). Assessment methods are the activities used to assess ongoing progress as well as achievement, for example, questions, discussions, observations, tests and assignments. All assessment methods should be suited to the level and ability of your learners. A level 1 learner might struggle to write a journal; a level 2 learner may not be mature enough to accept peer feedback; a level 3 learner may feel a puzzle is too easy, and so on.

Assessment types

Depending upon the subject you are assessing and any relevant qualification requirements, you might carry out various *types* of assessment with your learners which could be on a formal or informal basis. Formal assessment means the results will count towards achievement, for example, a qualification. Informal assessment helps you see how your learners are progressing at a given point. Assessment types relate to the *purpose* of assessment, i.e. the reason assessment is carried out. During formative assessment, which is usually informal, it is important that your learners are prepared for the way in which they will be formally assessed. This will ensure they are familiar with the methods to be used. Please see Table 4.2 for examples.

Example

Sara plans to use a holistic type of assessment with her learners who are working towards the Level 3 Award in Education and Training. This ensures several assessment criteria from the three units can be assessed at the same time when the learners each deliver a micro teach session. The methods she will use include observation and questioning which will be formal as they will count towards achievement of the qualification. The learners are familiar with these methods as they have been used regularly during sessions.

Assessment methods

All assessment methods should be suited to the level and ability of your learners. Assessment methods will be either formal or informal. You will need to know what formal assessments your learners must do to achieve the programme or qualification, as well as what informal assessments you can use to check ongoing progress and performance. Often it is your decision as to what assessment methods to use, as long as you follow the requirements of the programme or qualification. Please see Table 4.3 at the end of the chapter.

> We have to remember to choose assessment methods that provide the best fit with the course or programme of study with which we are involved ... For many adult education tutors, a considerable degree of professional autonomy is allowed, and assessment methods, perhaps even assessment outcomes, may be left entirely at their own discretion.

(Tummons, 2011, page 49–50)

Informal assessment

Informal assessment activities can take place at any time you are in contact with your learners, for example, oral questions during a tutorial review, or a quiz or a discussion at the end of a taught session. Informal activities might not always count towards your learners' achievement of their qualification, but will inform you how much learning is taking place and what progress is being made.

Informal methods can include:

- crosswords
- discussions
- gapped handouts (sentences with missing words)
- journals/diaries
- peer and self-assessment
- puzzles and crosswords
- practical activities
- questions: oral, written, multiple choice
- quizzes
- role plays
- worksheets

Formal assessment

Formal assessment activities usually count towards your learners' achievement of their qualification, for example, successful completion of an assignment, examination or test. The criteria for these will be stated in the qualification handbook and will probably be known as assessment criteria and linked to the learning outcomes of the qualification. Formal assessments are usually completed with certain constraints such as a time limit or the number of resources that can be used by learners.

Assessment should be a regular process; it might not always be formalised, but you should be observing what your learners are doing, asking questions and reviewing their progress throughout their time with you. Even if you are not assessing towards a qualification, for example, you are training and assessing a colleague regarding a new working procedure on the job, you should assess their ongoing progress and achievement.

Formal methods can include:

- assignments
- case studies
- essays
- examinations
- multiple-choice questions
- observations
- professional discussions and questions
- projects
- tests
- witness testimonies

Depending upon the situation, some methods could be classed as informal and formal, for example, a case study could be used informally during a session, but formally at the end of a unit of learning.

Table 4.2 Assessment types

Assessment type/ terminology	Description
Academic	Assessment of theory or knowledge.
Adaptive	Questions are selected during the test on the basis of their difficulty, in response to an estimate of the learner's ability.
Analytic scoring	A method of scoring grades for tests such as speaking and writing. For example, a writing test would have an analytic score based on grammar and vocabulary.
Aptitude	A diagnostic test to assess a learner's ability for a particular job or vocation.
Assessor-led	Assessment is planned and carried out by the assessor, for example, an observation.
Benchmarking	A way of evaluating learner performance against an accepted standard. Once a standard is set, it can be used as a basis for the expectation of achievements with other groups/learners.
Blended	Using more than one assessment method in different locations, for example, observation in the work environment backed up with online assessments.
Competence based	Criteria that learners need to perform in the work environment.
Criterion referencing	Assessing prescribed aspects a learner must achieve to meet a certain standard.
Diagnostic	A specific assessment relating to a particular topic or subject and level, which builds on initial assessment. Sometimes called a skills test. The results determine what needs to be learnt or assessed in order to progress further. Some types of diagnostic assessments can also identify learners with dyslexia, dyspraxia, dysgraphia, dyscalculia, etc.
Differentiation	Organising teaching, learning and assessment to suit learners' abilities and needs.
Direct	Evidence provided by a learner towards their qualification, for example, products from their work environment.
Evidence	Assessment is based upon items a learner provides to prove their knowledge and competence.
External	Assessments set and marked externally by an awarding organisation.
Formal	Assessment that involves the recognition and recording of achievement, often leading to certification of an accredited qualification.
Formative	Ongoing, interim or continuous assessment. Can be used to assess knowledge and/or skills and understanding in a progressive way, to build on topics learnt and plan future learning and assessments. Often referred to as assessment for learning, allowing additional learning to take place prior to further assessments.
Holistic	Assessing several aspects of a qualification, programme or job specification at the same time.

Assessment type/ terminology	Description
Independent	An aspect of the qualification is assessed by someone who has not been involved with the learner for any part of their learning or assessment.
Indirect	Evidence provided by others regarding a learner's progress, for example, a witness statement from their supervisor.
Informal	Assessment that is in addition to formal assessment, for example, questioning during a review of progress with a learner, or an observation during a group activity.
Initial	Assessment at the beginning of a programme or unit, relating to the subject being learnt and assessed, to identify a learner's starting point and level. Initial assessment can also include learning preferences tests, and English, maths and ICT tests. The latter can be used as a basis to help and support learners.
Integrated	Information acquired in a learning context is put into practice and assessed in the learner's work environment.
Internal	Assessments carried out within an organisation, either internally set and marked, or externally set by the relevant awarding organisation and internally marked.
Ipsative	A process of self-assessment to recognise development. Learners match their own achievements against a set of standards, or their own previous achievements. This is useful for learners to consider their progress and development. However, they do need to work autonomously and be honest with themselves.
Learner-led	Learners produce evidence and let their assessor know when they are ready to be assessed.
Norm referencing	Comparing the results of learner achievements, such as setting a pass mark to enable a certain percentage of a group to achieve or not. For example, the top 20 per cent would achieve an A, the next 20 per cent a B, and so on. This type of assessment is useful to maintain consistency of results over time; whether the test questions are easy or hard, there will always be those who achieve a higher grade or a lower grade.
Objective	An assessment decision that is based around the criteria being assessed, not a personal opinion or decision.
Predictive	An indication of how well a test predicts future performance in a relevant skill.
Process	The assessment of routine skills or techniques, for example, to ensure a learner is following a set process or procedure.
Process (as in teaching)	Teaching more than is required for the learner to achieve, for example, teaching keyboard skills to a learner who is taking a word-processing qualification (i.e. it is not in the syllabus but it is helpful).

Assessment type/ terminology	Description
Product	The outcome is assessed, not the process of making it, for example, a painting or a working model.
Product (as in teaching)	Only teaching the minimum amount required to pass an assessment.
Proficiency	An assessment to test ability or skills without reference to any specific programme of learning, for example, riding a bicycle.
Profiling	A way of recording learner achievements for each individual aspect of an assessment. Checklists can be a useful way to evidence these. More than one assessor can be involved in the process.
Psychometric	A test of psychological qualities, for example, intelligence and personality.
Qualitative	Assessment is based upon individual responses to open questions given to learners. Clear criteria must be stated for the assessor to make a decision as questions can be vague or misinterpreted.
Quantitative	Assessment is based upon yes/no or true/false responses, agree/ disagree statements or multiple choice tests, giving a clear right or wrong answer. Totals can be added to give results, for example, 8 out of 10. Learners could pass purely by guessing the correct answers.
Screening	A process to determine if a learner has a particular need, for example, in English or maths.
Subjective	A personal decision by the assessor, where the assessment criteria might not be clearly stated. This can be unfair to a learner.
Summative	Assessment at the end of a programme or unit, for example, an exam. If a learner does not pass, they will usually have the opportunity to retake. Often known as assessment of learning, as it shows what has been achieved from the learning process.
Triangulation	Using more than one assessment method, for example, observation, oral questioning and a test. This helps ensure the reliability and authenticity of a learner's work and makes the assessment process more interesting.
Vocational	Job-related practical assessment, usually in a learner's work environment.

Questioning techniques

Questions are often the best way to assess knowledge and understanding. If you are asking questions orally to a group of learners, ensure you include all learners. Don't just let the keen learners answer first as this gives the ones who don't know the answers the chance to stay quiet. Pose a question, pause for a second and then state the name of a learner you would like to answer. This way, all learners are thinking about the answer as soon as you have posed the question, and are ready to speak if their name is asked. This technique is often referred to as *pose, pause, pick* (PPP). To ensure you include everyone throughout your session with a question, you could have a list of their names handy and tick each one after you have asked them a question. If a learner doesn't know the answer or gets it wrong, state it was a good attempt and then ask another learner.

When questioning:

- allow enough time for your questions and your learners' responses
- ask open questions, i.e. those beginning with *who, what, when, where, why* and *how*
- avoid trick or complex questions
- be aware of your posture, gestures and body language
- be conscious of your dialect, accent, pitch and tone
- don't ask more than one question in the same sentence
- make sure you don't use closed questions to illicit a *yes* response; learners may feel that is what you want to hear but it doesn't confirm understanding
- use active listening skills
- try not to say *erm, yeah, okay, you know,* or *does that make sense?*
- use eye contact
- use learners' names
- watch your learners' reactions

When asking questions, use only one question in a sentence, as more than one may confuse your learners. Try not to ask *Does anyone have any questions?* as often only those who are keen or confident will ask, and this doesn't tell you what has been learnt. Try not to use questions such as *Does that make sense?* or *Do you understand?*, as your learners will often say *yes* as they feel that's what you expect to hear, but it does not tell you what they know or understand.

There are different ways of asking questions such as:

Open: 'How would you ...?'	Leading: 'So what you are saying is ...?'
Closed: 'Would you ...?'	Hypothetical: 'What would you do if ...?'
Probing: 'Why exactly was that?'	Reflecting: 'If you could do that again,
Prompting: 'What about ...?'	how would you approach it?'
Clarifying: 'Can you go over that again?'	

Try to use *open questions* which require an answer that demonstrates knowledge and understanding. For example, *How many days are there in September?* This ensures your learner has to think about their answer. Using a closed question such as *Are there 30 days in September?* would only give a yes/no answer which doesn't show you if your learner has the required knowledge and understanding.

If you are having a conversation with your learner, you can ask probing questions to obtain more information. These can begin with: *Why was that?* You can then prompt your learner to say more by asking *What about ...?* You can also clarify what your learner is saying by asking *Can you go over that again?*

Activity

Write a few questions based on your subject, for example, using open, closed, probing etc. Try them out with your learners and evaluate which were the best to use and why.

When writing questions for learners, think about how you will do this, i.e. short questions, essay-style questions, open, closed or multiple choice. If you are giving grades, for example, A, B, C, or pass/merit/distinction, you need clear grading criteria to ensure your decisions are justified, otherwise your learners may challenge your decisions. You may need to rephrase some questions if your learners are struggling with an answer, as poor answers are often the result of poor questions. For essay and short-answer tests you should create sample answers to have something to compare your learners' answers with. Be careful with the use of jargon – just because you understand it doesn't mean your learners will.

You need to be aware of plagiarism, particularly now that so much information is available via the internet. Learners should take responsibility for referencing any sources of all work submitted, and may be required to sign an authenticity statement. If you suspect plagiarism, you could type a few of their words into an internet search engine or specialist computer software and see what appears. You would then have to challenge your learner as to whether it was intentional or not, and follow your organisation's plagiarism procedure.

If you are using the same questions for different learners at different times, be careful as they may collude and share their answers with each other. Therefore, you will need to satisfy yourself that the work is that of each learner.

Extension Activity

Decide upon a type of assessment, for example, initial, formative, summative or holistic. Design an assessment activity based on it, and use the activity with your learners. Analyse the effectiveness in relation to meeting individual needs.

Peer and self-assessment

Peer assessment involves a learner assessing another learner's progress. Self-assessment involves a learner assessing their own progress. Both methods encourage learners to make decisions about what has been learnt so far, take responsibility for their learning and become involved with the assessment process. This approach gives your learners responsibility in the assessment *for*, and *of* their learning. Assessment *for* learning involves finding out a starting point for future learning and assessment. Assessment *of* learning involves making a decision regarding what has been learnt so far. Your learners will need to fully understand what needs to be assessed, and how to be fair and objective with their decisions and any feedback given to others. Throughout the process of peer and self-assessment, learners can develop skills such as listening, observing and questioning. The results of peer and self-assessment are usually not counted towards meeting the requirements of a qualification as you should make the final decision regarding achievement. However, in the workplace, peer assessment might be counted as proof the learner has met the requirements of a job role, for example, if the peer is a colleague.

Activity

How can you promote the use of peer and self-assessment activities with your learners to give them personal responsibility in the assessment for, and of, their learning?

Peer assessment

Peer assessment involves a learner assessing another learner's progress. This would actively involve your learners. However, you would need to ensure everyone was aware of the assessment criteria, how to reach a decision and how to give constructive feedback.

> *This assessment method requires a good level of self criticism and personal awareness and may need to be 'taught' before embarking on as a reliable method of assessment ... Authenticity is the main risk associated with this method of assessment in that candidates may not be familiar with the units of competence or be as confident in deciding sufficiency.*

> (Wilson, 2012, page 49)

Peer assessment can be useful to develop and motivate learners. However, this should be managed carefully, as you may have some learners who do not get along and might use the opportunity to demoralise one another. You would need to give advice to your learners as to how to give feedback effectively. If learner feedback is given skilfully, other learners may think more about what their peers have said than about what you have said. If you consider peer assessment has a valuable contribution to make to the assessment process, ensure you plan for it to enable your learners to become accustomed and more proficient at giving it. The final decision as to the achievement of your learner will lie with you.

Examples of peer assessment activities include:

- assessing each other's work anonymously and giving written or verbal feedback

- giving grades and/or written or verbal feedback regarding peer presentations and activities

- holding group discussions before collectively agreeing a grade and giving feedback, perhaps regarding a learner's presentation

- suggesting improvements to their peers' work

- producing a written statement of how their peers could improve and/or develop their practice in certain areas

Self-assessment

Self-assessment involves learners assessing their own progress, which can lead to them setting their own goals. It can give them responsibility and ownership of their progress and achievements. However, learners might feel they have achieved more than they actually have; therefore you will still need to confirm their achievements or otherwise.

Examples of self-assessment activities include:

- awarding a grade for a presentation they have delivered

- suggesting improvements regarding their skills and knowledge

- compiling a written statement of how they could improve their work

Example

Design two activities to use with your learners based on peer and self-assessment. Use the activities and analyse how effective they were. What would you change and why?

Making decisions and giving feedback

Throughout your time with your learners, you will constantly be making decisions regarding their progress and achievement. You will need to give constructive feedback on an individual basis to ensure each learner is aware of this, and what they need to develop or improve upon. Keeping records is important to prove what has been achieved. Table 4.1 earlier in this chapter is an example of a template which could be used to plan assessment activities as well as to give feedback to your learners.

Making decisions

The decisions you make regarding your learners' progress can affect them both personally and professionally. It is important to remain factual about what you have assessed and to be *objective* with your judgements. You should not be *subjective* and let other aspects influence or compromise your decision, for example, passing a learner just because you like them, feel they have worked hard or are under pressure to meet certain targets. When making a decision, refer to the principles of VACSR and SMART as stated in the first section of this chapter. You should always inform your learners when they can expect to receive any feedback or formal recognition of their achievements.

You will need to complete relevant records to prove that assessment took place. If you are keeping hard copies, usually, you will keep the original document and give your learner a copy. This is because it is more difficult to forge a copy than an original document.

Giving feedback

Feedback is a way of boosting learners' confidence, encouraging, motivating and reassuring them. All learners need to know how they are progressing, and what they have achieved; giving feedback will help them realise this. Feedback can be given formally, i.e. in writing, or informally, i.e. orally, and should be given at a level which is appropriate for each learner. Feedback can be direct, i.e. to an individual, or indirect, i.e. to a group. It should be more thorough than just a quick comment such as *Well done*. It should be given in a constructive way and include specific facts which relate to progress, achievement or otherwise in order to help your learners develop.

> *Feedback is such a powerful means of development that we must not ignore its potential to transform your learners' achievement. It therefore needs to be clear and jargon free – just as you check learning when you are teaching a new concept, you also need to check that they understand the feedback.*

(Machin et al., 2013, page 76)

It is therefore important when giving feedback, either orally or in writing, that your learners understand what progress and achievement they have made. However, they need to understand the feedback you have given too, as this should include information regarding how they can improve and develop further.

If you are giving oral feedback, you could always ask your learners first how they think they have done. For example, if you have just observed them perform a task and they made a mistake, it gives them the opportunity to say so before you need to, providing they realised it. If you are giving feedback in written form, it might be that your learner misinterprets something. Therefore, if possible, give them the opportunity to ask questions and clarify any points.

Activity

Think about the last time you gave feedback to a learner. Was it oral or written and why? What could you have done differently and why?

If possible, feedback should be a two-way process, allowing a discussion to take place to clarify any points. If you are giving oral feedback, be aware of your body language, facial expressions and tone of voice. Don't use confrontational words or phrases likely to cause offence such as racist or stereotypical remarks. Take into account any non-verbal signals from your learners; you may need to adapt your feedback if you see they are becoming uncomfortable. If you are giving written or electronic feedback consider that how your learner reads it may not be how you intended it to be interpreted.

Feedback should never just be an evaluative statement like *Well done, or That's great, you've passed.* This doesn't tell your learner what was done well, or what was great about it. Your learner will be pleased to know they have passed; however, they won't have anything to build upon for the future.

Descriptive feedback lets you describe what your learner has done, how they have met the requirements and what they can do to progress further. It enables you to provide opportunities for your learner to make any adjustments or improvements to reach a particular standard.

Most people need encouragement, to be told when they are doing something well and why. When giving feedback it can really help your learner if you tell them first what they have done well, followed by what they need to improve, and then end on a positive note to keep them motivated. This is known as the *praise sandwich*. Often, the word *but* is used to link these points; replacing this with the word *however* can make it much easier for your learner to accept.

Example

Start with something positive, for example, 'George, I really liked the way you delivered your presentation. You came across as very confident.'

Link with 'however' to anything that needs improving, for example, 'However, I feel if you had faced the group a bit more rather than looking at the screen I could have heard your voice better.'

End on a positive note, for example, 'It was a very interesting topic and I feel I've learnt something new.'

Using your learner's name makes the feedback more personal. Making the feedback specific enables your learner to know what they have achieved and what they need to do to improve and/or progress further. You will need to find out from your organisation how they require you to give feedback, for example, writing in the first, second or third person. You also need to know whether it should be given orally and/or written; formally or informally; how much detail should be given; what forms must be completed; and what records must be maintained.

The advantages of giving feedback are that it:

• creates opportunities for clarification and discussion

• emphasises progress rather than failure

- enables the learner to know what they have achieved

- helps improve confidence and motivation

- identifies further learning opportunities or any action required

Extension Activity

How does the way in which you give feedback contribute to the learning process? How can you remain objective and not become subjective with your judgements?

Maintaining records

It is important to keep records, otherwise how can you prove what progress your learners have made and exactly what they have achieved? You also need to satisfy any external requirements, for example, awarding organisation or regulatory authorities. Records will usually need to be kept for a set period, for example, three years. If a learner loses their work, without any assessment records you will have nothing to show what was assessed, and quality assurers need to sample the records along with the learners' work.

Activity

Find out what the requirements are for assessment record keeping at your organisation. What is the time period they must be maintained for, and can they be kept electronically?

Keeping full and accurate factual records is also necessary in case one of your learners appeals against an assessment decision you have made. If this happens, don't take it personally; providing you have been objective, they will be appealing against your decision, not you as a person. You will also need to pass records to your internal quality assurer if necessary, and any other authorised colleagues who have an interest in your learner's progress and achievement. Table 4.3 lists examples of assessment records; however, you might not need to use all of them depending upon your job role.

If you are teaching a programme which does not lead to an accredited qualification, i.e. non-accredited, you will still need to record learner progress. This is known as recognising and recording progress and achievement (RARPA). Please see Chapter 2 for more details. Records are often required for quality assurance purposes. For example, internal quality assurance is necessary to monitor the practice of assessors and the decisions they make. *It is important to make sure that assessment procedures are carried out fairly and consistently* (Tummons, 2011, page 82). If records are not maintained, it makes the assessment and quality assurance process very difficult as there is no proof of what took place.

Table 4.3 Examples of assessment records

Assessment records	
• achievement dates and grades • action plans • appeals records • application forms • assessment plan and review records • assessment tracking sheet showing progression through a qualification for all learners • authentication declarations/statements • checklists • copies of certificates • diagnostic test results • enrolment forms • formative and summative records • feedback records	• initial assessment records • learning preference results • observation checklists • observation reports • performance and knowledge records • professional discussion records • progress reports • receipts for submitted work • records of achievement • records of oral questions and responses • retention and achievement records • standardisation records • tutorial reviews • witness statements

Records must be up to date, accurate, factual and legible whether they are stored manually or electronically. If you are saving to a computer or cloud-based application, always ensure you have a backup copy in case any data is lost. You must always maintain confidentiality and follow relevant legislation such as the Data Protection Act (1998), which is mandatory for all organisations that hold or process personal data.

Extension Activity

Make a list of all the assessment records you need to use for your subject and state why you would need to keep them. What internal and external requirements must you follow regarding the assessment process and why?

Implementing the minimum core

The minimum core consists of four elements: literacy, language, numeracy and ICT. As part of your teaching role you should be able to demonstrate these elements to at least level 2. This will enable you to support your learners with English, maths and ICT (known as functional skills). It will also ensure you teach your area of specialism as effectively as possible.

Activity

Look at the four elements of the minimum core in Appendices 6, 7 and 8. Analyse the ways in which you feel you can demonstrate them when assessing learning. Tick off the ones you can use, and make a note of how you will demonstrate them within your practice.

If possible, obtain a copy of the supporting document: *Addressing literacy, language, numeracy and ICT needs in education and training: Defining the minimum core of teachers' knowledge, understanding and personal skills – A guide for initial teacher education programmes* (LSIS, 2007, revised 2013). Have a look at the content to help you see how you can demonstrate the minimum core elements.

The full document is available to download at: http://repository.excellencegateway.org.uk/fedora/objects/import-pdf:93/datastreams/PDF/content

Example: Literacy

- Reading and annotating the qualification guidance to ascertain what the assessment requirements are for your subject

- Creating assessment activities and materials such as assignments, tests or questions

- Completing templates and forms, and checking spelling, grammar and punctuation

Example: Language

- Speaking to learners about the assessment process and how it will be conducted

- Asking questions to check a learner's knowledge and understanding, and listening to their responses

- Listening to questions and answering them appropriately

Example: Numeracy

- Calculating how long various assessment activities will take

- Interpreting how long learners are actually taking to carry out an activity, and what time they have left to complete

- Evaluating grades, for example, how many achieved a pass, merit or distinction. Analysing retention and achievement rates

Example: ICT

- Preparing online assessment materials and uploading them to a VLE or other system

- Using a computer program or application to create assessment materials

- Using e-mail or social networking to communicate appropriately

- Using new technology for assessment activities such as online live observations, video conferencing, polls and surveys

- Using digital media for visual/audio recording and playback of assessment activities

Demonstrating your own skills regarding the minimum core should enable you to consider ways of improving the skills in your learners too. Ways of improving your learners' skills in these areas could include encouraging them to demonstrate skills similar to those you have used. You can also correct any mistakes, for example, in speech and written work.

You can play an important part in providing opportunities to develop your learners' skills in literacy, language, numeracy and ICT. However, it is your responsibility to continually update your own skills in these areas by undertaking professional development.

Evaluating own practice

You should always evaluate the effectiveness of your own assessment practice to enable you to develop and improve for the future. The process should take into account the views of your learners and others you come into contact with, for example, workplace supervisors. Reviewing your practice will also help you identify any problems or concerns, enabling you to do things differently next time. Never assume everything is going well just because you think it is. Please see Chapter 2 for further information regarding evaluating your practice and obtaining feedback.

What works with one learner or group might not work well with others, perhaps due to their learning preferences or other influences. However, don't change something for the sake of it; if it works, hopefully it will continue to work.

When evaluating the assessment process, ask yourself the following.

Did I ...?

☐ devise formative assessment activities to take place during sessions

☐ use the summative assessment activities from the awarding organisation (if applicable)

☐ ensure the validity and reliability of all assessment activities and decisions

☐ ask open questions to all learners at some point during the session

☐ assess learners on an individual basis, even if they were partaking in a group activity

☐ plan to use different types and methods of assessment

☐ differentiate assessment activities to meet any particular learner needs

☐ ensure assessment evidence is sufficient, authentic and correct

☐ give feedback to learners on an individual basis in a constructive manner

☐ review learner progress, for example, through tutorial reviews and discussions

☐ keep records of individual progress and feedback given

☐ track the progress of all learners' grades and dates of achievement

☐ communicate with others, for example, the internal quality assurer and/or workplace supervisors (if required)

After evaluating your practice, you should be able to make any necessary changes. Don't forget to ask for feedback from your learners as they are best able to inform you how effective the assessment process was.

Reflection

Reflection is about becoming more self-aware, which should give you increased confidence and improve the links between the theory and practice of teaching, learning and assessment.

Kolb (1984) proposed a four-stage continuous learning process. His theory suggests that without reflection, people would continue to make mistakes. When you are assessing, you may make mistakes; you should therefore consider why they happened and what you would do differently next time, putting your plans into practice when you have the opportunity.

This model of learning suggests that the cycle can be started at any stage; that reflection is as important as the experience; and that, once the cycle is started, it should be followed through all the stages for learning to be effective.

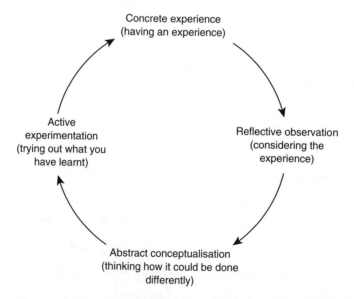

Figure 4.1 Kolb's (1984) four-stage model of learning

Aisha had planned to assess her learners using an assignment she had created. She issued the assignments to her learners (concrete experience); however, most learners were unable to complete it within the timeframe. Aisha reflected upon the experience (reflective observation), considering what she could have done differently regarding the assignment (abstract conceptualisation). With her next group, she used a revised assignment with fewer questions which worked well (active experimentation).

Activity

Think of a critical incident that has happened lately during the assessment process. Work through Kolb's theory to reflect upon it and see if you can reach an alternative solution.

Reviewing your progress will help you learn about yourself and what you could improve, for example, how you react to different situations or learners, how patient you are and what skills you may need to develop. You might also decide you need further training or support to improve your subject knowledge, teaching skills and/or English, maths and ICT skills.

Extension Activity

Based on your evaluation of your assessment practice, what areas have you identified as needing improvement? How can you act on what you have identified and what will you do differently as a result? Do you need any further training and/or support? If so, how will you go about obtaining it?

Summary

In this chapter you have learnt about:

- assessment in education and training
- assessment types and methods
- peer and self-assessment
- making decisions and giving feedback
- maintaining records
- implementing the minimum core
- evaluating own practice

Cross-referencing grid

This chapter contributes towards the following assessment criteria of the units which form the Certificate in Education and Training, along with aspects of the Professional Standards for Teachers and Trainers in England. Full details of the learning outcomes and assessment criteria of each unit can be found in the appendices.

Certificate units	Assessment criteria
Understanding roles, responsibilities and relationships in education and training	1.1, 1.4 3.1
Planning to meet the needs of learners in education and training	1.1, 1.2, 1.3 2.5
Delivering education and training	2.3 3.1, 3.2
Assessing learners in education and training	1.1, 1.2, 1.3, 1.4, 1.5 2.1, 2.2, 2.3, 2.4, 2.5 3.1, 3.2 4.1, 4.2
Using resources for education and training	

Area	Professional Standards for Teachers and Trainers in England
Professional values and attributes	1, 2, 3, 4, 5, 6
Professional knowledge and understanding	7, 8, 9, 10, 11, 12
Professional skills	13, 14, 15, 16, 17, 18, 19, 20

Theory focus

References and further information

Appleyard, N and Appleyard, K (2010) *Communicating with Learners in the Lifelong Learning Sector.* London: Learning Matters SAGE.

Gravells, A (2014) *Achieving your Assessment and Quality Assurance Units (TAQA).* London: Learning Matters SAGE.

Gravells, A and Simpson, S (2014) *Passing Assessments for the Certificate in Education and Training.* London: Learning Matters SAGE.

Hill, C (2008) *Teaching with e-learning in the Lifelong Learning Sector* (2nd edn). London: Learning Matters SAGE.

Holmes, B and Gardner, J (2006) *e-learning Concepts and Practice.* London: SAGE Publications Ltd.

Kolb, DA (1984) *Experiential Learning: Experience as the Source for Learning and Development.* New Jersey: Prentice-Hall.

LSIS (2007, revised 2013) *Addressing literacy, language, numeracy and ICT needs in education and training: Defining the minimum core of teachers' knowledge, understanding and personal skills – A guide for initial teacher education programmes.* Coventry: LSIS.

Machin, L, Hindmarch, D, Murray, S and Richardson, T (2013) *A Complete Guide to the Level 4 Certificate in Education and Training.* Northwich: Critical Publishing Ltd.

Ofqual (2009) *Authenticity – A Guide for Teachers.* Coventry: Ofqual.

Read, H (2011) *The Best Assessor's Guide.* Bideford: Read On Publications Ltd.

Read, H (2012) *The Best Quality Assurer's Guide.* Bideford: Read On Publications Ltd.

Read, H (2013) *The Best Initial Assessment Guide.* Bideford: Read On Publications Ltd.

Roffey-Barentsen, J and Malthouse, R (2013) *Reflective Practice in Education and Training* (2nd edn). London: Learning Matters SAGE.

Rushton, I and Suter, M (2012) *Reflective Practice for Teaching in Lifelong Learning.* Maidenhead: OU Press.

Skills for Business (2007) *Inclusive learning approaches for literacy, language, numeracy and ICT: Companion Guide to the Minimum Core.* Nottingham: DfES Publications.

Tummons, T (2011) *Assessing Learning in the Lifelong Learning Sector.* London: Learning Matters SAGE.

Wilson, LA (2012) *Practical Teaching: A Guide to Assessment and Quality Assurance.* Andover: Cengage Learning.

Wood, J and Dickinson, J (2011) *Quality Assurance and Evaluation in the Lifelong Learning Sector.* London: Learning Matters SAGE.

Websites

Assessment methods in higher education – www.brookes.ac.uk/services/ocsld/resources/methods.html

Assessment tools (literacy, numeracy, ESOL, dyslexia) – www.excellencegateway.org.uk/toolslibrary

Chartered Institute of Educational Assessors – http://ciea.co.uk/

COSHH – www.hse.gov.uk/coshh/

Developing Assessment Feedback – http://escalate.ac.uk/4147

Initial Assessment Tools – http://archive.excellencegateway.org.uk/page.aspx?o=toolslibrary

Ofqual – http://ofqual.gov.uk/

Plagiarism – www.plagiarism.org and www.plagiarismadvice.org

QCF – http://ofqual.gov.uk/qualifications-and-assessments/qualification-frameworks/

RARPA – www.learningcurve.org.uk/courses/ladder4learning/resources/rarpatoolkit

SWOT analysis – www.mindtools.com/pages/article/newTMC_05.htm

Table 4.4 Assessment methods, approaches and activities: strengths and limitations

Method/approach/activity	Description	Strengths	Limitations
Activities – group or individual	Different tasks carried out by learners to demonstrate their skills, knowledge, understanding and/or attitudes	Can be individual, paired or group tasks Ideal as a formative assessment approach to establish progress at a given point during a session, or as a summative approach for workplace tasks Could involve people external to the group, i.e. for a specific theme or purpose	If paired or grouped, assessor must establish achievement of individuals Can be time-consuming for the assessor to devise and organise
Assignments	Can be practical or theoretical tasks which can assess various aspects of a subject or qualification over a period of time	Consolidates learning Several aspects of a qualification can be assessed Some assignments are set by the awarding organisation which will give clear marking criteria Learners might be able to add to their work if they don't meet all the requirements first time	Everything must have been taught beforehand or be known by the learner Questions can be misinterpreted Can be time-consuming for learners to complete Must be individually assessed and written feedback given Assessor might be biased when marking
Blended assessments	Using more than one method of assessment, usually including technology	Several methods of assessment can be combined, enabling all learning preferences to be reached	Not all learners may have access to the technology
Buzz groups	Short topics to be discussed in small groups	Allows learner interaction and focuses ideas Checks understanding Doesn't require formal feedback	Learners may digress Specific points could be lost Checking individual learning may be difficult

Method/approach/ activity	Description	Strengths	Limitations
Case studies/ scenarios	Can be a hypothetical situation, a description of an actual event or an incomplete event, enabling learners to explore the situation	Can make topics more realistic, enhancing motivation and interest Can be carried out individually or in a group situation Builds on current knowledge and experience	If carried out as a group activity, roles should be defined and individual contributions assessed Time should be allowed for a debrief Must have clear outcomes Can be time-consuming to prepare and assess
Checklists	A list of criteria which must be met to confirm competence or achievement	Can form part of an ongoing record of achievement or job profile Assessment can take place when a learner is ready Ensures all criteria are documented	Learners may lose their copy and not remember what they have achieved
Controlled assessment	An activity or test which occurs in a number of stages with varying levels of control to ensure reliability Usually timed	Can be formative to assess progress or summative to assess achievement Can be used for knowledge and/or performance Is flexible and modification is possible Ensures the same conditions for everyone Makes assessment activities manageable	Can be stressful to learners Learners might study just to pass the assessment requirements
Discussions with learners *also known as a professional discussion*	A one-to-one conversation between the assessor and learner based around the assessment criteria	Ideal way to assess aspects which are more difficult to observe, are rare occurrences, or take place in restricted or confidential settings Useful to support observations to check knowledge Learners can describe how they carry out various activities	A record must be kept of the discussion, for example, audio/digital/visual along with notes Needs careful planning as it is a discussion not a question and answer session Learners need time to prepare

(Continued)

Table 4.4 (Continued)

Method/approach/ activity	Description	Strengths	Limitations
Discussions with learners (continued)			Assessor needs to be experienced at questioning and listening skills Assessor needs to be experienced at using open and probing questions, and listening carefully to the responses
Discussions/ debates	Learners talk about a relevant topic either in groups or pairs	Allows freedom of viewpoints, questions and discussions Develops communication skills, i.e. challenging a different viewpoint in an appropriate way Can contribute to meeting assessment criteria	Easy to digress Assessor needs to keep the group focused and set a time limit Some learners may not get involved; others may dominate Assessor needs to manage the contributions of individuals and know what has been achieved by each learner Can be time-consuming Learners may need to research a topic in advance Can lead to arguments
e-assessments/ online assessments	*Electronic assessment –* assessment using ICT *Synchronous –* assessor and learner are simultaneously present, communicating in real time	Teaching, learning and assessment can take place in a VLE Assessment can take place at a time to suit learners Participation is widened Results and feedback can be instantly generated Ensures reliability	Learners need access to a computer or suitable device and need to be computer literate Reliable internet connection needed Self-discipline is needed Clear targets must be set Authenticity of learner's work may need validating Technical support may be required

Method/approach/ activity	Description	Strengths	Limitations
e-assessments online assessments (continued)	Asynchronous – assessor and learner are interacting at different times	Less paperwork for the assessor Improves computer skills Can be blended with other assessment methods Groups, blogs, forums and chat rooms can be set up to improve communication	
Essays	A formal piece of written text, produced by a learner, for a specific topic	Useful for academic subjects Can check a learner's English skills at specific levels Enhances a learner's knowledge by using research and reading	Not suitable for lower level learners Marking can be time-consuming Plagiarism can be an issue Doesn't usually have a right or wrong answer therefore difficult to grade Learners need good writing skills
Examinations	A formal activity which must be carried out in certain conditions	Can be *open book*, or *open notes*, enabling learners to have books and notes with them Some learners like the challenge of a formal examination and cope well	Invigilation required Security arrangements to be in place prior to, and afterwards for examination papers Learners may have been taught purely to pass expected questions by using past papers, therefore they may forget everything afterwards Some learners may be anxious Can be *closed book*, or *closed notes* not allowing learners to have books and notes with them Results might take a while to be processed If a learner fails, they may have to wait a period of time before a retake

(Continued)

Table 4.4 (Continued)

Method/approach/ activity	Description	Strengths	Limitations
Group work	Enables learners to carry out a specific activity, for example, problem-solving Can be practical or theoretical	Allows interaction between learners Encourages participation and variety Rotating group members enables all learners to work with each other	Careful management by the assessor is required regarding time limits, progress, and ensuring all group members are clear about the requirements Could be personality problems with team members or large groups One person may dominate Difficult to assess individual contributions Time is needed for a thorough debrief
Holistic	Enables learners to demonstrate several aspects of a programme or qualification at the same time	Similar criteria from different units can be assessed at the same time Makes evidence collection and demonstration of achievement and competence much more efficient	Could confuse the learner if aspects were assessed which were not planned for
Homework	Activities carried out between sessions, for example, answering questions to check knowledge	Learners can complete at a time and place that suits them Maintains interest between sessions Encourages learners to stretch themselves further Consolidates learning so far	Clear time limits must be set Learners might not do the homework, or might get someone else to do it for them Must be marked/assessed and individual feedback given
Interviews	A one-to-one discussion, usually before a learner commences a programme, or part way through to discuss progress	Enables the assessor to determine how much a learner knows Enables the assessor to get to know each learner, and discuss any issues	Not all learners may react well when interviewed Needs careful planning, and consistency of questions between learners

Method/approach/ activity	Description	Strengths	Limitations
Learner statements	Learners write how they have met the assessment criteria	Enables learners to take ownership of their achievements	Learners might misinterpret the assessment criteria and/or write too much or too little Another assessment method should be used in addition to confirm practical skills
Learning journal/diary	Learners keep a record of their progress, their reflections and thoughts, and reference these to the assessment criteria	Helps assess English skills Useful for higher level programmes	Should be specific to the learning taking place and be analytical rather than descriptive Content needs to remain confidential Can be time-consuming and/or difficult to read
Observations	Watching learners perform a skill and demonstrate their knowledge or a change in behaviour	Enables skills to be seen in action Learners can make a mistake (if it is safe) enabling them to realise their errors Learners can be observed again if they didn't fully achieve the requirements Can assess several aspects at the same time (holistic assessment)	Timing must be arranged to suit each learner Communication needs to take place with others (if applicable) No permanent record unless visually recorded Questions must be asked to confirm knowledge and understanding Assessor might not be objective with decision Learner might put on an act for the assessor which isn't how they normally perform
Peer assessments	Learners give feedback to their peers after an activity	Promotes learner and peer interaction and involvement Learners may accept comments from peers better than those from the assessor Enables learners to assess each other	Everyone needs to understand the assessment criteria and requirements Needs to be carefully managed to ensure no personality conflicts or unjustified comments Assessor needs to confirm progress and achievements as they might differ

(Continued)

Table 4.4 (Continued)

Method/approach/ activity	Description	Strengths	Limitations
Peer assessments (continued)		Activities can often correct misunderstandings and consolidate learning without intervention by the assessor	Some peers may be anxious about giving feedback Should be supported by other assessment methods Needs careful management and training in how to give feedback
Portfolios of evidence	A formal record of evidence (manual or electronic) produced by learners towards a qualification	Ideal for learners who don't like formal exams Can be compiled over a period of time Learner-centred therefore promotes autonomy Evidence can be left in its natural location to be viewed by the assessor	Authenticity and currency to be checked Computer access required to assess electronic portfolios Tendency for learners to produce a large quantity of evidence All evidence must be cross referenced to the relevant criteria Can be time-consuming to assess Confidentiality of documents within the portfolio must be maintained
Practical activities/ tasks	Assesses learners' skills in action	Actively involves learners Can meet all learning preferences if carefully set	Some learners may not respond well to practical activities Can be time-consuming to create Questions must be asked to ascertain knowledge and understanding
Presentations	Learners deliver a topic, often using ICT	Can be individual or in a group Can assess skills, knowledge, understanding and/or attitudes	If a group presentation, individual contributions must be assessed Some learners may be nervous or anxious in front of others

Method/approach/ activity	Description	Strengths	Limitations
Products	Evidence produced by learners to prove competence, for example, paintings, models, video, audio, photos, documents	Assessor can see the final outcome Learners feel a sense of achievement, for example, by displaying their work in an exhibition	Authenticity needs to be checked if the work has not been seen being produced
Projects	A longer-term activity enabling learners to provide evidence which meets the assessment criteria	Can be interesting and motivating Can be individual or group led Can meet all learning preferences Encourages research and creativity skills Learners could choose their own topics and devise tasks	Clear outcomes must be set, along with a time limit; must be relevant, realistic and achievable Progress should be checked regularly If a group is carrying out the project, ensure each individual's input is assessed Assessor might be biased when marking
Puzzles, quizzes, word searches, crosswords, etc.	A fun way of assessing learning in an informal way	Fun activities to test skills, knowledge and/or understanding Useful backup activity if learners finish earlier than planned Useful way to assess progress of lower level learners Good for assessing retention of facts	Can seem trivial to mature learners Does not assess a learner's level of understanding or ability to apply their knowledge to situations Can be time-consuming to create and assess
Questions	A key technique for assessing understanding and stimulating thinking; can be informal or formal	Can be short answer or long essay style Can challenge and promote a learner's potential A question bank can be devised which could be used again and again for all learners Can test critical arguments or thinking and reasoning skills	Closed questions only give a yes or no response which doesn't demonstrate knowledge or understanding Questions must be written carefully, i.e. be unambiguous, and can be time-consuming to prepare

(Continued)

Table 4.4 (Continued)

Method/approach/ activity	Description	Strengths	Limitations
Questions (Continued)	Questions can be open, closed, hypothetical, leading, prompting, probing, multiple choice and reflective	Oral questions suit some learners more than others, for example, a learner who is dyslexic might prefer to talk through their responses	If the same questions are used with other learners, they could share their answers Written responses might be the work of others, i.e. copied or plagiarised Expected responses or grading criteria need to be produced beforehand to ensure consistency and validity of marking
Recognition of prior learning (RPL)	Assessing what has previously been learnt, experienced and achieved to find a suitable starting point, or to claim equivalent or exemption units on the QCF	Ideal for learners who have achieved aspects of the programme prior to commencement No need for learners to duplicate work, or be reassessed Values previous learning, experiences and achievements	Checking the authenticity and currency of the evidence provided is crucial Previous learning, experiences and achievements might not be relevant in relation to current requirements Can be time-consuming for both learner to prove, and the assessor to assess
Reports, research and dissertations	Learners produce a document to inform, recommend and/or make suggestions based on the assessment criteria	Useful for higher level learners Encourages the use of research techniques and analytical skills	Learners need research and academic writing skills Time-consuming to mark Plagiarism and authenticity can be an issue
Role plays	Learners act out a hypothetical situation	Enables the assessor to observe learners' behaviour Encourages participation Can lead to debates Links theory to practice	Can be time-consuming Clear roles must be defined Not all learners may want, or be able to participate Some learners may get too dramatic Individual contributions must be assessed Time needed for a thorough debrief

Method/approach/ activity	Description	Strengths	Limitations
Self-assessment	Learners decide how they have met the assessment criteria, or how they are progressing at a given time	Promotes learner involvement and personal autonomy Encourages learners to check their own work Encourages reflection	Learners may feel they are doing better or worse than they actually are Assessor needs to discuss progress and achievements with each learner to confirm their decisions Learners need to be specific about what they have achieved and what they need to do to complete any gaps
Skills tests	Designed to find out the level of skill or previous experience/knowledge towards a particular subject or vocation	Could be online or computer based to enable a quick assessment, for example, English Results can be used as a starting point for learning or progression	Learners might be apprehensive of formal tests Feedback might not be immediate
Simulation	Imitation or acting out of an event or situation	Useful when it is not possible to carry out a task for real, for example, to assess whether learners can successfully evacuate a building in the event of a fire	Only enables an assessment of a hypothetical situation; learners may act very differently in a real situation Not usually accepted as demonstration of competence
Team building exercises/energisers	A fun and light-hearted way of re-energising learners after a break Can be used to informally assess skills, knowledge and attitudes	A good way of learners getting to work with each other Can revitalise a flagging session	Not all learners may want to take part Some learners may see them as insignificant and time-wasting Careful explanations are needed to link the experience to the topic being assessed

(Continued)

Table 4.4 (Continued)

Method/approach/activity	Description	Strengths	Limitations
Tests	A formal assessment situation	Cost effective method as the same test can be used with large numbers of learners Some test responses can be scanned into a computer for marking and analysis Other tests can be taken at a computer or online which give immediate results	Needs to be carried out in supervised conditions or via a secure website Time limits usually required Can be stressful to learners Does not take into account any formative progress Feedback might not be immediate Learners in other groups might find out the content of the tests from others Identity of learners needs confirming
Tutorials	A one-to-one, or group discussion between the assessor and learner, with an agreed purpose, for example, assessing progress so far	A good way of informally assessing a learner's progress and/or giving feedback An opportunity for learners to discuss issues or for informal tuition to take place	Needs to be in a comfortable, safe and quiet environment as confidential issues may be discussed Time may overrun Records should be maintained and action points followed up
Video/Audio	Recorded evidence of actual achievements	Direct proof of what was achieved by a learner Can be reviewed by the assessor and internal quality assurer after the event	Can prove expensive to purchase equipment and storage media Can be time-consuming to set up and use Technical support may be required Storage facilities are required

Method/approach/ activity	Description	Strengths	Limitations
Walk and talk	A spoken and visual way of assessing a learner's competence	Enables a learner to *walk and talk* through their product evidence within their work environment Gives an audit trail of the evidence relating to the assessment criteria Saves time producing a full portfolio of evidence; the *walk and talk* can be recorded as evidence of the discussion Useful where sensitive and confidential information is dealt with	Can be time-consuming Difficult for quality assurers to sample the evidence
Witness statements/ testimonies	A statement from a person who is familiar with the learner (they could also be an expert in the standards being assessed and the occupation of the learner in the work environment)	The witness can confirm competence or achievements for situations which might not regularly occur, or when the assessor cannot be present	The assessor must confirm the suitability of the witness and check the authenticity of any statements Learners could write the statement and the witness might sign it not understanding the content
Worksheets and gapped handouts	Interactive handouts to check knowledge (can also be electronic) Blank spaces can be used for learners to fill in the missing words	Informal assessment activity which can be done individually, in pairs or groups Useful for lower level learners Can be created at different degrees of difficulty to address differentiation	Mature learners may consider them inappropriate Too many worksheets can be boring Learners might not be challenged enough

5 USING RESOURCES

In this chapter you will learn about:

- resources and their use for teaching, learning and assessment
- people as resources
- handouts and visual presentations
- selecting, adapting and using resources
- meeting the individual needs of learners
- implementing the minimum core
- evaluating own practice

There are activities and examples to encourage you to reflect on the above which will help you develop and enhance your understanding of using resources.

At the end of each section within the chapter are extension activities to stretch and challenge your knowledge and understanding. A list of useful references, further information and website links can be found at the end of the chapter in case you would like to research the topics further.

At the end of the chapter is a cross-referencing grid showing how the chapter's contents relate to the units of the Certificate in Education and Training, and the Professional Standards for Teachers and Trainers in England.

Resources and their use for teaching, learning and assessment

Resources are all the aids, books, handouts, items of equipment, objects, technology and people that you can use to support the teaching, learning and assessment process. They should stimulate learning, add impact and promote interest in the subject. Resources should be accessible and inclusive to all learners, while enabling them to acquire new skills, knowledge and understanding in a safe way. When using or creating resources, you will need to ensure they promote equality of opportunity, reflect diversity and challenge stereotypes. For example, text and pictures in a handout should portray all aspects of society as well as a diverse range of environments.

Resources should be appropriate in terms of level, quality, quantity and content, and be relevant to the subject, the methods of delivery and expected learning. Handouts and visual presentations should be checked for spelling, grammar, punctuation and syntax (sentence construction) errors, as you don't want to give a bad example to your learners by making a mistake. A resource should therefore be relevant to learning, clearly laid out or described, well presented, up to date, adaptable and purposeful. *Well designed resources should enhance perception: by involving more than one sense there is a greater likelihood that the learner will perceive what is intended. For example the touch and smell of a piece of wood can be more effective than reading about it* (Reece and Walker, 2007, page 157).

The resources you use should be varied and take account of the different needs of your learners as well as the type of programme they are taking. You should want your learners to find the learning experience interesting and enjoyable. You will find there is a wealth of resources already available, for example, via specialist websites, publishing companies, awarding organisations and external agencies, and many of these are free.

Resources come in many different guises and you need to find out what is already available to you within your organisation, and how they can be accessed and used. If you are involved in delivering work-based learning programmes, perhaps on the job, there may be a wealth of highly relevant or specialist resources accessible to both you and your learners. There is no point wasting time creating resources which might already be available and accessible. If you are visiting a learner in their workplace, make sure that the visit is well planned in advance, for example, if particular resources need to be available.

Designing and creating your own resources, such as a model to demonstrate a topic, can be time-consuming. Often it is easier and quicker to adapt an existing resource than to create a new one. You could ask experienced colleagues within your organisation which resources they use and what they would recommend. Ask them if you can go along and observe the way in which they use a particular resource. This should give you some ideas. Make contact with the support staff in your organisation, for example, to help word process, print or photocopy work for you. If you need to use reprographic equipment yourself, always err on the side of caution; check that the equipment is working, and allow time to use it. You might be allocated a budget for copying and when this has run out you can't do any more. If your learners have access to e-mail, an online shared file, or a virtual learning environment (VLE), you could encourage them to access or print the resources they need as necessary.

Table 5.1 on page 190 lists examples of resources and media which could be used with learners.

Activity

Consider the resources and equipment you currently use. Are you only using them because you feel confident and familiar with them? What other resources could you use to engage and motivate your learners, and bring your subject to life? Are there any resources your learners, colleagues or mentors could provide? If you need any extra training or support to create resources, you should ask for this at your organisation.

Table 5.1 Examples of resources and media

Information and communication technology	Objects
• Audio, visual and digital recorders • Calculators • Camcorder • CDROMs/DVDs • Computers/laptops/netbooks/tablets • Digital cameras • Epidiascope • Graphic organisers • Interactive whiteboards • Internet • Intranet • Microscope • Mobile phones and smart phones • Personal digital assistants • Photocopier • Printers • Projectors and data projectors • Radio • Recording devices • Robotics • Scanners • Social networking • Television • Video conferencing • Video recorder • Virtual learning environment • Voting technology • Webcam • Webpages • Webinars	• Animals • Apparatus • Costumes and hats • Games • Models • Pens, pencils, highlighters, rubbers, rulers • Plants • Puppets • Puzzles • Samples of products • Specimens of items • Sports equipment • The *real thing* • Tools • Toys **People** • Colleagues, teachers, trainers, managers, mentors, technicians, administrative staff, support staff, employers, supervisors • Friends and relatives • Information, guidance and careers staff • Learners (past and current) • Manufacturers/suppliers • Other professionals: internal/external agency staff, quality assurers, awarding organisation personnel, subject experts and advisors • Specialist speakers • Volunteers and teaching assistants • Yourself
External	**Visual aids**
• Cinema/theatre/concert • Conferences • Events and workshops • Exhibitions • Field trips • Jobs fairs • Lectures • Libraries • Museums • Specialist shops • Sports/leisure centres	• Charts/posters • Display board and pins • Flannel/sticky/magnetic boards • Flip chart, paper and pens • Maps • Overhead or slide projector • Photographs • Presentation equipment • Sticky notes • Whiteboard/chalk board • Year planner, calendar, diary
Other resource materials	
• Advertisements • Books • Catalogues • Comics • Handouts • Information leaflets • Journals • Magazines • Manuals • Newspapers	• Original documents • Periodicals • Photocopies of documents • Promotional literature • Publicity materials • Quizzes • Reports • Textbooks • Wordsearches/crosswords • Worksheets

The use of resources

During a session, you should always have relevant resources such as stationery, pens, paper, board markers and other items to ensure it runs smoothly. You could create a *teacher's toolkit*, of resources which you can carry around with you. The kit could contain the above items, plus extra activities for learners to carry out in case you have spare time during a session. This demonstrates to your learners that you are well organised, for example, if you have different coloured board markers to hand, you don't need to leave the room to locate them.

If you are working in venues away from the main building, you may have to transport heavy resources, which can be difficult and time-consuming. A portable trolley might be a useful resource to help you, for example, to move heavy textbooks or small items of equipment. You would need to plan ahead to ensure you have enough time to move them. Advance booking may also be required for some types of equipment and resources, for example, a portable projector and screen. You should also consider what resources you can access electronically, such as online quizzes and voting technology, which will make your sessions more interesting.

There will be times when the resources you planned to use are not available or not working. Preparing for unforeseen circumstances comes with experience. Whenever you are due to meet your learners, ask yourself, *What would I do if something wasn't available or doesn't work?* For example, you might prepare a computerised presentation and want to give a hard copy as a handout to your learners. However, if you can't get copies made in time, you can still deliver your presentation and offer to e-mail a copy to your learners, upload it to a VLE, or get photocopies made later. Try not to rely totally on presentation software when teaching: use different approaches and activities to add variety. Activities during a session can be differentiated, for example, according to learning preferences. One learner may prefer to read a handout but another may prefer to watch and listen to a video clip; therefore try to incorporate a variety of resources when you can.

If you give a handout at the beginning of the session, you may find your learners fiddle with it and become distracted. If you can, issue handouts at an appropriate time and talk through the content, asking questions to ensure your learners have understood the topic. Otherwise, issue them at the end of the session and ask learners to read them later to help reinforce what has been covered. Alternatively, to aid sustainability, you could upload handouts to a VLE or e-mail them to your learners. Handouts can also be used as activities; for example, a gapped handout can contain sentences with missing words that learners need to fill in. These are useful to assess lower level or new learners, as a fun team activity, or to fill in time at the end of a session. However, don't get too reliant on the use of handouts or worksheets as learners could become bored of them. If a resource you are using is not effective with some learners, try changing the experience rather than the resource, for example, change a group activity to become an individual one. Wherever possible, try to use resources which involve your learners actively, rather than just passively reading or watching something. You could involve them by creating a resource which they will all benefit from, such as a glossary of terms relating to the subject they are taking.

Activity

Begin to create a glossary of terms for your specialist subject, which could also include relevant abbreviations and acronyms. This will become a useful resource for yourself, and for your learners. It could be added to at any time, for example, by your learners as they progress through the programme. If it is created electronically via a VLE or as a shared file, all learners can have access and add to it.

Interactive whiteboards can be very effective when used to demonstrate topics, as learners can participate in activities such as online surveys. When using the whiteboard, be careful that the focus is on the learner and not on you as the teacher. If it is used for too long, the learners might not maintain their interest and may lose motivation. If you are using board markers for another activity, don't be tempted to use them on a whiteboard as they can damage it and writing is not always erasable.

Electronic equipment, i.e. computers, media players, televisions, digital equipment etc., can be used as tools for engaging with learners and offering choice about the way in which they learn. Many subject areas now use digital cameras, smart phones and tablets to enhance learning and captivate the learners' interest. Such equipment encourages the learners to be more independent in their learning, also enabling them to access information and materials in their own time via the internet.

The internet is a wonderful resource. However, information is not always accurate; therefore, learners need to be warned about this. It is always worth mentioning plagiarism when learners have access to the internet, for example, copying and pasting text into an assignment. Your organisation should have a plagiarism policy of which everyone needs to be aware. It could be that the venue you wish to use does not have wi-fi or internet enabled devices. Knowing this in advance will help with your planning, as learners might bring their own devices and be frustrated if they can't have access. If you plan to use other types of equipment you might find it is old and out of date, and sometimes it just won't work. Always check in advance what resources are available and whether they are working.

The resources you use will depend on your subject and the learning environment, and should link to the different teaching, learning and assessment activities you have planned to use. If you are teaching in the workplace or in a workshop, using genuine objects and materials from the vocational setting can make the learning more relevant and meaningful. This addresses the concept of *purposeful learning*: activities with a purpose which enable learners to use a wide range of skills, to work in a team and to gain real experiences. When teaching a skill, a handout or worksheet may not be as useful as the *real thing* or something which closely resembles it.

Dawn was delivering a First Aid programme and the current session was based on cardiac compression. She could not demonstrate this on real people, but used a mannequin instead. It had been designed to mimic a real person's response. Her learners were able to use the mannequin to try out the procedure. Prior to this, Dawn had shown a video to her group, and afterwards asked questions. This prompted an interesting discussion as one of her learners had witnessed the procedure between a paramedic and a relative of theirs.

Resources which are related to the vocational area and which can be contextualised will support the learner in applying their skills, knowledge and understanding outside of the learning environment. These are known as *transferable skills* as they can be transferred from one setting to another. It may be more of a challenge to select, adapt and use a range of resources in a work-related context; however, differentiating learning in this way is critical to meeting the needs of your learners.

Your organisation might have an environmental or sustainability policy; therefore you will need to take this into account regarding the use of resources. Can any current resources be reused or adapted in any way, rather than new ones purchased? Can handouts, activities and visual presentations be used electronically rather than being printed? It might be worth asking your colleagues what resources they use to see if you could share or adapt them.

Extension Activity

After your next session, analyse the resources and equipment you used by evaluating how effective they were, how well they engaged your learners, and how they met any individual needs. What would you change and why?

People as resources

Teachers are one of the most effective resources available to learners. You may not know everything about your specialist subject; however, you should always be honest with your learners. If you don't know something, assure them that you will find out and get back to them. Having a passion for your subject can be infectious and can create enthusiasm in your learners and increase their motivation to learn. When you are with your learners, you need to provide a stimulating and interesting environment in which learning can take place. Using a variety of resources can aid this. Learners who have a good learning experience usually state that this is because they have a good teacher. Where there is a poor experience, this might also be due to their teacher.

Wallace states:

Three important things [that] were missing from their learning experience ... were:

1. something to capture their interest

2. something to provide variety

3. an appropriate means of communicating knowledge or skills

(2011, page 121)

You could ask experts to speak to your learners to add variety to your sessions. They are known as *visiting speakers* and can provide additional knowledge as they are an authority on their subject. For example, people working in industry, authors, politicians and journalists who can bring a different and new approach. You might even learn something new yourself. If you know of, or can get in touch with, someone who is an authority in the subject area you are teaching, why not get in touch? You might need to seek approval from your organisation for them to attend, and to find out whether they can be paid for their time and expenses. You will need to remain present with them while they are with your learners, as your organisation will have safeguarding procedures to follow.

Colleagues and mentors in your organisation are a vital source of expertise in developing both your teaching skills and knowledge in your specialist subject area. Ensure that you establish relationships with others in your organisation as well as from other organisations, so that both you and your learners benefit from the exchange of expertise.

Witnesses and mentors, for example, in the workplace, can provide a vital source of support for your learners who are undertaking work experience. They are people who are experts in the subject area and are willing to give support and advice. It might be your responsibility to ensure they have the time to commit to the role, and that they are appropriately experienced. It is important that your learners feel comfortable with these people and that they have the time to commit to this. They need to have some knowledge of the programme content and be able to apply it to a workplace context.

Example

Haseem was delivering a Level 4 Diploma in Accounting programme to a group of 16 learners. As part of the programme, each learner had the opportunity to spend one day a week in a local accountancy firm. Haseem ensured each firm had a named mentor who was appropriately experienced to give support and advice. He gave them a copy of the qualification criteria to enable them to make sure they knew what each learner was working towards. Most mentors also offered to be a witness and give a statement as to how the learner was progressing towards the qualification.

Support staff, teaching assistants and volunteers can also give help to learners, perhaps to those who declare they have a learning difficulty or disability. It is important that they are included and kept informed regarding the individuals and the programme they are taking. However, support staff should be wary of the learner becoming too dependent or reliant upon them as they should try to develop their independence.

Make a list of all the people you could use as a resource to support your specialist subject, for example, support staff, authors and journalists. How can you include and involve them in the learning process?

Handouts and visual presentations

Handouts and visual presentations are useful resources to add variety to your session and focus attention. You should always check the spelling, grammar and punctuation of any materials you use, otherwise you could come across as unprofessional. If a learner does see an error, don't make excuses but thank them and say you will amend it for future use. Hard copies of your materials will enable your learners to refer to them during and after the session to go over important points. However, you might not always be able to get them copied in time. You could consider uploading them to a shared drive, shared cloud-based folder, or a VLE to aid sustainability, or you could e-mail them to your learners.

Learning doesn't have to stop just because the session has. You could therefore enable your learners to access materials outside of the session time. You could also give your learners access to a list of useful texts, websites, videos and other sources of information and research to help them with their studies.

Example

Philip wanted his learners to continue with the topic after they had left the class. He gave them a project to complete in small groups and e-mailed them a link to an interactive website. They were able to communicate and collaborate with each other via the website to create a short visual presentation. Philip could then access the completed presentation to show to everyone at the next session.

Creating handouts and presentations

The following are some hints which you could refer to when creating handouts and visual presentations. However, try not to rely on them too much during a session; make sure you add variety with different activities to ensure all learners are engaged and included.

Handouts

- Make the text easily readable, in an appropriate font and size. Don't put too much text or too many pictures on one page and don't mix fancy fonts. It might look good to you, but might not be easily readable by your learners. Keep plenty of *white space* (the blank area around the text/pictures). This makes the information stand out clearly and will allow your learners to make notes if necessary. If there is too much on a handout your learners may find it difficult to read and not absorb all the information.

- A single sheet, one sided or double sided, is best; too many pages will take too long for your learners to read and assimilate the information. If you do use more pages, always staple them in the top left corner and number each page at the bottom right.

- If you have created the handout yourself, include your name, filename, version number and date as a footer. This will enable you to find it easily to make future changes, ensures you are using the most recent version, and acknowledges you as the author of the work.

- Make sure the information is up to date. You may need to revise something if there have been changes to your subject.

- Consider numbering paragraphs or using numbers instead of bullet points. That way you can direct your learners to important points.

- If you have a learner who has dyslexia they might prefer handouts on pastel coloured paper. If so, use the same colour for everyone so that no one is singled out. If you can't get coloured copies made, give the learner a coloured plastic wallet within which they can place the handout. This will change its colour and hopefully make it easier to read. You could also check if there is a better type of font to use, i.e. Comic Sans, and whether left justified text is easier for them to read than fully justified text.

- If you are issuing several handouts during a session, you could print them on different coloured paper for ease of reference when you are talking about their content.

- If you use pictures of people, make sure they represent all aspects of society and that you have the relevant permissions first.

- If you use any quotes, make sure you reference them correctly. A list of relevant references or websites is useful to encourage your learners to research further after the session. Using them correctly will also help your learners with their own referencing skills if need be.

- If possible, give handouts towards the end of the activity they refer to. If you give them too early, your learners may read through them rather than concentrating on the topic.

Activity

Create a handout for your subject, taking into account the previous bulleted points. Use the handout with your learners and then evaluate its effectiveness.

Visual presentations

- Always check the equipment and data projector are connected and working. As a backup, store your work to an external drive or a memory stick as well. Check that the software and version in which you originally saved your presentation are compatible with the one to be used.

- Add variety by using different presentation software such as those available as online applications, some of which are free, rather than relying on traditional slides such as PowerPoint. Prezi is a useful application as users can collaborate via the internet to create interesting displays (www.prezi.com).

- Don't include too much text or use fancy fonts, colours and animations as this could distract from the points you want to make.

- Check if you need to insert your organisation's logo on each slide as a footer, or use a particular font and size for consistency throughout the organisation.

- Large, bold plain fonts are easier to read than smaller type, for example, Arial, Comic Sans or Verdana. Serif and script fonts are thought to be more difficult to read, for example, Times New Roman and *Brush Script*. The font size should be readable from the back of the room. Using combined upper and lower case text is preferable (not joined writing) as learners can recognise the shapes of letters. This is visually better than UPPER CASE, as the latter can also appear as though you are shouting.

- Blue-eyed people often struggle to see red, orange, green or yellow text, particularly if on a coloured background. Red and green can cause confusion for learners who are colour blind. Be consistent with the colours and backgrounds you use. For example, use dark text on a light pastel background which most learners, including those with dyslexia, should be able to read. Check which colours your learners prefer. How you see the colours may be very different to how your learners see them.

- Use bullet points, three or four per slide, and don't read them verbatim. Schedule them to come in line by line otherwise your learners will be reading ahead. Expand on each point and discuss it with your learners. Involve them where possible by asking open questions to make the presentation a two-way process and use anecdotes to bring your subject to life.

- Graphs and diagrams are often easier for learners to understand than tables; however, don't make them too complex. It is better to use several slides with a few pieces of information rather than one slide with too much.

- If you have time, incorporate a short video to bring your topic to life and add variety (do check for copyright restrictions or fair use policies). If you are connected to the internet you can insert the website link into your slide for easy access. Always check in advance that the website is still current and accessible.

- If you need to refer to the same slide more than once, copy it rather than moving back and forth through your presentation, otherwise you could lose your place.

- Use a remote control for moving through your slides. This enables you to move around the room holding and using a pointer rather than standing next to the keyboard. The remote control communicates via a device which plugs into a slot in the computer. Don't forget to unplug it at the end of the session or you may lose it.

- Press the letter B on the keyboard to black out the screen, or W to white out, for example, if you don't want a slide on display for a few minutes while you focus on something else or check your notes. Pressing B or W again will restore it.

- If your presentation is given via an electronic whiteboard, you could use features such as writing on the slides with a special pen-like device. You can then save, print or e-mail it to your learners, or upload it to a VLE.

- Involve your learners; ask them to use the presentation equipment and/or interactive whiteboard whenever possible.

- Have a hard copy of the presentation for yourself in case something goes wrong. You can then refer to it rather than having nothing. You can also hold it during the presentation and remain facing your learners, rather than looking at and talking to the full screen. Alternatively, you can stand near your computer or laptop where you can see your electronic notes on your own screen, and not be in the way of the full screen.

- If you want your learners to make notes throughout the presentation, you can print a copy using the *handout* function. That way, they can have several slides on one A4 page with room for making notes. Printing one slide per A4 sheet is just a waste of paper. If you are not sure how to do this, ask someone to show you.

- Supporting handouts can be given at the end which include further information, such as textbooks and websites, rather than squashing the information onto the slides.

Extension Activity

Create a visual presentation for your subject, taking into account the previous bulleted points. If possible, embed a short video and some website links. Use the presentation with your learners and then evaluate its effectiveness.

Selecting, adapting and using resources

At some point, you may need to create your own or adapt someone else's resources. Therefore, your first approach will be to research and find out what is already available. This could be a handout of useful information, a practical activity, a worksheet or a complex working model used to demonstrate a topic. If you can access and search the internet, you might find resources such as handouts for your subject area are freely available. Publishers are often happy to give away free inspection copies of textbooks for your subject, providing you give feedback and/or recommend them to your learners. You will find details on their websites of the latest books, which is useful if you need to use a new edition and are not sure when it was published.

Whatever resources you use, it is important to ensure they meet the differing needs of your learners and relate to your subject. For example, putting posters on the wall of the room will help to reinforce points as learners may not always look at them consciously, but subconsciously will glance at them, taking in the information. You might have to acknowledge your organisation's resource constraints and make best use of what is available. You should always evaluate the effectiveness of any resources you use, so you can modify or change them for future use.

Too often teaching is worksheet and handout driven. Using resources and materials effectively in order to support learning is challenging. However, it can be exciting for you as a teacher, and engaging and motivating for your learners. Try to be creative and innovative when selecting and/or developing resources for your programme. For example, could you make a recording of your session and upload it to a VLE for learners to watch again later? This would be useful if a learner was absent, enabling them to see the session they missed. However, it could lead to absenteeism as learners might feel they don't need to attend. Powell and Tummons state: *Make the session resources accessible outside of the classroom and make them as multi-sensory as possible, for example, using classroom capture (a video of your teaching session) and providing interactive activities* (2011, page 34).

You might be able to upload resources to a VLE for access before, during or after a session. You should select and use resources which centre around the learner and the purpose of learning. If they can also be fun, they will help ensure that learning is interesting and memorable. A holistic approach to the use of resources will ensure that they are realistic and relevant to the learner and their reasons for learning.

Selecting, developing and/or adapting learning materials require an in-depth knowledge of the programme and subject you are delivering. If learners are taking a qualification, there will be certain criteria that they will be required to achieve. If you are teaching a programme which doesn't lead to a qualification, there will be a curriculum to follow with a syllabus stating the content. This might be produced by your organisation, or you may have to produce it yourself. You will need to obtain all this information before considering what resources to use.

Wherever possible, resources should reflect your learners' interests as well as the subject. For example, enabling learners to choose projects that reflect their own interests will help their motivation, progress and achievement. These could include a range of occupational, vocational, community, cultural and/or family interests.

It is possible you may have updated or revised many of your resources in the past, either based on feedback, the success (or otherwise) of their use, or to meet any individual learner needs. However, you will need to make sure they are still fresh and professional looking, and current, i.e. reflecting the latest developments regarding the subject.

Example

Maureen teaches the Level 1 Award in Information and Communication Technology (ICT) to a group of unemployed young people who are all keen on sport. During the first few sessions, Maureen used standard worksheet resources and experienced a lack of motivation and a lot of disruption from her learners. She decided to redesign the worksheets so that they were sports related, but still met the qualification criteria. These materials provided a combined approach to ICT and the area of interest of her learners. The learners became much more motivated and there was less disruption as a result.

Information and communication technology resources

Technology as a resource is fast becoming the norm in education and training. Most teachers use a computer or a tablet for preparing programme materials, documenting assessment decisions, completing a record of attendance, and using e-mail and the internet. Nearly all organisations have computer facilities available for teachers and learners to use, either in a specific area, in a learning resource centre, or in the actual learning environment. Most learners expect to use ICT and to have internet access, and often bring along their own smart phone or tablet to sessions. You could therefore try to incorporate their use within your sessions to help make topics more active and interesting. Please see Chapter 3 for more information regarding using ICT during sessions.

Learners in the Further Education and Skills Sector in the UK are very diverse; you might, for example, have a learner whose first language is not English and who needs more time to understand the generic language, before using ICT. Initial assessment should have helped identify this and enable you to differentiate your resources to suit.

Activity

Research software and applications that could be used as a resource with your learners for your specialist subject. Devise an activity using the software or application you have found during your research. Use the resource and activity with your learners and then evaluate how effective it was.

When developing and/or using resources, consider that there may be a need for:

- more than one level of difficulty – you could produce activities which meet the qualification's learning outcomes, with additional, more complex activities to challenge more able learners, for example, extension activities which help extend the scope of capable learners by stretching and challenging them further

- the use of different media, including ICT and interactive resources – you could integrate these during your sessions, keeping the format and content varied and interesting, for example, using video clips, online quizzes, live surveys and voting technology

- relevant support for individuals or small groups as required – if some learners are progressing quite quickly, you will need to ensure the others are not left behind

- a learning support worker – if possible they could work with learners who declare they have a learning difficulty or disability

- English, maths and ICT support as appropriate – this might be identified during initial assessment, or as the programme progresses

- It may be that you feel you require some training in developing and using resources yourself. There might be continuing professional development (CPD) opportunities for you to access within your team, your organisation or via national bodies like the National Institute of Adult Continuing Education (NIACE) and professional associations such as the Institute for Learning (IfL). It might be useful to find out if there is specialist help available in your organisation such as an E-Guide or ICT support worker, and if they could support a couple of your sessions to help build your confidence at using ICT.

Extension Activity

Make a list of resources you have either created or adapted in the past. What was the focus of each? Was it relevant to the individual needs of your learners as well as your specialist subject? How could you adapt the resources to meet the individual needs of your current learners? Adapt one of the resources to use with your learners, try it out and then evaluate how effective it was.

Meeting the individual needs of learners

When designing resources, any individual needs of your learners should be taken into account, for example, dyslexia, dyspraxia, a hearing impairment, a visual impairment, a physical or mental disability. You may need to produce handouts in a larger sized font, print them on different coloured paper, or ensure there is plenty of white space surrounding the text (the blank area around the text/pictures). You also need to consider the location, cost, challenges and benefits of using certain resources. It might be that your organisation is very proactive with regard to providing resources, or you might have to be creative with what is available. You also need to consider the fact that some learners might not have access to certain resources away from your sessions, for example, computers, the internet or relevant textbooks. There are other aspects such as shift work, travel, childcare and financial concerns which could all impact upon the learning process and any homework you issue.

Activity

Thinking about your current learners, what individual needs or concerns do they have? How could you address these with the use of differentiated resources?

If you are using, adapting or copying work, you will need to check you are not in breach of copyright legislation. The Copyright, Designs and Patents Act (1998) covers copying, adapting and distributing materials, including applications and materials found via the internet. It may be that you will have to ask the author's permission to use their materials, and they may need to be acknowledged for their work on your resource.

Using pictures as well as text and not putting too much information on a handout will make it easier to read. If you were given one handout with a lot of written information in small text, and another with text in a larger more pleasing font with a few pictures, which one would you prefer to read? It would probably be the latter, therefore the same will apply to your learners.

You will need to consider how adaptable your resources can be for use in other contexts with other learners. One size does not fit all; therefore resources may need to be adapted to suit current and future particular learner needs. Everyone is different, but all your learners deserve to be treated with an equal level of respect and have equal access to all the resources. Be proactive in coping with differences by talking to your learners and finding out exactly what they require, so that their learning is effective from the start of their programme. When you are considering any required changes or alterations to resources, you must make sure they are reasonable. You should keep in mind that your organisation has a legal responsibility to comply with the Equality Act (2010) and the Welsh Language Act (1993). The latter placed the Welsh language on an equal footing with the English language in Wales with regard to the public sector.

If you have not yet identified the way your learners learn, i.e. their learning preferences, they could take a short online questionnaire to find out if they are predominantly visual, aural, read/write or kinaesthetic. A free questionnaire is available at www.vark-learn.com. Hill states:

> Give your learners choices, so they can select the ways of learning they like best. For example, where at one time you might have set an essay to write, now you could encourage them to choose alternatives such as an audio recording, a PowerPoint presentation or a mind map ... It helps too if you raise your learners' awareness of how they learn.

(Hill, 2008, page 31)

Health and safety with regard to the use of equipment and training materials is imperative, and you should always follow the Health and Safety at Work etc. Act (1974). Please see Chapter 1 for further details, and check your organisation's requirements too. It may be that you are using resources which have not previously been used; you may therefore need training, or be required to carry out a risk assessment to ensure their safe use. You should be aware that your learners also have a personal responsibility to be mindful of their own and other people's safety, and that you have a duty of care while they are with you.

Example

John is teaching a Do-It-Yourself programme to a mixed group of adults in a community learning centre. He has been teaching this group for a while and knows most of them really well. In this session, the learners are using battery-powered drills to make holes in pieces of wood. They have used these drills before and John therefore assumed they knew the procedures regarding health and safety, and did not recap them at the beginning of this session. One particularly important health and safety point is that only one learner operates a drill at any one time. One drill was not working properly and John was busy elsewhere; a learner held the drill bit while another learner tried to switch it on. Fortunately, John saw what was happening and yelled across the room. A serious accident was averted – this time.

Always be careful with any equipment both you and your learners will use, and recap the safety advice each session.

Activity

Take a look at the Ofsted (2012) Handbook for the Inspection of Further Education and Skills, *available: www.ofsted.gov.uk/resources/handbook-for-inspection-of-further-education-and-skills-september-2012*

You might find it useful to see what their current views are regarding the use of resources.

There may be other resources and help available in your organisation, for example, support for the production of word-processed handouts, use of library facilities for borrowing books and accessing other useful resources such as journals, digital recordings, newspapers, etc. Perhaps you can book a session for your learners with a member of staff who can explain and demonstrate how the system works. Not all organisations have library or resource facilities and you may have to find out from a public library or resource centre what books, ICT facilities and other useful resources they have available for learners to borrow or use.

Always have a clear rationale to justify the resources you have chosen, and evaluate them afterwards. Using the *who, what, when, where, why* and *how* rationale is a good basis for determining how relevant, purposeful and effective your resource will be.

Extension Activity

Create a new resource for use with your learners which promotes equality and values diversity. When deciding what to use, consider the wide range of resources available, and try to be creative and imaginative. Don't be afraid of trying something different. Use the resource with your learners and then evaluate how effective it was.

Implementing the minimum core

The minimum core consists of four elements: literacy, language, numeracy and ICT. As part of your teaching role you should be able to demonstrate these elements to at least level 2. This will enable you to support your learners with English, maths and ICT (known as functional skills). It will also ensure you teach your area of specialism as effectively as possible.

Activity

Look at the four elements of the minimum core in Appendices 6, 7 and 8. Analyse the ways in which you feel you can demonstrate them when using resources. Tick off the ones you can use, and make a note of how you will demonstrate them within your practice.

If possible, obtain a copy of the supporting document: *Addressing literacy, language, numeracy and ICT needs in education and training: Defining the minimum core of teachers' knowledge, understanding and personal skills – A guide for initial teacher education programmes* (LSIS, 2007, revised 2013). Have a look at the content to help you see how you can demonstrate the minimum core elements.

The full document is available to download at: http://repository.excellencegateway.org.uk/fedora/objects/import-pdf:93/datastreams/PDF/content

Example: Literacy

- Reading books and handouts for your subject
- Creating resource materials such as handouts, visual presentations, activities and quizzes
- Checking spelling, grammar and punctuation

Example: Language

- Speaking to learners about how to use the resources
- Asking questions to check a learner's understanding of using the resources and listening to their responses
- Listening to questions and answering them appropriately

Example: Numeracy

- Calculating how much money and how long various resources will take to create and use
- Interpreting how long learners are actually taking to use the resources

Example: ICT

- Preparing resource materials using ICT and uploading them to a VLE or other system
- Using a computer program or application to create resource materials
- Using e-mail or social networking to communicate appropriately
- Using new technology for activities such as online live observations, video conferencing, polls and surveys
- Using digital media for visual/audio recording and playback of resource activities

Demonstrating your own skills regarding the minimum core should enable you to consider ways of improving the skills in your learners too. Ways of improving your learners' skills in these areas could include encouraging them to demonstrate skills similar to those you have used. You can also correct any mistakes, for example, in speech and written work.

You can play an important part in providing opportunities to develop your learners' skills in literacy, language, numeracy and ICT. However, it is your responsibility to continually update your own skills in these areas by undertaking professional development.

Evaluating own practice

You should always evaluate the resources you use to enable you to develop and improve for the future. The process should take into account the views of your learners and others you come into contact with, for example, workplace supervisors. Reviewing your practice will also help you identify any problems or concerns, enabling you to do things differently next time. Never assume everything is going well just because you think it is. Please see Chapter 2 for further information regarding evaluating your practice and obtaining feedback.

What works with one learner or group might not work well with others, perhaps due to their learning preferences or other influences. However, don't change something for the sake of it; if it works, hopefully it will continue to work.

When evaluating the resources you have used, ask yourself the following.

☐ Could everyone see and hear what I was doing?

☐ Did I carry out any necessary risk assessments?

☐ Did I check that all my learners could access and use the resource?

☐ Did I encounter any problems setting up the resource and using it? Was it too time-consuming?

☐ Did it motivate the learners to learn more and make progress?

☐ Did it reach all learning preferences, i.e. was there something to look at (visual), did I talk about it and could learners discuss it (aural), was there something written and/or could learners make notes (read/write), was there something practical for learners to do (kinaesthetic)

☐ Did it support and reinforce learning effectively?

☐ Did it meet individual needs?

☐ Did it promote equality and value diversity?

☐ Did the resource do what I expected? If not why not?

☐ Was it active or passive? Do my learners prefer to be actively engaged when using resources, such as a working model, rather than passively reading a handout?

☐ Was it easy for me to create? Can I update or amend it easily?

☐ Was it of a high quality and professional looking?

☐ Was it up to date and relevant to the subject?

☐ Were all learners able to use it with ease?

☐ Were there enough resources for everyone?

After evaluating your practice, you should be able to make any necessary changes. Don't forget to ask for feedback from your learners as they are best able to inform you how effective it was.

Reflection

Griffiths and Tann (1992) introduced a model of reflection with different time frames. They state that, without a conscious effort, the most immediate reactions to experiences can overwhelm the opportunity for deeper consideration and learning. They describe their reflective cycle as:

Figure 5.1 Griffiths and Tann's (1992) model of reflection

These aspects go through five levels or time frames:

1. rapid reaction (immediate)

2. repair (short pause for thought)

3. review (time out to reassess, over hours or days)

4. research (systematic, focused, over weeks/months)

5. retheorise/reformulate (abstract, rigorous, over months/years)

Example

Val had adapted a colleague's handout to give to her learners. When she used it, she realised the content was set at too high a level as her learners were asking a lot of questions. She therefore told them she had issued the handout far too early in the programme and facilitated a discussion based on the topic instead. This was a rapid reaction to the situation and was therefore immediate reflection.

Schön (1983) suggests two methods of reflection:

- reflection in action
- reflection on action

Reflection in action happens at the time of the incident, is often unconscious, is proactive and allows immediate changes to take place. For example, if you see that some learners are confused by a handout you have given them, you will explain it in more detail straight away.

Reflection on action takes place after the incident, is a more conscious process and is reactive. This allows you time to think about the incident, consider a different approach, or to talk to others about it before making any changes. However, it might not allow you to deal with a situation as it occurs: for example, if you chose not to explain the handout in more detail but to reflect on how you would use it differently with future learners.

Activity

Think of a critical incident that has happened lately when using resources. Work through Griffiths and Tann's, or Schön's theory to reflect upon it and see if you can reach an alternative solution.

Reviewing your progress will help you learn about yourself, and what you could improve, for example, how you react to different situations or learners, how patient you are and what skills you may need to develop. You might also decide you need further training or support to improve your subject knowledge, teaching skills and/or English, maths and ICT skills.

Extension Activity

Based on your evaluation of using resources with learners, what areas have you identified as needing improvement? How can you act on what you have identified and what will you do differently as a result? Do you need any further training and/or support? If so, how will you go about obtaining it?

Summary

In this chapter you have learnt about:

- *resources and their use for teaching, learning and assessment*
- *people as resources*
- *handouts and visual presentations*
- *selecting, adapting and using resources*
- *meeting the individual needs of learners*
- *implementing the minimum core*
- *evaluating own practice*

Cross-referencing grid

This chapter contributes towards the following assessment criteria of the units which form the Certificate in Education and Training, along with aspects of the Professional Standards for Teachers and Trainers in England. Full details of the learning outcomes and assessment criteria of each unit can be found in the appendices.

Certificate units	Assessment criteria
Understanding roles, responsibilities and relationships in education and training	1.1, 1.4
Planning to meet the needs of learners in education and training	2.3, 2.5
Delivering education and training	1.1, 1.3 3.1, 3.2
Assessing learners in education and training	Not applicable
Using resources for education and training	1.1, 1.2, 1.3 2.1, 2.2 3.1, 3.2

Area	Professional Standards for Teachers and Trainers in England
Professional values and attributes	1, 2, 3, 4, 5, 6
Professional knowledge and understanding	7, 9, 10, 11, 12
Professional skills	13, 14, 15, 16, 19, 20

Theory focus

References and further information

Armitage, A, Evershed, J, Hayes, D, Hudson, A, Kent, J, Lawes, S, Poma, S and Renwick, M (2012) *Teaching and Training in Lifelong Learning.* Maidenhead: OU Press.

Becta (2009) *Harnessing Technology Review 2008: The Role of Technology and its Impact on Education.* Coventry: Becta.

Gravells, A and Simpson, S (2012) *Equality and Diversity in the Lifelong Learning Sector* (2nd edn). London: Learning Matters SAGE.

Gravells, A and Simpson, S (2014) *Passing Assessments for the Certificate in Education and Training.* London: Learning Matters SAGE.

Griffiths, M and Tann, S (1992) Using reflective practice to link personal and public theories. *Journal of Education for Teaching,* 18(1): 69–84.

Hill, C (2008) *Teaching with e-learning in the Lifelong Learning Sector* (2nd edn). London: Learning Matters SAGE.

LSIS (2007, revised 2013) *Addressing literacy, language, numeracy and ICT needs in education and training: Defining the minimum core of teachers' knowledge, understanding and personal skills – A guide for initial teacher education programmes.* Coventry: LSIS.

Powell, S and Tummons, J (2011) *Inclusive Practice in the Lifelong Learning Sector.* London: Learning Matters SAGE.

Reece, I and Walker, S (2007) *Teaching, Training and Learning: A Practical Guide* (6th edn). London: Business Education Publishers Ltd.

Schön, DA (1983) *The Reflective Practitioner.* San Francisco: Jossey-Bass.

Wallace, S (2011) *Teaching Tutoring and Training in the Lifelong Learning Sector* (4th Edn). London: Learning Matters SAGE.

Websites

Copyright – www.copyrightservice.co.uk

Dyslexia Association – www.dyslexia.uk.net

English and Maths free support – www.move-on.org.uk

Facebook – www.facebook.com

Games to download for activities – www.npted.org/schools/sandfieldsComp/games/Pages/default.aspx

Health and Safety at Work etc. Act (1974) – www.legislation.gov.uk/ukpga/1974/37

Learning and Skills Network (2008) *Getting Ahead with Personal Learning and Thinking Skills: Lessons from the wider key skills* – http://archive.excellencegateway.org.uk/media/post16/files/keyskillspltspublication.pdf

Learning preference questionnaire – www.vark-learn.com

LinkedIn – www.linkedin.com

NIACE: *Readability: How to produce clear written materials for a range of readers* – http://shop.niace.org.uk/media/catalog/product/R/e/Readability.pdf

Ofsted (2012) Handbook for the Inspection of Further Education and Skills – www.ofsted.gov.uk/resources/handbook-for-inspection-of-further-education-and-skills-september-2012

Online free courses in various subjects – www.vision2learn.net

Online games – www.npted.org/schools/sandfieldsComp/games/Pages/Game-Downloads.aspx

Online presentations – www.prezi.com

Plagiarism – www.plagiarism.org

Prezi online presentation application – http://prezi.com/

Puzzle software – www.crossword-compiler.com

www.educational-software-directory.net/game/puzzle

http://hotpot.uvic.ca

www.mathsnet.net

Resources Centre – www.heacademy.ac.uk/resources

Twitter – www.twitter.com

Video e-mail – http://mailvu.com/

Welsh Language Act (1993) – www.legislation.gov.uk/ukpga/1993/38/contents

Unit title: Understanding roles, responsibilities and relationships in education and training

Level 3 (3 credits)

Learning outcomes The learner will:	Assessment criteria The learner can:	
1. Understand the teaching role and responsibilities in education and training	1.1	Explain the teaching role and responsibilities in education and training
	1.2	Summarise key aspects of legislation, regulatory requirements and codes of practice relating to own role and responsibilities
	1.3	Explain ways to promote equality and value diversity
	1.4	Explain why it is important to identify and meet individual learner needs
2. Understand ways to maintain a safe and supportive learning environment	2.1	Explain ways to maintain a safe and supportive learning environment
	2.2	Explain why it is important to promote appropriate behaviour and respect for others
3. Understand the relationships between teachers and other professionals in education and training	3.1	Explain how the teaching role involves working with other professionals
	3.2	Explain the boundaries between the teaching role and other professional roles
	3.3	Describe points of referral to meet the individual needs of learners

APPENDIX 2

Unit title: Planning to meet the needs of learners in education and training

Level 4 (3 credits)

Learning outcomes The learner will:	Assessment criteria The learner can:	
1. Be able to use initial and diagnostic assessment to agree individual learning goals with learners	1.1	Analyse the role and use of initial and diagnostic assessment in agreeing individual learning goals
	1.2	Use methods of initial and diagnostic assessment to negotiate and agree individual learning goals with learners
	1.3	Record learners' individual learning goals
2. Be able to plan inclusive teaching and learning in accordance with internal and external requirements	2.1	Devise a scheme of work in accordance with internal and external requirements
	2.2	Design teaching and learning plans that meet the aims and individual needs of all learners and curriculum requirements
	2.3	Explain how own planning meets the individual needs of learners
	2.4	Explain ways in which teaching and learning plans can be adapted to meet the individual needs of learners
	2.5	Identify opportunities for learners to provide feedback to inform inclusive practice
3. Be able to implement the minimum core in planning inclusive teaching and learning	3.1	Analyse ways in which minimum core elements can be demonstrated in planning inclusive teaching and learning
	3.2	Apply minimum core elements in planning inclusive teaching and learning
4. Be able to evaluate own practice when planning inclusive teaching and learning	4.1	Review the effectiveness of own practice when planning to meet the individual needs of learners, taking account of the views of learners and others.
	4.2	Identify areas for improvement in own planning to meet the individual needs of learners

 # APPENDIX 3

Unit title: Delivering education and training

Level 4 (6 credits)

Learning outcomes The learner will:	Assessment criteria The learner can:
1. Be able to use inclusive teaching and learning approaches in accordance with internal and external requirements	1.1 Analyse the effectiveness of teaching and learning approaches used in own area of specialism in relation to meeting the individual needs of learners 1.2 Create an inclusive teaching and learning environment 1.3 Demonstrate an inclusive approach to teaching and learning in accordance with internal and external requirements
2. Be able to communicate with learners and other learning professionals to promote learning and progression	2.1 Analyse benefits and limitations of communication methods and media used in own area of specialism 2.2 Use communication methods and media to meet individual learner needs 2.3 Communicate with other learning professionals to meet individual learner needs and encourage progression
3. Be able to use technologies in delivering inclusive teaching and learning	3.1 Analyse benefits and limitations of technologies used in own area of specialism 3.2 Use technologies to enhance teaching and meet individual learner needs
4. Be able to implement the minimum core when delivering inclusive teaching and learning	4.1 Analyse ways in which minimum core elements can be demonstrated when delivering inclusive teaching and learning 4.2 Apply minimum core elements in delivering inclusive teaching and learning
5. Be able to evaluate own practice in delivering inclusive teaching and learning	5.1 Review the effectiveness of own practice in meeting the needs of individual learners, taking account of the views of learners and others 5.2 Identify areas for improvement in own practice in meeting the individual needs of learners

Unit title: Assessing learners in education and training

Level 4 (6 credits)

Learning outcomes The learner will:	Assessment criteria The learner can:	
1. Be able to use types and methods of assessment to meet the needs of individual learners	1.1	Explain the purposes of types of assessment used in education and training
	1.2	Analyse the effectiveness of assessment methods in relation to meeting the individual needs of learners
	1.3	Use types and methods of assessment to meet the individual needs of learners
	1.4	Use peer and self-assessment to promote learners' personal responsibility in the assessment for, and of, their learning
	1.5	Use questioning and feedback to contribute to the assessment process
2. Be able to carry out assessments in accordance with internal and external requirements	2.1	Identify the internal and external assessment requirements and related procedures of learning programmes
	2.2	Use assessment types and methods to enable learners to produce assessment evidence that is valid, reliable, sufficient, authentic and current
	2.3	Conduct assessments in line with internal and external requirements
	2.4	Record the outcomes of assessments to meet internal and external requirements
	2.5	Communicate assessment information to other professionals with an interest in learner achievement
3. Be able to implement the minimum core when assessing learners	3.1	Analyse ways in which minimum core elements can be demonstrated in assessing learners
	3.2	Apply minimum core elements in assessing learners
4. Be able to evaluate own assessment practice	4.1	Review the effectiveness of own assessment practice taking account of the views of learners and others
	4.2	Identify areas for improvement in own assessment practice

Unit title: Using resources for education and training

Level 4 (3 credits)

Learning outcomes The learner will:	Assessment criteria The learner can:
1. Be able to use resources in the delivery of inclusive teaching and learning	1.1 Analyse the effectiveness of resources used in own area of specialism in relation to meeting the individual needs of learners
	1.2 Use resources to promote equality, value diversity and meet the individual needs of learners
	1.3 Adapt resources to meet the individual needs of learners
2. Be able to implement the minimum core when using resources in the delivery of inclusive teaching and learning	2.1 Analyse ways in which minimum core elements can be demonstrated when using resources for inclusive teaching and learning
	2.2 Apply minimum core elements when using resources for inclusive teaching and learning
3. Be able to evaluate own use of resources in the delivery of inclusive teaching and learning	3.1 Review the effectiveness of own practice in using resources to meet the individual needs of learners, taking account of the views of learners and others
	3.2 Identify areas for improvement in own use of resources to meet the individual needs of learners

Minimum Core: Language and literacy personal skills

	Demonstrated by:
Speaking	
☐ Expressing yourself clearly, using communication techniques to help convey meaning and to enhance the delivery and accessibility of the message	
☐ Showing the ability to use language, style and tone in ways that suit the intended audience, and to recognise their use by others	
☐ Using appropriate techniques to reinforce oral communication, checking how well the information is received and supporting the understanding of those listening	
☐ Using non-verbal communication to assist in conveying meaning and receiving information, and recognising its use by others	
Listening	
☐ Listening attentively and responding sensitively to contributions made by others	
Reading	
☐ Finding, and selecting from, a range of reference material and sources of information, including the internet	
☐ Using and reflecting on a range of reading strategies to interpret texts and to locate information or meaning	
☐ Identifying and recording the key information or messages contained within reading material using note-taking techniques	
Writing	
☐ Writing fluently, accurately and legibly on a range of topics	
☐ Selecting appropriate format and style of writing for different purposes and different readers	
☐ Using spelling and punctuation accurately in order to make meaning clear	
☐ Understanding and using the conventions of grammar (the forms and structures of words, phrases, clauses, sentences and texts) consistently when producing written text	

Minimum Core: Numeracy personal skills

Communication	Demonstrated by:
Communication	
☐ Communicating with others about numeracy in an open and supportive manner	
☐ Assessing own, and other people's, understanding	
☐ Expressing yourself clearly and accurately	
☐ Communicating about numeracy in a variety of ways that suit and support the intended audience, and recognising such use by others	
☐ Using appropriate techniques to reinforce oral communication, checking how well the information is received and supporting understanding of those listening	
Processes	
☐ Using strategies to make sense of a situation requiring the application of numeracy	
☐ Processing and analysing data	
☐ Using generic content knowledge and skills	
☐ Making decisions concerning content knowledge and skills	
☐ Understanding the validity of different methods	
☐ Considering accuracy, efficiency and effectiveness when solving problems and reflecting on what has been learned	
☐ Making sense of data	
☐ Selecting appropriate format and style for communicating findings	

Minimum Core: Information and communication technology (ICT) personal skills

Communication	Demonstrated by:
☐ Communicating with others with/about ICT in an open and supportive manner ☐ Assessing own, and other people's, understanding ☐ Expressing yourself clearly and accurately ☐ Communicating about/with ICT in a variety of ways that suit and support the intended audience, and recognising such use by others ☐ Using appropriate techniques to reinforce oral communication, checking how well the information is received and supporting understanding of those listening **Processes** ☐ Using ICT systems ☐ Finding, selecting and exchanging information ☐ Developing and presenting information	

Further information

LSIS (2007, revised 2013) *Addressing literacy, language, numeracy and ICT needs in education and training: Defining the minimum core of teachers' knowledge, understanding and personal skills – A guide for initial teacher education programmes.* Coventry: LSIS.

The full document is available at: http://repository.excellencegateway.org.uk/fedora/objects/import-pdf:93/datastreams/PDF/content

A companion guide: *Inclusive learning approaches for literacy, language, numeracy and ICT (2007)* is available at: www.excellencegateway.org.uk/node/12020

Professional Standards for Teachers and Trainers in England

Professional standards

As a professional teacher or trainer you should demonstrate commitment to the following in your professional practice.

Professional values and attributes

Develop your own judgement of what works and does not work in your teaching and training

1. Reflect on what works best in your teaching and learning to meet the diverse needs of learners

2. Evaluate and challenge your practice, values and beliefs

3. Inspire, motivate and raise aspirations of learners through your enthusiasm and knowledge

4. Be creative and innovative in selecting and adapting strategies to help learners to learn

5. Value and promote social and cultural diversity, equality of opportunity and inclusion

6. Build positive and collaborative relationships with colleagues and learners

Professional knowledge and understanding

Develop deep and critically informed knowledge and understanding in theory and practice

7. Maintain and update knowledge of your subject and/or vocational area

8. Maintain and update your knowledge of educational research to develop evidence-based practice

9. Apply theoretical understanding of effective practice in teaching, learning and assessment drawing on research and other evidence

10. Evaluate your practice with others and assess its impact on learning

11. Manage and promote positive learner behaviour

12. Understand the teaching and professional role and your responsibilities

Professional Skills

Develop your expertise and skills to ensure the best outcomes for learners

13. Motivate and inspire learners to promote achievement and develop their skills to enable progression

14. Plan and deliver effective learning programmes for diverse groups or individuals in a safe and inclusive environment

15. Promote the benefits of technology and support learners in its use

16. Address the mathematics and English needs of learners and work creatively to overcome individual barriers to learning

17. Enable learners to share responsibility for their own learning and assessment, setting goals that stretch and challenge

18. Apply appropriate and fair methods of assessment and provide constructive and timely feedback to support progression and achievement

19. Maintain and update your teaching and training expertise and vocational skills through collaboration with employers

20. Contribute to organisational development and quality improvement through collaboration with others

http://www.et-foundation.co.uk/supporting/programmes/professional-standards-review/ date accessed 11.04.14

INDEX

Development or DESTRUCTION?

The Oil Industry

Richard and Louise Spilsbury

WAYLAND

Published in paperback in 2014 by Wayland
Copyright © 2014 Wayland

Wayland
338 Euston Road
London NW1 3BH

Wayland Australia
Level 17/207 Kent Street
Sydney NSW 2000

Editor: Julia Adams
Designer: Elaine Wilkinson
Picture researcher: Julia Adams
Proofreader and indexer: Sarah Doughty
Map illustrators: Adrian Stuart and Martin Sanders

Spilsbury, Richard, 1963-
  The oil industry. -- (Development or destruction?)
  1. Petroleum industry and trade--Case studies--Juvenile literature. 2. Petroleum industry and trade--
  Environmental aspects--Juvenile literature.
  I. Title II. Series
  338.2'7282-dc22

ISBN 978 0 7502 8085 3

Picture acknowledgements:
The author and publisher would like to thank the following agencies for allowing these pictures to be
reproduced:
Alamy/Christine Osborne Pictures: p14; Alamy/Friedrich Stark: p23; Alamy/WoodyStock: p28; Alamy/
AlamyCelebrity: pp40–41; Corbis/Ed Kashi: p22, p24; Corbis/Thomas Ashby/Reuters: p25; Corbis/George
Steinmetz: p26, p35; Corbis/Natalie Fobes/Science Faction: p36; Getty/Arnulf Husmo: front cover, p29;
Getty: p13, p18 (top), p13 (top); Getty/Bloomberg: p16, p18 (bottom); Getty/AFP: p19; Getty/National
Geographic: p21; iStock: p4, p5, p8, p13 (bottom), p38; KPA/Zuma/Rex Features: p. 17 (bottom);
ESA: p24; Rex/Actionpress: p32; Sciencephoto/Dr Davidhall: p42; Shutterstock: p5, p9, p11, p12, p14,
p17, p20, pp36–37, p43; Statoil: all images pp30–31;
All locator maps: Shutterstock.
Images used throughout for creative graphics: iStockphoto, Shutterstock.
Should there be any inadvertent omission, please apply to the publisher for rectification.

Note: The website addresses (URLs) included in this book were valid at the time of going to press. However, because
of the nature of the Internet, it is possible that some addresses may have changed, or sites may have changed or closed
down since publication. While the author and publishers regret any inconvenience this may cause to the readers, no
responsibility for any such changes can be accepted by either the author or the publishers.

Printed in Malaysia
10 9 8 7 6 5 4 3 2 1

Wayland is a division of Hachette Children's Books,
an Hachette UK company.
www.hachette.co.uk

Contents

The importance of oil

Oil has made a bigger impact on our world in the last 100 years than any other natural resource. It is the major fuel for vehicles, allowing the transport of goods and people globally. It is also a vital raw material for many industries. The use and trade of oil has had a major influence on the economic development of countries around the world. Oil has often been called black gold – because crude oil taken from the ground is thick and black and because oil is such a valuable commodity.

▲ Oil fuels the global fleet of airplanes, lorries, cars, motorcycles and ships.

Uses of oil

Crude oil contains a mix of different useful substances that are extracted in industrial plants, called oil refineries. About 60 per cent of all crude oil is refined into petroleum fuels, which are burned in engines to power anything from cars to chainsaws. Other refined products include asphalt, important for surfacing roads, and petrochemicals. For example, the petrochemical ethylene is used to make the common plastic polyethylene, PVC and also polyester, which is used in fabrics. Other petrochemicals are made into a wide range of products including polystyrene, rubber, dyes, paints, fertilizers, bullet-proof vests and even some medicines, such as aspirin.

Where is oil found

Oil is not distributed evenly around the world, as it's only found in certain types of rocks. Areas of rock where oil is found in large quantities that can be accessed by people are called oil reserves. More than half of the

North America

South America

world's crude oil reserves are found in the Middle East, and Saudi Arabia has the largest oil reserves of any country – about 20 per cent of the world's total. The other main oil reserves are found in Canada, the US, Latin America, Africa, and Russia.

Who owns oil reserves?

In general, oil reserves are owned by the country on whose territory they are found. Oil is extremely valuable and countries with large reserves are often rich. Usually countries divide up their land and ocean areas where there might be oil into portions called concessions. Oil companies with skills and expertise in finding and extracting oil pay for licences to explore particular concessions. The companies sell the oil they produce on a concession and pay taxes to the country on the amount they extract. Oil companies may be wholly owned by countries, such as Saudi Aramco of Saudi Arabia, or privately owned, such as BP and ExxonMobil.

Europe

Asia

Africa

The blue areas on this world map show oil fields that have been discovered to date.

Australasia

Antarctica

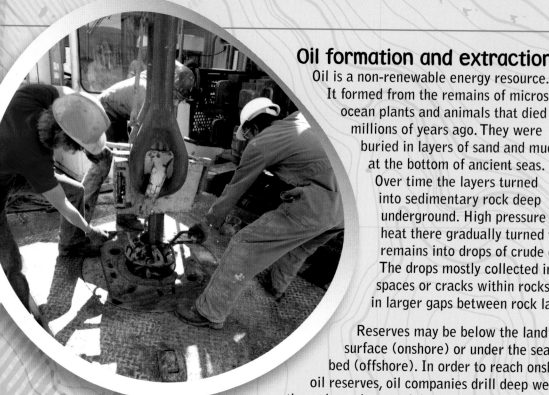

Oil formation and extraction

Oil is a non-renewable energy resource. It formed from the remains of microscopic ocean plants and animals that died millions of years ago. They were buried in layers of sand and mud at the bottom of ancient seas. Over time the layers turned into sedimentary rock deep underground. High pressure and heat there gradually turned the remains into drops of crude oil. The drops mostly collected in spaces or cracks within rocks or in larger gaps between rock layers.

Reserves may be below the land surface (onshore) or under the sea bed (offshore). In order to reach onshore oil reserves, oil companies drill deep wells through or along rock layers. Offshore oil companies drill from oil platforms (or rigs) built on stilts or floating on the sea surface. In order to retrieve the oil, platforms use pipes called risers. High pressure underground often forces oil out of the rock to the surface. If there isn't enough pressure, liquids are injected into the reserves or pumps are used to suck out the oil. Some oil is found at the surface, soaked into soft rocks called oil shale and tar sands. These are mined, crushed and heated to release the oil inside them. Once oil has been extracted, it is usually transported to an oil refinery across land by long-distance pipes or by sea on massive ships called tankers.

Oil drilling is much safer than it was in the past, but there is still a risk that oil will catch fire, and high underground pressure can blow out drills and underground pipes.

Very hard rock

Porous rock containing gas

Porous rock containing oil

Porous rock containing water

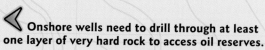
Onshore wells need to drill through at least one layer of very hard rock to access oil reserves.

Destruction fact

One litre (2 US pints) of oil is enough to pollute 900,000 litres (1,900,000 US pints) of drinking water.

The downside of oil

Burning oil-based fuels to release energy also releases waste gases. Carbon dioxide collects in the atmosphere, stores heat, and most scientists believe it contributes to climate change. Other gases cause air pollution, affecting human health. The extraction and transport of oil may also damage the environment. Accidents as well as regular oil company activities cause water and land pollution. These impacts and the uneven distribution of oil profits cause conflicts.

Do the benefits of oil production balance out destruction of these sorts? And are there more sustainable solutions, lessening the impact of the oil industry? This book considers this question by examining five international case studies.

▽ Oil exploration and production brings benefits and problems all over the world. The five case studies in this book look at some of the major issues and impacts today.

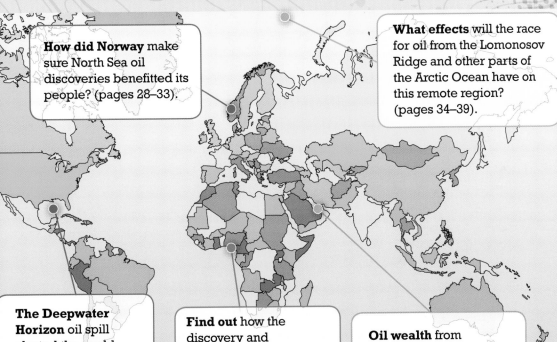

How did Norway make sure North Sea oil discoveries benefitted its people? (pages 28–33).

What effects will the race for oil from the Lomonosov Ridge and other parts of the Arctic Ocean have on this remote region? (pages 34–39).

The Deepwater Horizon oil spill alerted the world to the risks of deep drilling. How has it impacted the Gulf of Mexico oil industry? (pages 16–21).

Find out how the discovery and exploitation of oil riches in the Niger Delta have created great environmental and social problems (pages 22–27).

Oil wealth from fields such as Zakum transformed Abu Dhabi, but can development continue? (pages 10–15).

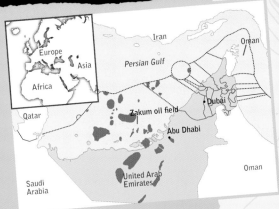

The United Arab Emirates (UAE) in the Middle East is a country about the size of Iceland that edges on the Persian Gulf. It is made up of seven states, or emirates, the largest of which is Abu Dhabi. It is also the richest emirate, mainly because it controls the country's biggest oil field – Zakum.

This map shows the oil fields that have been discovered in the UAE. The dotted lines mark the concession borders.

A brief history of Middle East oil

Oil had been used in small quantities in the Middle East for millennia, for example for lamps, but at the start of the twentieth century oil was increasingly in demand. Major world powers such as Britain, Germany and the US needed oil-based fuel, especially for their fleets of military ships. Britain, France and Germany had long had political influence over and even controlled parts of the Middle East because of its ideal position for trade with Asia and Africa. Therefore, their oil companies, including Anglo-Persian oil, which later became BP, explored for oil in concessions across the region.

The first major oil discovery in the Middle East was made in Iran in 1908. During the following decades, oil was found throughout the Persian Gulf region, including Abu Dhabi in 1953. Global demand for oil grew because of the increasing use of cars and aircraft, and the large reserves of the Middle East, especially Saudi Arabia, could meet that demand. Today the Middle East produces more oil than any other region in the world.

Oil exports

Around two thirds of the world's crude oil reserves are located in the countries bordering the Persian Gulf. The oil is exported by fleets of oil tankers and pipelines to countries around the world, such as China and India. The pie chart below shows the share of oil produced by different Gulf countries.

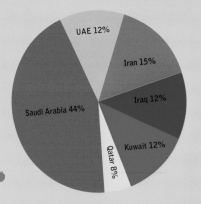

Chapter 2

ON THE SCENE

'Beneath the glistening waters off the coast of Abu Dhabi lies one of the world's largest oil fields...an estimated 50 billion barrels of oil sit below the sea.'

Morten Mauritzen, ExxonMobil, Abu Dhabi, 2010

The Zakum oil field

In 1955 the ruler of Abu Dhabi sold exploration rights for offshore Abu Dhabi to the Abu Dhabi Marine Areas (ADMA) company, owned by the foreign oil companies BP and Total. Their geologists drilled into the seafloor from ships in order to get rock samples and check them for oil content. Some oil was found in 1958, but the giant Zakum reserve was discovered in 1963. Over the next four years, BP and Total built platforms to drill for Zakum oil. They installed pipelines taking the oil to nearby Zirku Island and built a port there so tankers could collect the oil.

The Abu Dhabi government got 50 per cent of ADMA profits on oil sales. In 1971 the government set up the Abu Dhabi National Oil Company to take more control, and profit more, from oil produced on their territory. They bought part of ADMA and its oil infrastructure. The government also worked in partnership with other oil companies to produce more oil from different parts of Zakum. Today there are tens of platforms and hundreds of wells which, together with the other infrastructure, form the enormous Zakum oil field – the fourth largest oil field in the world.

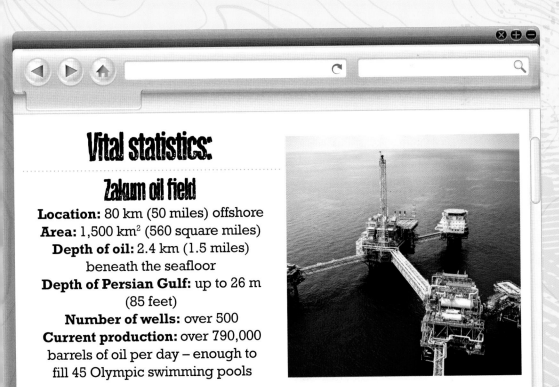

Vital statistics:

Zakum oil field

Location: 80 km (50 miles) offshore
Area: 1,500 km^2 (560 square miles)
Depth of oil: 2.4 km (1.5 miles) beneath the seafloor
Depth of Persian Gulf: up to 26 m (85 feet)
Number of wells: over 500
Current production: over 790,000 barrels of oil per day – enough to fill 45 Olympic swimming pools

▽ The oil wealth of Abu Dhabi has paid for the development of a high standard of living for its citizens and access to a luxury lifestyle.

Transformation of a city-state

Abu Dhabi is both the capital city and an emirate of the UAE. Until the 1950s, the major industry in the small island town of Abu Dhabi was pearl fishing and there were no paved roads in the UAE. Abu Dhabi developed from the 1970s onwards because the government was earning increasing oil revenue from oil companies operating wells in its concessions. The government spent a large amount of the revenue on improving infrastructure both for the oil industry and for Abu Dhabi citizens. They invested in a network of roads linking the city with onshore oil fields, and installed running water, a sewerage system and electrical supply to households. They also built schools and government buildings.

Today Abu Dhabi is the richest city in the world. It has many modern high-rise buildings, international hotels, multi-lane highways and luxury shopping malls. Abu Dhabi's population of around 650,000 is seven times larger than in 1975, partly because of migrant workers in the oil industry. International influences have caused some cultural change. For example, in the past, it was not acceptable for women to work in the UAE. Today women make up over 60 per cent of the workforce in state jobs such as in government and teaching.

Zakum oil field, Abu Dhabi (UAE)

Migrant workers in Abu Dhabi who have contributed to its economic development are sometimes forced to live in hostel rooms with up to 20 other people.

Downsides of development

Drilling and transporting oil always causes some oil spills. Some are accidental while others are caused by washing out tankers. Because of the high volume of oil tanker traffic around Abu Dhabi, 1 million barrels of oil are spilled each year. Spilled oil and other chemicals used by the oil industry can poison or choke many marine organisms and damage plants such as seagrass, which are important wildlife habitats. Dredging the seabed to deepen channels for boats also destroys seagrass. Populations of dugongs are dwindling, partly because they do not have enough seagrass to eat.

Oil has made most UAE citizens rich. They rarely take on the low-paid jobs in oil or construction industries. Around 95 per cent of such jobs are carried out by migrant workers from Asian countries such as Nepal and India. They can earn more in the UAE than they can at home, but they are exploited by working long hours for low wages which are often not paid for months on end. Rents are so high in the city that migrant workers usually live in poor housing.

EXPLORE FURTHER

Find out how the neighbouring UAE Dubai became rich even though it has little oil. Why did the global financial crisis affect its growth?

Dugongs were once hunted but are now officially protected by the Abu Dhabi government. However, they are threatened by the environmental impact of oil development.

13

Abu Dhabi investments

Abu Dhabi's future success relies in part on continuing oil and also gas revenues from Zakum. However, it is costly to get oil from Zakum due to the low pressure of oil in parts of the field and the high cost of drilling new wells or extending existing ones to reach it. This is why Abu Dhabi is also investing in oil and gas developments in other parts of the world such as Indonesia, Thailand and Canada, as well as in non-oil industries overseas. These industries range from part ownership of Gatwick Airport in the UK to mines in Africa.

▲ The Abu Dhabi government has invested some of its oil wealth in properties worldwide, including an estimated US$800 million in 2008 to buy the famous Chrysler Building in central Manhattan.

Artificial Islands

The World Islands are formed by sand dredged from the floor of the Gulf. To complete the formation of these islands 300 million cubic m (390,000,000 cubic yards) of sand will have to be deposited, in an area where the seabed is between 10 and 17 m (11 and 18 yards). The sand needed for the project is dredged from the open sea. Each island will be up to 3 m (10 feet) above sea level. The main contractors for The World Islands are Van Oord ACZ Marine Contractors Gulf FZE – Dubai who are responsible for land reclamation, dredging works and the breakwaters. This is the largest project Van Oord has undertaken in the region.

▲ A ship sprays out sand mined from the open sea to create an artificial island in shallow Persian Gulf waters.

Zakum oil field, Abu Dhabi (UAE)

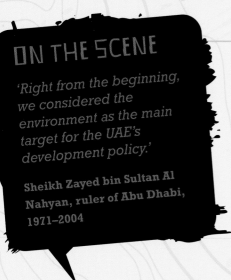

Individuals, banks and other organisations in Abu Dhabi are also investing in a range of industries to create work and revenue, so the emirate is not completely dependent on oil. These include the largest aluminium processing facility in the world and Saadiyat Island, an artificial island built for tourism. It will be home to world-class museums, such as a new Louvre. A further project is Masdar, a sustainable city. This is a revolutionary, solar-powered settlement for 50,000 people on the outskirts of Abu Dhabi city. It includes electric cars, and is planned for completion by 2025. However, Abu Dhabi citizens are some of the highest users of energy in the world, from electricity to power air conditioning, to fuel for their gas-guzzling cars. Reducing Abu Dhabi's energy consumption would have a bigger impact on climate change than building Masdar.

Development or Destruction?

Development:

* Abu Dhabi's Zakum field has contributed to making the UAE the 7th biggest exporter of oil in the world.
* Abu Dhabi offers a high standard of living for its citizens.
* The emirate is using its oil wealth to diversify industry and to invest in sustainable energy use, ready for a future when less oil will be available.

Destruction:

* Oil development in Abu Dhabi has caused coastal pollution and environmental damage.
* Abu Dhabi citizens have among the largest carbon footprints in the world.
* Oil wealth has created higher living standards for Abu Dhabi citizens, but some of its migrant workers face social injustice.

Oil has been vital to the development of the US as a whole, as well as to particular regions, such as the Gulf of Mexico. In 2010, the industry there changed overnight following a catastrophic accident on a single rig. This highlighted the dangers of offshore drilling.

Development fact

Cheap oil from Spindletop spurred the Texan Santa Fe railway to change fuel from coal to the more efficient oil. There was one oil-driven locomotive in 1901, but 250 by 1905.

US oil development

Individuals and their small companies first drilled for oil in the US in the mid- to late nineteenth century. Back then oil was mostly refined to make kerosene for burning in lamps, but little else. In spring 1901, enormous quantities of oil were found in Texas, in a location called Spindletop. By the end of the year there were 200 wells operated by 100 private companies at Spindletop. Some of these turned into the major oil companies of today, including Gulf Oil.

There are thousands of oil rigs dotting the coastal waters of the Gulf of Mexico.

Oil states took taxes from oil companies based on how much oil was found, but there was no law preventing companies claiming public land where they found oil as their own until 1920.

Up to the 1940s the major oil producing states were Texas and California. However, as onshore reserves dwindled, oil companies focused on searching for offshore oil in the Gulf of Mexico.

Chapter 3

Rigs of the Gulf of Mexico (indicated by red dots on this map) are mostly located in the shallowest water where reserves are easiest to exploit. However, the largest, most lucrative new reserves are in deeper parts, further out to sea.

Into the Gulf

Gulf of Mexico oil was first found seeping from the marshes of Louisiana. Oil companies brought in experienced oil workers from Texas to find oil reserves and employed locals who knew how to find their way through the dense marshes. The companies built piers from solid land to drill from the marshes, and in 1911 Gulf Oil created the first offshore rig to drill under a lake. In the 1940s to 50s, oil rigs gradually spread from the coastal edge further out into the deeper water in the Gulf, because geologists had located large reserves of high-pressure oil there. By then, oil companies had developed rigs that could remain stable in deep water, drill down into the seabed for many kilometres, and survive strong waves and storms.

By 2010 there were around 4,000 rigs in the Gulf of Mexico, one of which was the Deepwater Horizon. This was a floating rig with motors that could move it to different parts of the Gulf to drill. Using a floating rig is cheaper and causes less seafloor damage than setting up a fixed rig.

Vital statistics:

Deepwater Horizon

Built: 2001
Owner: Transocean Ltd, a specialist offshore drilling company
Length: 114 m (374 feet) – the length of a big football pitch
Height: 41 m (134 feet)
Weight: 32,500 tonnes
Record: Drilled deepest well in history at 10.6 km (6.6 miles)

Blowout

From February 2010, Deepwater Horizon had been rented by the oil company BP. On the night of 20 April 2010 the crew on the rig had just spent weeks drilling down over 5 km (3 miles) into a possible oil producing reserve called Macondo. They had sealed the drill hole with mud and concrete until BP was ready to collect the oil. But then a surge of gas and oil broke through the seal and shot up the riser. The blow-out set the rig on fire, killing and injuring workers, and it sank. With no seal, up to 60,000 barrels of oil poured out of the hole each day.

BP used submarine robots to lower a heavy dome over the hole to stop the leak, but gas emerging from the drillhole floated it off. They put a giant steel funnel over the hole, attached to a pipe that took some oil up to a waiting tanker. Eventually, in September they managed to drill another hole and forced concrete into the Macondo well to plug it. By then, 5 million barrels of oil had spilled into the Gulf of Mexico – enough to fill nearly 300 Olympic swimming pools.

▷ **Fire boats battle to stop the ferocious flames on the remaining section of the Deepwater Horizon, shortly before it sank.**

Innovations: Blowout preventer

Blowout preventers (BOPs) are special heavy valves placed over oil wells. They have hydraulic rams that automatically cut through and shut off the riser when high-pressure oil moves through it. This should prevent a blowout. However, the BOP on the Macondo well failed, possibly because the hydraulics did not work.

◁ **A blowout preventer similar to the one that failed on Deepwater's Macondo well.**

Environmental impacts

The oil spill from Deepwater Horizon's well formed a vast floating slick that gradually moved towards the shores of Louisiana and adjoining states. Sticky crude oil coated many coastal shores, killing plants and sealife, such as crabs and oysters, and blackened beaches. Thousands of oiled animals including pelicans and sea turtles could not move or feed, and many died as a result.

A response team organised by the US Government and partly funded by BP cleaned up the oil. They dug tar from beaches and rescued oiled animals. Wildlife rescue experts carefully used detergent to clean off oil, fed the animals and released them back into the wild. They skimmed oil from the water surface using booms dragged by boats. They also sprayed millions of litres of chemicals called dispersants on the slick. These broke the oil up into small pieces that sank before more oil reached the coasts. However, tiny young of fish such as tuna or shrimp that breed in the Gulf may die when they accidentally eat the oil pieces. This could impact on the future stocks of these economically important fish.

▽ **Volunteers clean an oil-covered brown pelican, affected by the BP Deepwater Horizon oil spill in the Gulf of Mexico, found off the Louisiana coast.**

Going deeper

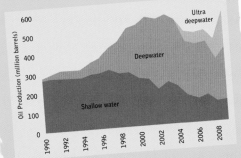

The Gulf of Mexico oil industry is important to the US – it supplies one-third of US domestic oil. This graph reveals that every year since the 1990s, more oil in the Gulf of Mexico has come from wells in deeper water. The reason is that supplies from wells closer to land are dwindling, yet US and global demand for oil is growing.

▽ **Baton Rouge oil refinery has developed from its first beginnings in 1909 to become the second largest in the US, employing around 6,000 people.**

The Louisiana economy

Gulf of Mexico oil changed the Louisiana economy in the mid-twentieth century. It created employment on rigs, boats supplying rigs and in refineries. The oil supplied raw materials for petrochemical factories. Oil revenue was used to drain the marshes to create coastal land for settlements and farming. It has funded state schools and public services, and the growth of big regional cities such as Baton Rouge, home to many oil companies. However, oil wealth does not benefit all Louisiana's citizens. The state has some of the highest proportions of people unemployed or living in poverty in the US. One reason for this is that since the late 1980s there have been fewer low-skill jobs available.

The Deepwater Horizon disaster put a further strain on the economy. President Obama suspended all deep drilling in the Gulf for six months afterwards owing to concerns about the safety of wells. Thousands of Louisiana citizens became temporarily unemployed because a third of jobs in coastal Louisiana are in the oil industry.

Recovery?

Fishing and shrimping were suspended in a third of the Gulf's waters because of possible oil contamination of seafood. Tourists were kept away from coastal resorts owing to tar-stained sands and the smell of oil in the air. Many affected individuals and businesses were helped out by compensation payments from BP and by an injection of government money.

By 2011, beaches were mostly clean and fishing and oil exploration had resumed. However, scientists have found a thick layer of oil on the seafloor in deep waters. This could have long-term pollution impacts for the Gulf of Mexico.

Unloading pink shrimp from the depths of the Gulf of Mexico on a trawler.

Development or Destruction?

Development:

* Oil has created employment and development in Louisiana and other Gulf of Mexico states.
* The Macondo well blowout happened because of equipment failure, but other deep wells are producing oil safely.
* Gulf of Mexico oil is essential for the US economy as a whole.

Destruction:

* The Deepwater Horizon disaster killed people and wildlife, and caused unemployment in the region.
* BP's response to the disaster was too slow, allowing too much oil to spill.
* The long-term pollution of the Gulf could impact fishing and the food industry for years to come.

Niger Delta, Nigeria

Nigeria is an oil-rich country, yet the majority of its people live in poverty. Most of its oil comes from the highly populated Niger Delta, where impacts of the industry such as pollution cause conflict.

Nigeria's oil fields and industry are concentrated in the south-east of the country.

A woman in a fishing village of the Niger Delta, overshadowed by the oil industry infrastructure.

Oil development

In the early twentieth century Nigeria was part of the British Empire and Britain controlled its resources, including oil. In 1938, the British government sold licences to explore concessions covering the whole country to oil company Shell D'Arcy. Shell, as it was later known, made its first large oil discovery under the Delta region of the Niger River in 1956. Two years later, it sold on licences for some concessions to other oil companies including, Mobil and Agip, in order to concentrate its resources on building wells and pipelines in the Delta oil fields. Nigeria became independent from Britain in 1960, but the foreign companies continued to control the oil exploration and production.

Chapter 4

Destruction fact

Drilling for oil in the Niger Delta releases lots of natural gas from underground. This is wasted and burnt off, as there is so little demand. The amount burnt each year is about one quarter of the total used for heating in the whole of the UK.

Following a civil war in the Delta region in the late 1960s, the Nigerian military government increased state participation in the oil industry to earn more money from oil than just concession rents. They took stakes in the foreign oil companies, so they earned a share of each company's profits in return for letting the companies continue to operate in the country. In the 1970s Nigerian oil exploration and production rose because its oil was cheaper than that from many other regions, and it was in demand from the US. Today Nigeria supplies 40 per cent of US oil. The Nigerian government used some of its oil revenue to build transport infrastructure.

Pollution in the oilfields

People in the Niger Delta oilfields live in a heavily polluted environment. Oil seeps from old, unused pipes and is spilled along with toxic chemicals from refineries, wells or tankers. Spills are an enormous problem. A report by Amnesty International claimed that nearly twice the amount of oil lost by Deepwater Horizon (see page 18) is spilled in Nigeria each year. The oil pollutes farmland, making crops unsafe to eat, and also contaminates water, killing fish and making it unsafe to drink.

In 2004 scientists sampled water from around the Delta and found it contained around five times the safe limit of cancer-causing toxins that is recommended by the World Health Organisation. Burning waste gas from the oil industry in Nigeria releases toxic gases and particles, which cause breathing problems and create more greenhouse gases than the rest of Africa south of the Sahara.

⚠ A boy stands in an oil-contaminated area in Ogoniland, Nigeria

Poverty in Nigeria

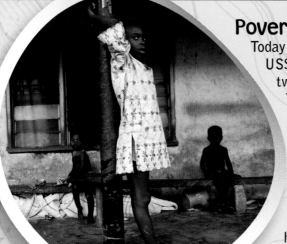

Today Nigeria oil exports are worth around US$70 billion per year. Nevertheless, two-thirds of Nigerians live in poverty. This is partly because of the Nigerian government. Some people claim that corrupt generals running the government, especially in the 1980s and 90s, stole hundreds of billions of dollars of oil revenue. In this period the government invested little in its country, so today there is inadequate healthcare and less than half of Nigerians have access to clean water and electricity. Although there is officially low unemployment in the country, few people can get well-paid jobs – the average income for a Nigerian citizen is the same as it was in 1960. Better paid oil industry jobs in the Niger Delta are mostly taken by foreign oil workers or people from particular Nigerian tribes with government influence.

Problems are made worse by dependency on oil. By the 1980s, revenue from oil overtook that from former major export crops like palm oil and peanuts. Farming declined because many Nigerians migrated to expanding cities, such as Lagos, in the hope of finding better-paid work.

Children play in their front porch in the village of Gbarantoru, which is the closest community to the massive Gbaran Gas project. This community lives in poverty even though there are more than a dozen wells in their vicinity.

Vital statistics:

Nigeria

Population: 160 million
Export earnings: 95 per cent from oil
Below poverty line: 66 per cent
Life expectancy in Niger Delta: 40 years
Health spending per person: US$2
(UN recommends US$34)

Subsistence farmers in the polluted Delta lands struggled to grow enough food for their families. With less farming, there was not enough food to feed the growing population. The Nigerian government has had to use oil revenue to import staple foods ever since.

Conflict and violence

During the 1980s ethnic groups including the Ogoni people in the Niger Delta began peaceful protests. These were directed at Shell, which produces half of Nigeria's oil, and the Nigerian government. They protested against pollution and the violence used to move villagers off their land to allow oil exploration. They also protested against poverty and unemployment in an oil-rich region. In 1996, for example, Shell employed just 88 Ogoni in their Delta operations – around two per cent of the workforce. Thousands of protestors occupied and forced closure of Shell facilities.

At the time, Shell and other oil companies had great influence on the Nigerian government, as the oil industry created such revenue for the country. The companies encouraged the government to stop protests. For example, Shell supplied weapons and paid for military missions against particular villages where protest leaders came from, while Chevron used its helicopters to bring in navy personnel who shot protesting youths. The Ogoni struggle became known internationally, following the trial and execution by the government of the popular Ogoni environmental leader Ken Saro-Wiwa in 1995. Government forces murdered over 2000 protestors and destroyed whole villages. Locals fought back and bombed oil pipelines and kidnapped oil workers.

◁ Militia groups in the Niger Delta region say that they are fighting for a fair share of the oil wealth. However, the Nigerian government and oil companies claim that these groups are trying to claim river routes which are used by oil smugglers to export stolen crude oil.

Changes in Nigeria

Since 2008 the Nigerian government has tried to stop violence in the Niger Delta. For example, it has offered money to armed militants to stop fighting and disrupting oil production, and has offered a percentage of regional oil revenue to local tribes. In 2010 President Jonathan announced that the government would use oil revenue to make improvements in power supply and in the roads of Nigeria, for the benefit of all Nigerians. However, the problems of pollution and poverty in Nigeria will take a long time to be rectified.

Learning from mistakes

The story of the impact of the oil industry in many African countries is similar to that in Nigeria. For example Lusaka, the capital of Angola, developed rapidly using oil revenue and foreign investment from countries such as China that import their oil, but remains totally dependent on oil exports.

Destruction fact

Nigeria's few oil refineries are badly maintained and inefficient so the government of this oil-rich country imports refined fuels from as far away as Europe. This transportation causes huge environmental damage.

In an almost daily routine, cars line up for petrol in Port Harcourt, Nigeria. Many of Nigeria's petroleum refineries are no longer functioning, as corrupt government officials find it more lucrative to export crude oil and import refined fuels from neighbouring countries.

EXPLORE FURTHER

Find out how Malaysia used its oil revenue from the 1970s onwards to develop different industries. What are its biggest exports today?

People living in oil-producing areas are in conflict with government forces over land and gain little benefit from oil. The government of Ghana, which discovered oil in 2010, hopes to learn from these mistakes. For example, they plan to invest some oil revenue in a range of industries, including the cocoa industry and aluminium production, as well as in health, education and other basic needs. They also want to work with foreign oil companies to extract oil while providing Ghanaians with oil industry jobs.

Development or Destruction?

Development:

* Oil from the Niger Delta increased Nigeria's GDP, funded development and made some Nigerians rich.
* Oil provides almost all of Nigeria's export revenue.
* In the twenty-first century Nigerian politicians are trying to share the benefits of oil more fairly, especially in the Delta region.

Destruction:

* Oil development has created ongoing conflict between people living on oil-rich land, the government and foreign oil companies, killing thousands of people.
* Oil development has caused environmental destruction in the Delta which has impacted on people's health and jobs.
* Oil revenue has benefitted only some Nigerians, while many live in worse poverty than 40 years ago.

Statoil, Norway

Norway, like Nigeria, discovered large reserves of oil in the late 1950s, yet while only few profit from oil revenue in Nigeria, the opposite is the case in Norway. The reason is that the Norwegian government, and the state oil company Statoil in particular, used oil revenue to carefully develop and sustain the industry.

▲ Western Europe's largest oil and gas reserves are under the North Sea. Norway controls about 57 per cent of them. This map shows both the oil reserves and pipelines (in blue) and the gas reserves and pipelines (in pink). Concession borders are in orange.

North Sea oil

In 1959 the Netherlands found a gas and oil field near Groningen that extended under the North Sea. This began a race by countries around the North Sea to discover their own offshore oil supplies. At first exploration was on parts of the continental shelf off Germany and Denmark, where drilling was easiest. Then its exploration moved further offshore into Norwegian and British waters. After years of expensive, largely unsuccessful test drilling in the late 1960s, oil companies were about to give up exploration.

But in December 1969, the Ocean Viking rig, operated by Phillips Petroleum on behalf of Norwegian oil company Norsk Hydro, discovered large amounts of oil 3 km (1.9 miles) beneath the sea floor in the Ekofisk field. Ekofisk started producing oil in 1971 and Norway made many more major oil and gas discoveries over the next two decades. The UK started production from its own offshore oil fields in 1975. In 2011 there were over 300 oil and gas fields in the North Sea, spreading from north of the Shetlands, Scotland, to around 640 km (499 miles) further south.

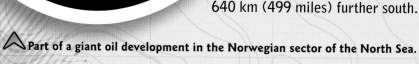

▲ Part of a giant oil development in the Norwegian sector of the North Sea.

Chapter 5

Development fact

From the 1970s onwards Stavanger grew from a small fishing town to Norway's oil capital. The population almost tripled and it has the nation's highest proportion of oil workers.

Taking control of oil

The Norwegian government realised that the North Sea could provide enormous amounts of revenue, so in 1972 it established a state oil company, Statoil, to develop Norwegian oil resources. It also set up the Norwegian Petroleum Directorate (NPD) to regulate how the oil companies, including Statoil, worked together and how the country spent oil revenue. For example, NPD decided to invest in non-oil industries providing long-term work. They created a welfare fund for Norwegians, as well as investing in technology to help preserve the environment when exploiting the oil. Unlike Nigeria, Norway invested in developing oil fields, using the technical skills of foreign oil companies such as Phillips, while also strongly regulating the industry. This prevented any one company or interest group from gaining too much power over Norwegian oil.

Gullfaks C oil platform being constructed in a Norwegian yard before being installed in the North Sea for operation.

Statoil

Statoil grew following discovery of the major fields Statfjord and Gullfaks in the 1970s. Today, Statoil controls around 80 per cent of Norway's oil and gas production. It has become a world leader in finding oil, aided by Norwegian investment in oil technology research at universities. Statoil has particular expertise in technology that helps extract oil from deep offshore fields. For example, it has developed units resting on the seafloor that can drill into oil fields and also create links into existing subsea pipelines.

Statoil uses robot submarines equipped with cameras and pressure sensors to operate this technology, controlled from computers on ships. It is much cheaper and less damaging to the seafloor to do this than to drill in deep water from surface rigs or lay new pipelines.

Oil drilling and production aided by robots reduces risks to personnel and costs.

Statoil uses cutting-edge computer technology to create high-resolution images of oil fields that can be used to improve drilling efficiency.

Innovations: Recovering more oil

When oil fields start to empty, oil companies try to extract or recover more oil from the rock in different ways. Statoil forces in gas and seawater to flush out oil and also injects bacteria to help extract the oil. It has automated systems that separate oil coming out of wells from water and sand at the bottom of the sea. Statoil has also developed sophisticated 3D computer images of oil fields so it knows exactly where to drill to find the most oil.

Oil and GDP

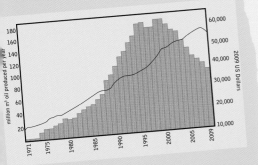

In order to find out whether oil industry development in a country is sustainable, it is important to look at data that will reveal whether the economy of a country is entirely dependent on the oil industry. This chart shows two things. The bar chart shows how North Sea oil production in Norway grew from the 1960s and peaked in 2001. Since then production has fallen, as reserves have started to run out. The line graph shows Norway's GDP – a measure of the wealth of a country divided by its number of citizens. Norway's GDP has continued to grow even when oil production has fallen. This means that Norwegian economic success is not entirely due to producing oil, but also relies on other industries.

Statoil, Norway

Norway and UK oil

Norway produces over half of all North Sea oil. Since the first oil discovery it has developed wells, refineries and other oil assets worth more than US$98 billion. Around one-tenth of government revenue comes from offshore oil and gas, and a quarter of a million people work in its oil industry. The UK produces far less oil, even though its fields are larger than Norway's, and UK citizens have benefitted less from oil revenue. This is partly because the UK government gave more control of oil production to independent companies, which reduced revenue. It also did not invest so much revenue in developing other UK industries.

The refinery at Mongstad has a capacity of 10 million tonnes of crude oil a year. The refinery is the largest in Norway and is part-owned by Statoil.

31

Existing oil infrastructure

Oil and gas rigs and wells often only last for around 50 or 60 years in the North Sea, either because oil fields dry up or the structure weakens in the rough conditions. The NPD is concerned that some older, less productive Statoil wells, such as those in the Gullfaks field, were not maintained properly and could be at risk of leaks or blowouts. However, it is very expensive to close up deep wells and it is often cheaper to sink old rigs into deep water than to dismantle them. This is a very controversial solution because residual oil and chemicals in the structures can cause ocean pollution. Statoil has many old rigs and faces some difficult decisions in the future about their disposal.

Greenpeace demonstrators occupying Brent Spar oil rig to prevent Shell disposing of the rig in the sea.

New frontiers

Norway's North Sea oil reserves are gradually decreasing, so it is searching for oil in deeper, more northerly regions. For example, in 2014 Statoil is due to start producing oil from the new Goliat field in the Barents Sea. Such Arctic exploration is very controversial, owing to pollution concerns (see page 36). The Norwegian government is also investing in the oil industry worldwide under the Oil for Development programme. This aims to help less economically developed countries with oil reserves to manage their oil resources in a sustainable way. Some people question whether the programme has been right to support the oil industry in places such as Nigeria where the oil industry has had severe negative impacts (see page 24).

Development or Destruction?

Development:

* Norway has used North Sea oil revenue to benefit its citizens through careful development of its state-run oil industry, Statoil.
* Statoil uses up-to-date technology to produce oil efficiently.
* Statoil shares its expertise worldwide with poorer countries. The environmental impact of oil production is carefully regulated in Norway.

Destruction:

* North Sea oil is running out and when Statoil invests in other countries it may have less control over production and revenue.
* Statoil has collaborated with countries such as Nigeria where most local people benefit little from oil revenue.
* Statoil is investing elsewhere when it has North Sea wells and platforms that need maintenance or disposal.

Lomonosov Ridge, Arctic Ocean

How much oil in the Arctic?

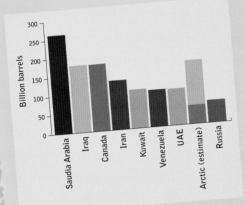

The bar chart above shows the major proven reserves of oil remaining worldwide. It also shows the estimate of Arctic oil. This refers to a 2009 US Geological Survey report based on oil found in the samples of rock drilled from around the region – both onshore and offshore – and the knowledge of where similar rocks are found. There is uncertainty about the exact amount of oil, so the estimate is a range of values.

The Lomonosov Ridge is a mountain range at the bottom of the Arctic Ocean. It runs underneath the North Pole and the rest of the Arctic ice cap. Countries bordering the ocean are claiming ownership of this ridge because there may be enormous oil reserves beneath it. They need this oil for development and revenue, yet the Arctic oil rush has the potential to harm the fragile environment of the Arctic Ocean.

The disputed Lomonosov Ridge is under deep polar water between Russia, the US, Canada and Greenland. In the winter, this part of the Arctic Ocean is frozen over.

Russian claims

Russia does not have the biggest oil reserves, yet is the world's biggest producer of crude oil, largely from oil fields in western Siberia. However, its onshore fields are running out because of high production of oil for both domestic use and export.

▽ A drilling ship in the pack ice of the Arctic Ocean carrying out a test drill to see whether underwater rocks contain oil. The guard is keeping a lookout for polar bears!

Chapter 6

ON THE SCENE

'It's a very important move for Russia to demonstrate its potential in the Arctic. It's like putting a flag on the Moon.'

Sergei Balyasnikov, Russian Arctic and Antarctic Institute, 2007

Therefore, the country is increasingly searching for oil in Russian sectors of the Arctic Ocean. Normally coastal countries can exploit subsea resources for up to 322 km (200 miles) away from their coasts. But Russian scientists had test-drilled the seafloor further out than this and found it potentially held large amounts of oil.

In 2007 a Russian submarine containing a small team of explorers voyaged to the Lomonosov Ridge and planted a Russian flag on it! This was to symbolically claim ownership of the Ridge and an area of surrounding seafloor, totalling the size of western Europe. The Russians claimed they could do this because the Ridge is an underwater extension of Russian Arctic lands. Controlling this area would potentially double Russian oil reserves as the scientists estimated there were up to 75 billion barrels of oil beneath the Ridge. Not surprisingly, Canada, Greenland and the US have also claimed that they should own this area of the Arctic Ocean because it is connected to their territories.

The Arctic environment

The Arctic Ocean is a harsh environment. It is so cold that part of it around the North Pole is permanently frozen, and large areas freeze each winter. In winter many months are permanently dark and there are thick sea fogs and strong winds. However, the waters are rich in wildlife. The nutrient-rich waters support large numbers of tiny algae, fed upon by plankton, which form an essential part of the food chain including larger fish, seabirds, and mammals such as seals and whales. The sea ice on the Arctic Ocean is also important for seals to give birth to their young and for polar bears to hunt on. Very few people live on the cold, treeless land edging the Arctic Ocean.

Oil impacts

For decades, oil has been drilled and produced from Arctic land, for example in Alaska, and also since the 1990s in shallow waters off Sakhalin Island, north-east Russia. There have been many impacts of the oil industry in the Arctic region already. For example, in 1989 an oil tanker called Exxon Valdez ran aground in Alaska and spilled 750,000 barrels of oil that killed hundreds of thousands of seabirds and polluted the coasts for decades.

The supertanker Exxon Valdez caused huge concern worldwide in 1989 when it spilled oil in the pristine Alaskan Arctic waters.

Development fact

An Alaskan study estimated that development of the oil industry in US Arctic waters could create over 50,000 jobs and generate nearly US$200 billion in government, state and local revenue.

At Sakhalin, a Russian island in the North Pacific, millions of tonnes of oil industry waste were dumped at sea in a major salmon fishing area. Only large-scale international protests convinced oil companies to re-route subsea oil pipelines away from the feeding and breeding grounds of endangered grey whales.

Hazardous potential

Offshore drilling in the deep Arctic Ocean started in 2010 off Greenland and in 2011 Russian state-owned oil company Rosneft was planning to start a major drilling operation by 2015. BP was a possible production partner partly because of its experiences with the Gulf of Mexico spill in deep waters. Oil companies and environmentalists consider the freezing and rough Arctic Ocean conditions more hazardous than those of the Gulf of Mexico, with high potential for accidents and environmental damage. Therefore, companies such as Statoil are carrying out careful environmental reviews of possible drilling sites and plan to drill narrower than normal wells to slow the speed of oil production and reduce the chance of rapid oil loss from spills.

Walruses are Arctic mammals which are already threatened by loss of sea ice due to climate change. Pollution and disturbance by the oil industry could severely endanger them.

Greenland waits

Russia, Canada and the US want to exploit their offshore Arctic waters, and Lomonosov, for oil to help meet their populations' existing demand for oil. Greenland has little domestic demand for oil as its population is only around 57,000, but oil revenue is very important to the future development of the country. The country's main industries of fishing, some tourism and gold mining provide insufficient money to run the country. It relies on financial help from Denmark, which partly controls Greenland. Greenlanders, who are mostly Inuit people, have only had legal rights to resources (minerals, as well as fish and whales) on and off their shores since 2009. Oil revenue from Greeland's Arctic Ocean sections and ideally Lomonosov would help it to become completely economically independent and to increase employment and the standard of living for its people.

∨ Arctic communities in Greenland and other countries would be transformed by oil development. But at what cost?

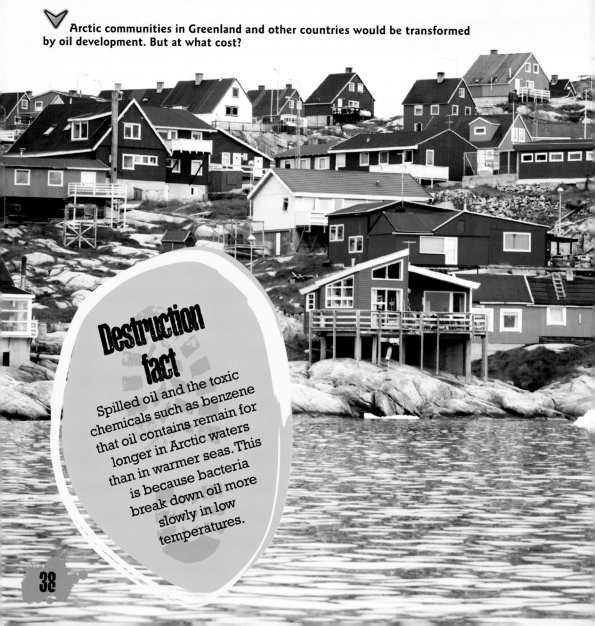

Destruction fact

Spilled oil and the toxic chemicals such as benzene that oil contains remain for longer in Arctic waters than in warmer seas. This is because bacteria break down oil more slowly in low temperatures.

Lomonosov Ridge, Arctic Ocean

The Inuit and other Arctic peoples, such as the Sami in northern Sweden and Dene in Canada, are trying to maximise oil revenue and minimise environmental damage, especially when it may affect their cultural traditions. For example, in 2010 Inuit people stopped Shell from drilling in Alaskan waters during periods when Bowhead whales visit coastal waters. This was to stop oil industry disturbance from scaring off the whales, partly because Bowhead hunting is an important part of Inuit culture.

Development or Destruction?

Development:

* Exploiting the oil reserves under the Lomonosov Ridge and other parts of the Arctic Ocean seafloor could increase global reserves by as much as one tenth.
* Arctic oil could speed development and independence for Inuit and other Arctic peoples.
* Oil companies are exploring and producing Arctic oil slowly in order to lessen the chance of environmental damage.

Destruction:

* The Arctic is a unique habitat whose wildlife could suffer long-term damage by oil spills.
* The cold conditions of the Arctic region cause pollution to stay in the water for longer.
* The Arctic reserves are estimates and it could take decades before large amounts of oil are actually recovered.

Sustainable futures

Destruction fact

Global energy use could increase by half of today's levels by 2030 according to the International Energy Agency. Meeting this increase mainly by burning fossil fuels, including oil, could release enough carbon dioxide to raise global temperatures significantly.

Using oil is the very opposite of sustainable. It is a finite, non-renewable natural resource that, once burnt to release, disappears, leaving dwindling oil reserves for future generations. The pollution and greenhouse gases released through its production and use is harming the environment and causing climate change. So how can the oil industry and its development ever be sustainable?

Immediate oil futures

Many scientists believe that the world is past the point of its highest output of oil and is now falling. Existing reserves may also not be as high as previously thought. In 2011 WikiLeaks published previously secret US documents that say Saudi Arabia's reserves may be 40 per cent smaller than previously estimated. Global demand for oil is also increasing, especially in fast-growing economies with large populations, such as India and China. For example, there were just 250,000 private cars in China in the 1990s, but in 2010 alone around 7 million cars were sold. Uncertainty about oil supplies, made worse by political problems in oil-producing countries such as Libya, caused oil prices to reach their highest ever levels in 2011.

Chapter 7

ON THE SCENE

'If I were emperor of the world, I would put the pedal to the floor on energy efficiency and conservation for the next decade.'

Stephen Chu, American Physicist, 2007

Oil companies have only just started to find crude oil in the Arctic Ocean (see page 34) and have also started drilling off the Falkland Islands, near Antarctica, another potentially large source of crude oil. The tar sands and oil shale of countries such as Canada may contain four trillion barrels of oil and satisfy demand in the near future. However, extracting oil from these sources uses lots of energy, releases large amounts of greenhouse gases, and pollutes land and rivers used by indigenous peoples. This oil production could be made less damaging by using technology to reduce emissions and environmental pollution.

▽ **The Aptera hybrid car uses newly developed materials and technology to achieve fuel efficiency. It uses about 1 litre per 100 km (1 gallon per 330 miles).**

More efficient

If we are going to continue to use oil beyond the next few decades, then we are going to have to use it much more slowly. This can be achieved by extracting the maximum oil possible from reserves (see page 30) and by reducing spills, for example from old pipes (see page 23). It can also be achieved in many other ways, for example by using energy-efficient vehicles such as hybrid cars that use less fuel, using public transport, car sharing and cycling.

Oil alternatives

Some people believe that remaining oil reserves should be left in the ground because of the threat from climate change and pollution caused by their extraction and use. The liquid fuels required by today's fleet of cars, aeroplanes, trains and ships could, in theory, be supplied in part by biofuels. Biofuels include bioethanol made from crops such as corn or sugar cane, and biodiesel made from palm seed oil. They are renewable resources and even though burning biofuel releases greenhouse gases, quantities are smaller than those released when burning oil. Crops also take in carbon dioxide as they grow.

EXPLORE FURTHER

Find out about the pros and cons of using different biofuels as oil replacements.

As growing crops use as much carbon when they grow as they release when they burn, they are considered carbon neutral. Biofuel crops are more sustainable than oil, but do cause environmental destruction, such as deforestation. Farmers cut down forests in some poorer parts of the world to create space for biofuels, because they can be a valuable export crop. This also means that they grow less food. In 2008 the World Bank calculated that increasing biofuel production caused three-quarters of worldwide price rises in foods.

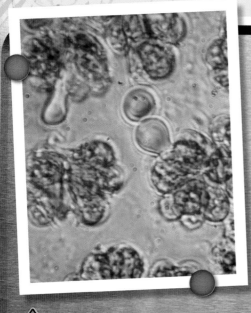

Innovations:
Oil from algae

Around half of the weight of some types of green algae is oil. Scientists worldwide are developing ways to grow such algae in open ponds or clear plastic bags. The algae may be harvested and pressed to release oil or treated with chemicals to extract oil without killing the algae. Potentially, algae could yield over 90,000 litres of biodiesel per hectare at around US$0.40 a litre, which is far cheaper than crude oil.

In this microscopic view, it is possible to see the alga **Botryococcus** (green spheres) secreting bubbles of clear oil.

Palm oil is sometimes called rainforest diesel because tropical forests are being destroyed to plant oil palms as biofuel crops.

A new world power?

A more sustainable alternative to oil and biofuel is to develop new renewable energy technologies that are virtually non-polluting, have fewer land impacts, and create no greenhouse gases. The world has been in the age of oil through the twentieth and early twenty-first century, when oil fuelled industrial growth, transport and other transformation. In future the driving force could be hydrogen.

Hydrogen cells are special batteries that release energy to power vehicles using liquid hydrogen fuel. At present hydrogen power is little used, partly because it is expensive to make hydrogen fuel using electricity from fossil-fuel power stations. In future, solar power might be used to create the fuel and there could be hydrogen filling stations in every town.

ON THE SCENE

'Ever since the car has been around we've been dependent on fossil fuels. What we need to do is to move on to electric power and in the long term, hydrogen. This is the seismic shift in terms of technologies under-pinning how we power our cars.'

Professor David Bailey, Coventry University Business School, UK

Debate club

Oil is discovered in the fields near a remote village. The people there have no electricity and most of them are subsistence farmers. Organise a debate to discuss drilling for oil in this village. You'll need six people to act as the characters below. They can use information from the book and the statements below to get started.

Each person should be given a chance to speak, without interruptions. Others in the class or group can listen to the speakers in the debate as if they are the developers. The developers have to decide at the end whose arguments are most convincing and why, and if they will proceed with the oil drilling.

STATE REPRESETIVE

'This region needs oil development and infrastructure because it will help raise the standard of living for people here to match that of people in other parts of the country.'

TEENAGER

'I don't want to struggle in the fields for a living like my parents. I could get a job building wells or pipe lines, maybe even training to get a better paid job in the oil industry.'

ENVIRONMENTALIST

'I have no doubt that drilling for and transporting oil will create spills and cause pollution. The soil and local rivers will never be the same again.'

OLDER MAN

'Our family has farmed this land for centuries and I don't want things to change. I can't eat oil and I'm sure it will be the oil company who gets rich, not me.'

OIL COMPANY REPRESENTATIVE

'We have lots of experience in getting oil out of the ground quickly and safely. Oil sales will benefit us all. Villagers can always find other farmland if needs be.'

LOCAL FACTORY OWNER

'I welcome the oil wells and local development. If there were new roads and power I could make and transport goods more easily, employ more workers and get richer!'

44

Glossary

algae simple, plant-like organisms that grow in or near water. Seaweed is a type of algae.

bacteria microscopic, single-celled organisms, some of which break down dead organisms and waste. Some kinds of bacteria can cause disease.

barrel unit of measurement in the oil industry, equal to 42 gallons (191 litres)

blowout sudden escape of oil from an oil well

carbon footprint the direct effect someone's actions and lifestyle have on the environment in terms of carbon dioxide emissions

climate change changes in the world's weather patterns caused by human activity

concession the right to use land or property for a specific purpose

contamination when something is dirty or impure due to pollution or poison

continental shelf shallow area of underwater land surrounding a continent to a depth of approximately 180 m (600 feet)

crude oil oil that has been extracted from the ground but not yet refined into a usable form

deforestation destroying or felling all the trees of a forest

delta area of land where a river splits into smaller rivers before entering the sea

dugong marine mammal that grazes on seagrass in warm, coastal waters

emirate territory ruled by a leader called an emir

GDP abbreviation for Gross Domestic Product – the total value of goods and services produced by a country in one year

geologist scientist who studies the rocks and soil from which Earth is made

greenhouse gas gas in the upper atmosphere that warms the lower atmosphere around Earth by trapping the sun's heat

hydraulic describes machines operated by liquid moving under pressure

infrastructure facilities that serve a community such as roads and water and sewer systems

Inuit people from northern Canada, parts of Greenland and Alaska

invest spend money on something to make it better, more successful or to make more money

migrant someone who moves from one place to live in another for a while

non-renewable something that cannot be replaced once consumed, such as the energy resources oil and coal

offshore in the sea, not far from land

oil field area overlying oil reserves with wells and/or rigs extracting oil

onshore on land

particle very small piece of something

petrochemical chemical or product made from crude oil

plankton tiny organisms that float in the sea

platform large structure used for workers and machinery to drill wells in the seabed and extract oil

refinery factory that makes petrol, diesel and petrochemicals from oil

reserve oil that's still in the ground

revenue income, or money earned from a particular activity, such as oil production

rig see platform

riser pipe carrying crude oil from reserve to surface

sedimentary rock type of rock formed by layers of sediment, such as sandstone

sustainable using natural resources to meet the needs of the present without jeopardising those resources for future generations

toxin poison

United Nations (UN) international organisation promoting peace, security and economic development

World Bank organisation that lends funds to provide help to poorer member countries

Index